Capital Mobility, Exchange Rates and Economic Crises

Capital Mobility, Exchange Rates and Economic Crises

George Fane

Senior Fellow, Department of Economics, Research School of Pacific and Asian Studies, Australian National University, Australia

Edward Elgar

Cheltenham, UK • Northampton, MA, USA

© George Fane 2000

Published by
Edward Elgar Publishing Limited
Glensanda House
Montpellier Parade
Cheltenham
Glos GL50 1UA
UK

Edward Elgar Publishing, Inc.
136 West Street
Suite 202
Northampton
Massachusetts 01060
USA

A catalogue record for this book
is available from the British Library

Library of Congress Cataloguing in Publication Data

Fane, George, 1944–
    Capital mobility, exchange rates and economic crises / George Fane.
    Includes bibliographical references and index.
        1. Capital movements. 2. Foreign exchange. 3. Financial crises.
    4. Currency question. I. Title.

    HG3891 .F36 2001
    332'.042—dc21   00-041736

ISBN 1 85898 784 9 (cased)

Typeset by Green Words & Images, Canberra, Australia.
Printed and bound in Great Britain by MPG Books Ltd, Bodmin, Cornwall

For Anne

Contents

Figures

Tables

Preface

I began work on this book while visiting the Development Centre of the Organisation for Economic Co-operation and Development in Paris and continued working on it at the Harvard Institute for International Development in Cambridge, Massachusetts. I completed the book after returning to the Australian National University in Canberra. I received much help and encouragement from colleagues and seminar participants in all three institutions and am especially grateful for the hospitality and facilities I received as a visitor in Paris and Cambridge.

I am very grateful for the data and patient help provided by many bankers, central bankers and government economists in Australia, Hong Kong, Indonesia, Korea, Malaysia, Singapore, Taiwan and Thailand. I also owe a large debt to my family and colleagues. Anne, Beatrice, Catherine, Jeff, Kate and Simon have been infinitely tolerant and supportive. Anne Daly, Warwick McKibbin and Kishen Rajan read and commented on early drafts of the entire manuscript; Changmo Ahn, Matt Benge, Soonthorn Chaiyindeepum, Max Corden, Ross McLeod, Guy Meredith, Kurt Schuler, Ted Sieper and K.K. Tang also provided many helpful comments, contacts and ideas. Catherine Mellors of Green Words & Images has been an exceptionally conscientious and competent typesetter.

Abbreviations and conventions

$	dollar (US dollar, unless otherwise specified)
ADB	Asian Development Bank
ADR	American Depository Receipt
AMF	Asian Monetary Fund
basis point	one hundredth of one per cent
Bht.	Thai baht
BI	Bank Indonesia
billion	one thousand million
BNM	Bank Negara Malaysia
BOK	Bank of Korea
BOT	Bank of Thailand
CAR	capital adequacy ratio
CBC	Central Bank of China (Taiwan)
CCL	Contingent Credit Lines
CEIC	CEIC Data Ltd., Hong Kong
CI	Certificate of Indebtedness
DF	delivery forward
EF	Exchange Fund
EFB	Exchange Fund Bill issued by HKMA
EFM	Emergency Financing Mechanism
EMS	European Monetary System
ERM	Exchange Rate Mechanism
EU	European Union
FDI	foreign direct investment
FDIC	Federal Deposit Insurance Corporation
FTC	foreign tax credit
FTD	foreign tax deduction
FTE	foreign tax exemption
G–7	Group of 7 (Canada, France, Germany, Italy, Japan, UK, USA)
G–10	Group of 10 (actually has 11 members: the G–7 plus Belgium, Netherlands, Sweden, Switzerland)
G–22	Group of 22 (G–7 plus Argentina, Australia, Brazil, China, Hong Kong, India, Indonesia, Korea, Malaysia, Mexico, Poland, Russia, Singapore, South Africa, Thailand)
GAB	General Arrangements to Borrow

GATS	General Agreement on Trade in Services
GDP	gross domestic product
HIBOR	Hong Kong Interbank Offered Rate on HK$
HK$	Hong Kong dollar
HKMA	Hong Kong Monetary Authority
HSI	Hang Seng stock market index
ICIC	International Credit Insurance Corporation
IET	interest equalization tax
IFIAC	International Financial Institution Advisory Commission
IMF	International Monetary Fund
Korea	Republic of (South) Korea
LAF	Liquidity Adjustment Facility
LIBOR	London Interbank Offered Rate (on US$, throughout this study)
M0	base money
M2	broad money
NAB	New Arrangements to Borrow
NDC	net domestic credit
NDF	non-delivery forward
NFA	net foreign assets
NT$	New Taiwan dollar
OECD	Organisation for Economic Co-operation and Development
QFII	Qualifying Foreign Institutional Investor (Taiwan)
RBNZ	Reserve Bank of New Zealand
RER	real exchange rate
Rgt.	Malaysian ringgit
Rp.	Indonesian rupiah
RR	reserve ratio
S&L	Savings and loan institution
SBI	*Sertifikat Bank Indonesia* (certificate of deposit issued by BI)
SDR	special drawing right
SRF	Supplemental Reserve Facility
trillion	one thousand billion
UK	United Kingdom
US	United States
USA	United States of America
VDR	variable deposit requirement
WTO	World Trade Organization

1. Introduction

1.1 OUTLINE OF THE BOOK

Capital account liberalisation has three major benefits. First, it allows capital to be moved from countries and sectors where its marginal productivity is relatively low to those where it is relatively high. This is particularly important because there are very widespread and stringent restrictions on international labour mobility; the inefficiencies and wage inequalities created by these restrictions can be reduced, if capital can be moved from industrialised to developing countries.[1] If capital always had to be used in the country of residence of its owners, it would be far more abundant relative to labour in the rich industrialised countries than in the poorer developing ones, for which capital inflows are an important source of growth.

The second major direct benefit of free capital mobility is that it allows portfolio risks to be diversified. Again, this is particularly important for developing countries, since they often have relatively small endowments of most factors other than labour, but relatively large endowments of a few very specific factors, such as particular minerals or export crops. Relaxing restrictions on international trade in factor ownership allows governments and private investors to diversify their portfolios and alleviates the problems created for many developing countries by the volatility of primary commodity prices.[2] The financial sector illustrates a particularly important instance of the need for portfolio diversification: it is argued in Chapter 6 that the observed fragility of the financial systems of developing countries results in part from the restrictions which their own governments have imposed on the entry of foreign banks – the result has been banking sectors dominated by domestic banks with asset portfolios which, rather than being globally diversified, are focused on the domestic economy and are therefore especially vulnerable to economy-wide shocks, such as terms of trade shocks or exchange rate crises.

The third main benefit to a small country of unrestricted access to world capital markets is that it allows aggregate spending to follow a smoother path than aggregate income. It therefore provides a form of inter-temporal partial insurance against events, such as droughts and adverse movements in the terms of trade, that would be costly to insure against by directly purchasing insurance.

Despite these benefits, developing countries have become increasingly reluctant to relax all controls on capital movements because of fears that doing so would increase the risk of speculative attacks on their exchange rates and financial systems. There were three major episodes of speculation and turbulence in foreign exchange markets in the 1990s: the 1992–93 crisis of the European

Exchange Rate Mechanism (ERM); the 1994–95 crisis that was dubbed the 'tequila crisis' because it initially involved an attack on the Mexican peso, although it subsequently spread to other Latin American and Asian currencies; and the Asian crisis that began in 1997 and became an emerging markets' crisis in 1998 when financial panic spread to Russia and Brazil. The European economies that were forced to devalue in 1992–93 were able to benefit from their increased competitiveness, but Mexico's gross domestic product (GDP) fell by 6 per cent between 1994 and 1995, and Argentina's fell by 5 per cent over the same period. The Asian crisis produced even more severe recessions: between 1997 and 1998 Indonesia's GDP fell by 14 per cent, Thailand's by 10 per cent, Korea's by 9 per cent and Malaysia's by 8 per cent. This spate of crises in the emerging market economies shows that something must be seriously wrong with their economic policies. This study surveys and analyses the main contending explanations and suggested remedies with particular emphasis on international capital mobility.

Controls on capital inflows and outflows and the relationship between capital controls and exchange controls are discussed in Chapter 2, which also analyses the effects of the main types of controls used in developing countries. Chapter 3 describes the detailed operations of controls in Taiwan, Korea, Malaysia and Chile. These four countries provide examples of all the main types of controls now used by emerging market economies. The conclusion of this chapter is that the experience of these four countries suggests that mild, or even moderate, restrictions on capital mobility are not effective devices for preventing financial and exchange rate crises.

Section 4.1 discusses the case for taxing capital inflows that is based on the existence of sovereign default risk. Section 4.2 deals with the international aspects of income taxation. The conclusion of these two sections is that, except in the case of tax havens, it would be in the self-interest of most developing countries to reduce the rates at which they currently tax the domestic earnings of foreign capital. Sections 4.3 and 4.4 survey some of the arguments that capital controls may be a 'second-best' way of coping with the problems created because some policies have been set badly and cannot be readily changed. The case for using capital controls to bolster government revenue from money creation, and to reduce interest payments on government debts is discussed in section 4.3. Section 4.4 discusses second-best arguments for capital controls based on the existence of tariffs and export taxes. A priori, one cannot rule out the possibility that, when trade is taxed, increased capital flows may reduce welfare by exacerbating the inefficiencies caused by trade taxes by enough to outweigh the direct benefits of capital account liberalisation; however, this section shows that two commonly used arguments which claim that this is normally the case are wrong. Section 4.5 criticises the argument that, although foreign direct investment (FDI) should be welcomed, portfolio and bank-financed capital flows should be discouraged.

The most important second-best arguments for restrictions on capital flows are those based on speculation and financial fragility; Chapter 5 deals with speculation and Chapter 6 with moral hazard, banking and bankruptcy procedures. Because speculation against an exchange rate system can be created by loss of credibility of the institutions and policies that underpin it, Chapter 7 deals with macroeconomic responses to capital flows and the choice between fixed and floating exchange rates in a world of high capital mobility. Chapter 8 deals with how to design institutions to make monetary and exchange rate policies credible. Chapter 9 reviews proposals for reforming the international financial system.

Readers willing to take assertions in the main text on trust can skip the endnotes. There is an overview section at the end of each chapter for those who wish to skim. The remainder of the present chapter surveys the gradual removal of all capital controls by the industrialised countries, the partial (but now stalled) liberalisation of capital controls in developing countries and the remarkable growth in international capital mobility.

1.2 CAPITAL ACCOUNT LIBERALISATION BY THE INDUSTRIALISED COUNTRIES

The medium-term objective of the Bretton Woods Agreement of 1944, which established the International Monetary Fund (IMF) and laid out the structure of the post-war international financial system, was to make currencies fully convertible on current account at exchange rates that would normally remain fixed. In contrast to its aim of liberalising current account transactions, the Agreement accepted, and even prescribed, the indefinite use of controls to limit speculative capital flows. Article VI of its Articles of Agreement prohibited the IMF from lending to a member to finance a 'large or sustained' capital outflow. Section 1(a) of this Article allowed the IMF to request a member to exercise controls to meet such an outflow and section 3 explicitly gave members the right to impose 'such controls as are necessary to regulate international capital movements', provided that in doing so they do not restrict payments for current account transactions, nor unduly delay transfers of funds in settlement of commitments.[3]

At the end of 1958, when convertibility on current account had been largely achieved by the industrialised countries, capital controls were still in use in the Sterling Area countries and in all of continental Europe, except West Germany, which had abolished its exchange controls even on capital account transactions.[4]

The liberalisation of international capital movements was one of the objectives of the Organisation for Economic Co-operation and Development (OECD) from its creation in 1960–61. Two OECD codes were used to promote this objective: the Code of Liberalisation of Capital Movements and the Code of Liberalisation of Current Invisible Operations.[5] Under these codes, 'liberalisation' means not merely the removal of government restrictions on foreign exchange transactions, but also the removal of government restrictions on the underlying transactions; for example, 'liberalisation' includes the removal of restrictions on foreign ownership of particular types of assets, and on foreign investment in particular sectors. However, the OECD codes did not compel members to remove restrictions on capital account transactions, they merely required them to justify the restrictions which they maintained.

Initially, little progress was made in capital account liberalisation by the OECD countries. Indeed, Britain tightened its controls on capital outflows in the period 1961–66 and the USA introduced capital controls in 1964 and then tightened them in 1965 and 1968. In 1961, Britain restricted the availability of foreign exchange at the official rate to finance FDI by British companies outside the Sterling Area and in 1965–66 it stopped providing any foreign exchange at the official rate for such FDI outflows, which had to be financed by borrowing abroad or by buying foreign exchange from residents who wished to sell foreign portfolio assets. In 1964 the USA imposed an 'interest equalization tax' (IET) on outflows of portfolio equity and bonds with more than three years to maturity. The effect of the IET was to impose a charge of 1 per cent per year on foreign borrowing by US residents. In 1965, the IET was extended to bank loans and quantitative guidelines were proposed on lending abroad by banks and other financial institutions and on outflows of capital from US corporations to their branches and subsidiaries in other industrialised countries. Initially, these quantitative guidelines were not legally binding, but they were made mandatory in 1968.[6]

There are two factors that make the use of exchange controls more prevalent under fixed than under flexible exchange rate systems. First, few fixed exchange rate regimes have been immune from speculation about devaluation or revaluation; and a frequent response of governments and central banks is to try to counter speculation by imposing controls on exchange transactions and capital movements. Second, when a country moves from a fixed to a floating exchange rate regime, the task of operating the foreign exchange market is transferred from the central bank to private banks and dealers; without the central bank's foreign exchange reserves to act as a buffer between day-to-day and month-to-month discrepancies in the supply and demand for foreign exchange by traders and long-term investors, private banks and dealers must provide this buffer. To do this, they need to be able to borrow, lend and hedge in international financial markets. It is therefore not surprising that the abandonment of the Bretton Woods fixed exchange rate system by the major industrialised countries in the period 1971–73 accelerated their progress towards capital account liberalisation. Nor was it coincidental that the problems caused by the move to fixed exchange rates among the currencies within the ERM coincided with the temporary return to capital controls in 1992 by several European countries, including Spain, Portugal and Ireland.

The USA removed its capital controls in 1974. Germany, which had reintroduced some controls in 1970, finally abolished all controls in 1974.[7] The UK removed its exchange and capital controls in 1979 and Japan completed the gradual removal of its exchange controls in 1980. Australia abruptly removed all its exchange controls in December 1983 and simultaneously floated its exchange rate, which had previously been pegged to a basket of the currencies of its main trading partners. A similar sequence of events occurred in New Zealand, where the removal of controls occurred in late 1984, and the decision to float the exchange rate was taken in March 1985. In the second half of the 1980s, most of the other OECD members removed their remaining exchange controls and the coverage of the OECD codes was extended to cover intellectual property rights and a wider range of service sector activities. In 1989, the OECD Invisibles Code was extended to ensure national treatment for foreign financial institutions, and their branches and agencies. The Capital Movements Code was extended to cover the provision of cross-border services by banks and international capital movements, including trade in money market instruments, forward foreign exchange, swaps and other derivatives.

European unification also provided an important stimulus to the removal of capital controls. Whereas the OECD codes allowed governments to provide justifications for not liberalising, the members of the European Union (EU) were obliged by the Single European Act of 1987 to remove all restrictions on the movements of goods, people, services and capital. The deadline for the removal of restrictions was set at the end of 1992 for most countries, but some were allowed additional grace periods. The final removal of restrictions on capital convertibility by industrialised countries occurred in 1993–95: Portugal, Spain and Greece completed the liberalisations required under their EU commitments by July 1994, and Iceland adopted full convertibility in January 1995.[8]

1.3 STALLED LIBERALISATION OF CAPITAL CONTROLS IN DEVELOPING COUNTRIES

Capital Flows to Developing Countries

In the last 30 years the developing countries have received two great waves of inflowing foreign capital. The first began in the mid-1970s and ended abruptly in 1982 with the onset of the debt crisis in Latin America. The second began in the early 1990s, stalled temporarily in 1995 at the time of the Mexican crisis, and ended abruptly in 1997 with the onset of the Asian crisis.

After the tripling of oil prices in 1973–74, the large current account surpluses of the oil-exporting countries were recycled, mainly through the international banks, to the oil-importing industrialised and developing countries. The further approximate doubling of oil prices in 1978 added to the current account surpluses of the oil-exporting countries and the corresponding deficits of the oil-importing countries. In the period 1977–82, net capital inflows to all developing countries (other than oil-rich capital exporting countries such as Kuwait and Saudi Arabia) averaged $31 billion per year, of which $26 billion per year went to Latin America. Most of the flows to Latin America were in the form of syndicated bank lending.

In mid-1982, this lending boom was brought to a painful halt by the Latin American debt crisis, which was triggered by a sudden very large increase in world real interest rates combined with a severe recession in the industrialised countries and a sharp deterioration in the terms of trade of most developing countries. Even before the occurrence of these adverse shocks, several economists and bankers had expressed unease about the extent to which the international banks were exposed to credit risk on their Latin American debts. The total debt of all developing countries was of the order of $600 billion; about one-third of the total was owed by Argentina, Brazil and Mexico and roughly another one-third by the next 10 largest debtors.[9] Unable to roll over their debts, and facing greatly increased debt service obligations, the major Latin American debtors suspended debt service payments.

Capital flows to developing countries during the next seven years, 1983–89, were dominated by the protracted negotiations between the international banks, the debtor governments, and the governments of the USA and the other industrial countries, whose stake in the negotiations arose from their concern for the political stability of Latin America and the financial viability of the international banks. During this period, developing country debt was traded in secondary markets at a fraction of its face value. By 1990 the average market value of these claims had fallen to a low point of only 30 per cent of their face value. Asian countries continued to receive net capital inflows during the period 1983–89 at the rate of $17 billion per year, which was roughly unchanged from the period 1977–82.[10] However, the net inflows to all developing countries (excluding the traditional capital exporters) during this period were very small, since the net inflow to Asia was matched by an almost equal net capital outflow from Latin America.[11]

The eventual resolution of the negotiations on developing country debt was achieved partly by a fall in world interest rates and partly by the Brady Plan of 1989, which restructured bank loans into Brady bonds using a combination of new lending, debt-for-equity swaps and debt forgiveness by the commercial banks and credit guarantees by the World Bank, the IMF and the governments of Japan and the USA. Following this resolution, the secondary market value of the debt of developing countries almost doubled from its low point of just over

30 cents per dollar of face value in 1990 to almost 60 cents per dollar by late 1993.[12] The optimism generated by the resolution of the debt crisis was reinforced by the success of economic liberalisation, particularly in Asia, but also in Latin America. Capital flows to 'emerging markets' – that is, developing countries with liberalised financial systems and at least partially open capital accounts – were both 'pulled' by optimism about their economic prospects and 'pushed' by the very large falls in interest rates in the industrial countries.[13] As a result, the early and mid-1990s saw renewed and even larger capital flows to developing countries.[14] In dollar terms, the average annual net inflows to developing countries in the period 1990–96 exceeded $150 billion, which is about five times larger even than those in the boom of 1977–82. In 1996 alone, the inflow to all developing countries was $235 billion, of which Asia received $107 billion.[15]

The tremendous growth in international capital flows to developing countries has been accompanied by radical changes in the ways that these flows are financed. In the early post-war period, most lending to developing countries was in the form of official loans from the governments of a handful of the major industrial countries. In the oil boom period, this concentration among lenders was reduced by the substitution of syndicated bank loans for official lending as the dominant form of lending to developing countries. Nevertheless, just 25 banks held a dominant share in Mexico's total foreign debts in 1982.[16] Growing technological sophistication, the removal of capital controls by the industrialised countries and the liberalisation of financial markets in both industrialised and developing countries facilitated the growth of lending to the developing countries through mutual funds and bond issues. In the 1990s, portfolio investment and FDI made up 79 per cent of the total net inflow to developing countries, whereas these two items had together made up only 2 per cent of total net inflows in the period 1977–82, when net portfolio outflows almost cancelled out the net inflows of FDI. These developments brought about further large reductions in the concentration among lenders to developing countries in the 1990s and made it harder to negotiate the rescheduling and reduction of debts when the Asian crisis broke.

Capital Account Opening in Developing Countries: the Role of the IMF

Once the Bretton Woods fixed exchange rate system had been abandoned in 1973, the IMF strongly supported the removal of capital controls by the industrial countries. Although it took a more cautious approach towards the removal of such controls by the developing countries, it nevertheless generally favoured gradual relaxation. For example, in response to the large inflows to developing countries in the early and mid-1990s, the IMF recommended adjusting fiscal, monetary and exchange rate policy rather than tightening capital controls.[17]

However, long after the collapse of the Bretton Woods system, almost all developing countries continued to try to manage the values of their currencies in terms of the dollar or some weighted average of the major currencies. Partly for this reason, the liberalisation of capital account transactions in developing countries has been much slower than in industrialised countries. Mathieson and Rojas-Suárez (1993) estimate that the number of developing countries with open capital accounts increased only from 20 to 21 over the period 1975–90.

In April 1997, the Interim Committee of the IMF proposed that the IMF should seek the approval of its members to amend its Articles of Agreement to make the promotion of capital account liberalisation a specific purpose of the Fund and to give the Fund appropriate jurisdiction over capital movements.[18] The proposed amendments would have extended to capital account transactions the arrangements for promoting convertibility on current account that are contained in the IMF's existing Articles VIII and XIV. Like the OECD codes, the IMF's proposed amendment would have promoted rather than compelled capital account liberalisation. It would have provided for a phasing-out of controls by allowing members to maintain existing exchange controls and to adapt them to changing circumstances until their currencies were strong enough to allow for the full removal of controls.[19]

The IMF's plans for accelerating the process of capital account liberalisation in developing countries were abruptly interrupted by the Asian crisis in 1997. Since the start of this crisis, proposals for the reform of international and national policies towards international capital flows have been increasingly focused on regulating short-term capital movements and exchange rate speculation, and on searching for mechanisms that would force private lenders to increase their lending to countries experiencing crises. Since 1998, both the World Bank and the IMF have canvassed the merits of controls on capital inflows as a temporary prudential measure, until more effective ones can be put in place.[20]

The next two chapters are concerned with the choice between using taxes or direct controls to regulate short-term capital flows or removing all such restrictions and directly attacking any market imperfections that might be exacerbated by increased capital mobility. The conclusions reached support the complete removal of capital and exchange controls because mild, or even moderate, controls have not proved to be a reliable way of preventing financial and exchange rate crises, while the long-term effects of very severe controls are worse than those of the crises that they are designed to cure.

NOTES

1.   Trade in goods and services is a partial substitute for the international mobility of capital and labour. Under the extreme assumptions that predict international factor price equalisation, it would be a perfect substitute. The very large capital flows of the post-war period, and the

very stringent immigration controls that the industrialised countries impose to limit labour mobility, demonstrate that trade in goods and services is still very far from having equalised international factor prices.

2. Nash (1990a, 1990b).
3. Rule and regulation H-1 of the IMF, adopted in September 1946, required it to keep all exchange controls 'under review'; however, the right of a member to use exchange controls to manage capital movements was fully accepted (see Horsefield, 1969, Vol. I, pp. 150–51 and Vol. III, p. 293).
4. de Vries (1969a, pp. 277–8) and IMF (1959).
5. OECD (1990).
6. Kindleberger (1987, p. 57), Yeager (1976, pp. 429, 561), de Vries (1969b, p. 296), Cairncross (1973, pp. 32–43).
7. From April 1970, banks' liabilities to non-residents were subject to a special reserve requirement in excess of the requirement on liabilities to residents. From March 1972, most forms of borrowing from non-residents had to be accompanied by placing a 40 per cent non-interest-bearing cash deposit at the Bundesbank. The deposit proportion was raised to 50 per cent in July 1972. In addition, regulations restricted sales of fixed interest securities to non-residents and the payment of interest on non-residents' bank deposits (Dooley, 1995b, pp. 261–2).
8. Quirk, Evans *et al.* (1995, p. 11).
9. These data are for mid-1983 and are taken from Sjaastad (1983, pp. 305, 322–3).
10. Folkerts-Landau, Ito *et al.* (1995, Table 1.1, p. 33).
11. The $17 billion per year net outflow from Latin America over the period 1983–89 itself comprised a much faster reduction in commercial bank exposure, partially offset by increased new lending by governments, and international agencies: the debts of developing countries with debt-servicing problems (which were predominantly Latin American countries) to official creditors rose over this period by about $20 billion per year in real terms (Dooley 1995a, p. 273).
12. Dooley (1995a, p. 275).
13. The annualised three-month London Interbank Offered Rate (LIBOR) on US dollar deposits fell from 11.9 per cent in the third quarter of 1984 to 3.2 per cent in the second quarter of 1993 (IMF, *International Financial Statistics* CD-ROM).
14. See Calvo *et al.* (1993) and World Bank (1997).
15. Fischer (1998).
16. Truman (1996, p. 12).
17. Quirk, Evans *et al.* (1995, p. 6).
18. Mohammed (1998).
19. Fischer (1998).
20. See, for example, Adams *et al.* (1998, Chapter III).

2.   Capital controls and exchange controls

This chapter defines capital controls and exchange controls, discusses why governments resort to them, describes the main types of controls used in the Asia-Pacific region to limit speculation and sets out a model of the effects of each main type.

2.1   CAPITAL CONTROLS AND EXCHANGE CONTROLS: CONCEPTS, PURPOSES AND EXAMPLES

Capital Controls

Capital flows can be separated into 'FDI', 'portfolio investment' and 'other'.[1] A country's FDI liabilities comprise the equity in domestic firms owned by non-residents who have a significant degree of managerial control over them. Its FDI assets comprise the equity owned by its residents in foreign firms over which they have a significant degree of control. Portfolio liabilities comprise the marketable securities and equity issued by domestic firms and owned by non-residents who do not have a significant degree of control over them. The 'other' category comprises everything else; the main components of 'other liabilities' are loans to residents from offshore banks, deposits of non-residents at domestic banks, trade credits to residents from non-residents and similar credits under leasing arrangements. 'Other assets' are defined analogously. For each of the three categories – FDI, portfolio and other – the net capital inflow is the net increase in liabilities to non-residents minus the net increase in assets of residents. Capital controls can be defined as regulations or taxes that restrict the freedom of residents and non-residents to buy or sell any of these assets and liabilities.

The most basic feature of capital controls is that by restricting international trade in assets they create artificial disparities between the real rates of return on some or all assets in the home country and those in the rest of the world. To understand the effects of actual examples of capital controls, it is useful to analyse simple extreme possible cases. A uniform tax on all capital inflows together with a uniform subsidy on all capital outflows would raise the rates of return to domestic savers and investors on all assets, both domestic and foreign, relative to the rates of return faced by non-residents. This would encourage savings, discourage investment and generate a current account surplus to match the reduced capital inflows and increased capital outflows. It would not directly discourage portfolio diversification, which involves trading in assets among residents and non-residents: the taxes resulting from sales of domestic assets to non-residents would be matched by the subsidies resulting from purchases of foreign assets by residents. Another way of seeing the same point is that domestic residents would not be discouraged from diversifying their portfolios because they would face increased rates of return on both domestic and foreign assets. Nor would a uniform tax on inflows and subsidy to outflows discourage the inter-temporal smoothing of consumption, since the tax on borrowing in bad times would be offset by the subsidy to lending in good times. A uniform tax on all capital outflows, together with a uniform subsidy to all inflows, would of course have exactly opposite effects on rates of return and would also have no direct effects on portfolio diversification or inter-temporal smoothing of consumption.

Actual systems of capital controls seldom, if ever, subsidise either inflows or outflows and often tax both. This obviously discourages both portfolio diversification and the inter-temporal smoothing of consumption: just as tariffs on goods imported on current account also discourage exports, so taxes on capital inflows, that are not matched by subsidies on outflows, also discourage capital outflows. Similarly, capital inflows are discouraged by taxes on outflows if they are not matched by inflow subsidies.

Comprehensive outflow controls can be administered by requiring central bank approval for all forms of payments to non-residents other than payments for exports and debt service payments on previously approved foreign borrowing. Even in developing countries that do not restrict other forms of outflow, it is common to find restrictions on lending to non-residents in domestic currency. The reason is that the major way in which non-residents can speculate against a currency is by borrowing in that currency – either directly, or indirectly through the swap or forward foreign exchange markets – to finance the acquisition of foreign currency assets.

Inflows are sometimes restricted by explicit taxes. An example of a tax on inflows is the tax that Malaysia has imposed since September 1999 on repatriating profits earned on portfolio investments. This tax is described in Chapter 3. A more common way of restricting inflows, and the one preferred by central banks, is to set a variable deposit requirement (VDR), which stipulates that domestic residents who borrow from non-residents, or sell securities to non-residents, must place a specified percentage of the gross inflow in a non-interest-bearing account at the central bank, which is returned at some specified date, such as after one year, or when the loan is repaid. The specified percentage is usually higher for short-term borrowings than for long-term ones – hence the 'variable' in VDR. While a VDR is not an explicit tax, it is like a tax, rather than a direct control, since it does not ration the amount borrowed but rather specifies a fixed per unit charge – the interest rate forgone multiplied by the ratio of non-interest-bearing deposits to borrowings, net of these deposits – that must be paid to the authorities by those who borrow from abroad. VDRs have been widely used by both industrialised and developing countries. They are used by industrialised countries that attempt to combine pegged exchange rates with lower rates of inflation than those of the countries to which they have pegged their currencies and by developing countries that wish to moderate spending booms.[2]

Most developing countries restrict inflows of FDI by licensing projects on a project-by-project basis; foreign investors are also often required to take on local partners. The access of foreign portfolio investors to the domestic share markets and bond markets is sometimes banned or rationed, and additional limits are sometimes set on the share of the equity of locally registered companies that may be held by non-residents.

Exchange Controls

Exchange controls restrict the use by domestic residents of foreign exchange, or the use of domestic currency by non-residents. By supplying or requisitioning foreign exchange at a price that differs from its open market price, governments can subsidise, or tax, any transactions between domestic residents and non-residents. Exchange controls can therefore be applied to current account transactions to achieve the same effects as tariffs, quotas and export taxes. There is in fact a one-to-one equivalence between systems of taxes on imports and exports and exchange controls on current account transactions that result in a system of multiple exchange rates.

There is a similar equivalence between systems of capital controls implemented by means of explicit taxes and systems of such controls implemented by means of exchange controls. For example, a 30 per cent non-interest-bearing deposit requirement is observationally identical to the following exchange control system:

1. the proceeds of foreign borrowing must be surrendered at a special capital account exchange rate that is 30 per cent below the rate (measured in domestic currency per unit of foreign exchange) that applies to current account transactions and capital outflows other than repayments of principal;
2. repayments of principal can be made at the same low rate that applies to foreign borrowing;
3. the foreign exchange needed for interest payments abroad must be bought at the current account rate.

Similarly, a dual exchange rate system in which the price of foreign exchange for all capital account transactions is twice the price paid at the 'official' rate applicable to current account transactions would cause the domestic interest rate to be half the world interest rate, given that interest receipts and payments are made at the current account exchange rate. This dual exchange rate system would therefore be equivalent to a 50 per cent tax – expressed as a proportion of the amount paid by the foreign borrower – on lending abroad, together with a 50 per cent subsidy on borrowing from abroad. If, as in the above example, the foreign exchange to finance new capital outflows had to be bought at the high capital account rate, but if, more realistically, the proceeds of inflows, other than repatriation of previous outflows, had to be surrendered at the current account rate, the system would be equivalent to a tax on outflows not accompanied by a subsidy to inflows.

The last of the dual exchange rate systems just described contains the essence of the most popular method for restricting capital outflows, although the details of actual exchange control systems are of course much more complicated. The controls on portfolio outflows used by the Sterling Area countries after World War II were very similar to this dual exchange rate system, except that rather than directly controlling the differential between the two exchange rates, and therefore the differential between onshore and offshore interest rates, the UK authorities prevented net outflows of portfolio capital from the Sterling Area by requiring residents who wished to buy dollar-denominated securities to buy the necessary foreign exchange from other residents who wished to sell dollar-denominated securities. As a result, the capital account exchange rate was determined by the supply and demand of residents for dollar-denominated securities, and the sterling price of dollars for offshore investment exceeded the sterling price of dollars at the official exchange rate by enough to equalise the expected returns to domestic residents on Sterling Area assets and other assets.

The tax elements in the dual exchange rate treatment of capital inflows and outflows arise only because borrowings, interest payments and repayments of principal are not all made at the same exchange rate. If, hypothetically, all capital inflows and outflows and all interest payments and receipts were made at an exchange rate (domestic currency per unit of foreign exchange) that was above the rate applicable to trade in goods and services, the implicit subsidy to repatriation of capital would exactly offset the implicit tax on capital outflows, and the implicit subsidy to new inflows would be exactly offset by the tax on repayments to non-residents of principal and interest. In practice, actual exchange control systems tax capital flows by deviating from this hypothetical system of uniform rates in three main ways.

First, new outflows are often either restricted, or banned, or must be made at a higher price of foreign exchange than the rate that applies to new inflows. A system that is designed to restrict outflows by forcing residents who wish to invest abroad to buy the necessary foreign exchange at a high price, may allow the eventual repatriation of the original principal at the same premium exchange rate, as was usually the case under the Sterling Area controls on portfolio investment, but will not also allow a non-resident who wishes to finance a new capital inflow to buy domestic currency at the premium exchange rate. Similarly, a system designed to tax inflows will certainly not provide corresponding subsidies to outflows. Even repatriation of all the original principal may not be permitted at the premium rate. For example, after 1965, residents of the Sterling Area who sold dollar securities could only repatriate 75 per cent of the proceeds at the premium exchange rate, and had to sell the remaining 25 per cent at the lower official sterling price of foreign currency.[3]

Second, interest and dividend payments are usually not made at the same exchange rates that apply to inflows and outflows of principal: interest and dividend receipts from abroad must typically be surrendered at a rate below the rate that applies to new outflows, and interest payments abroad must typically be made at a rate in excess of that at which receipts of new inflows must be surrendered.

Third, the differences between capital account and current account exchange rates vary over time. In a crisis situation when outflow controls have just been tightened, the capital account premium will be abnormally high and investors are likely to expect that it will eventually fall. Such an anticipated reduction operates like a tax on outflows: because new offshore investments are expected to incur a capital loss due to the anticipated depreciation of the capital account premium, the domestic real interest rate can fall below the world real interest rate.

Why Controls Are Used

The two most important purposes of controls on capital flows are 'fiscal' and 'prudential'. The fiscal purpose is the most obvious, and often the most important: directly or indirectly, most controls on capital flows help to raise or conserve government revenue. The prudential purpose is interpreted broadly to mean anything designed to reduce the severity and frequency of financial and exchange rate crises. A third objective of some systems of capital controls is to boost the domestic capital stock, and thereby raise the demand for labour, by allowing inflows but restricting outflows. This objective is probably no longer very important because most countries have realised that in the long run, in which this kind of development strategy might be relevant, outflow controls can do more to discourage inflows than to reduce outflows.[4] One might cite a fourth purpose of capital controls: to conserve official foreign exchange reserves. However, this purpose is a hybrid of the fiscal and prudential purposes: by imposing capital controls, governments hope to be able to finance expenditure by running down official foreign exchange reserves for longer, without provoking a crisis, than if no controls are in place.

The fiscal purpose is most evident in the case of outflow controls: if successful, they reduce the burden of servicing government debt by allowing domestic real interest rates to be depressed below world real interest rates, they bolster other sources of government revenue and they allow governments to run down their foreign exchange holdings in crisis periods, without being forced to devalue. Because it is difficult to predict the quantitative effects of taxes on trade and capital flows, governments faced by acute shortages of foreign exchange at the official exchange rate – as a result of war, economic collapse or excessive use of inflationary finance – usually prefer licensing and quantitative controls to taxes. Outflow controls that prevent domestic residents substituting offshore or onshore holdings of foreign money for onshore holdings of domestic money add indirectly to the revenue that the government derives from being able to issue its own fiat money. Controls that stop residents substituting offshore investments for onshore ones raise the revenue from taxing the earnings of the capital owned by domestic residents, since it is much harder for a government to monitor and tax offshore income than onshore income. Dual exchange rate systems on either current or capital account contribute directly to government revenue since inflows of foreign exchange generally have to be surrendered to the authorities at a lower average price, in terms of domestic currency, than that paid by private sector purchasers of foreign exchange.

The importance of capital controls as a fiscal device for bolstering the revenue from money creation and for depressing the interest burden of government debt is demonstrated by the findings of Grilli and Milesi-Ferretti (1995). They construct a capital control variable for 61 industrialised and developing countries for the period 1960–89. This variable is defined to be one or zero depending on whether the country is classified by the relevant issue of the IMF's *Annual Report on Exchange Arrangements and Exchange Restrictions* as having, or not having, 'restrictions on payments for capital transactions'. They found that capital controls were relatively more likely to be adopted by countries with high ratios of government consumption to GDP; low ratios of imports and exports to GDP; central banks that lack independence; high current account deficits relative to GDP; low levels of per capita GDP; 'left-leaning' governments, and fixed exchange rates. However, only the first three of these effects were statistically significant in developing countries alone. In part, this lack of statistical significance may be due to the lack of variation among developing countries in the measure of capital controls used by Grilli and Milesi-Ferretti: their 'on–off' measure does not distinguish between mild and severe controls and only 11 out of the 40 developing countries in their sample in 1979 and only 6 out of 40 in 1989 did not apply some form of capital controls.

Grilli and Milesi-Ferretti (1995) also found that in the period 1966–89 inflation was relatively high and *ex post* real interest rates were relatively low in countries with capital controls and multiple exchange rates, after controlling for measures of central bank independence, political stability, the level of GDP, the openness of the country to international trade, the ratio of the government budget deficit to GDP and the exchange rate system (whether managed or flexible).

The findings that inflation is relatively rapid in countries with capital controls and that controls tend to be used by countries with fixed exchange rates are consistent with the view that one of their purposes is to prevent speculative attacks on currencies. This is clearly the rationale for controls that stop residents making domestic currency denominated loans to non-residents.

The main purpose of inflow controls is prudential, in the broad sense of the term used here: they are intended to moderate spending booms – and the real exchange rate appreciation that they cause – and to prevent both financial and non-financial enterprises from building up foreign debts that the authorities judge to be excessive. In good times, when the authorities may wish to slow down the rate of capital inflow, they usually allow exchange controls to lie dormant and use VDRs. In crisis situations, new capital inflows are likely to be very small and governments are glad to get whatever inflows are available. VDRs are therefore relaxed in such periods.

Common Patterns in Asian Controls on Foreign Exchange Markets

The types of exchange controls that countries use determine the types of off-shore deposit and forward foreign exchange markets that emerge. This is illustrated by the patterns observed in the Asia-Pacific region, as summarised by the following lists:

- list A: Australia, Hong Kong, Japan and New Zealand;
- list B: Indonesia, Malaysia (before September 1998), Singapore and Thailand;
- list C: China, India, Korea, Philippines and Taiwan;
- list D: Bangladesh, Laos, Malaysia (after September 1998), Pakistan, Sri Lanka and Vietnam.

Banks in offshore financial centres accept deposits in the currencies of the countries on lists A and B, but do not accept significant amounts of deposits in the currencies of the countries on lists C and D. The same country groupings characterise the arrangements of the offshore forward foreign exchange markets: the offshore and onshore forward markets for the currencies of the countries on lists A and B are 'delivery forward' (DF) markets; in contrast, for countries on list C the offshore forward markets are 'non-delivery forward' (NDF) markets, while the onshore forward markets are mainly DF markets, although in Taiwan there is both an onshore DF market and an onshore NDF market. The distinction between DF and NDF contracts is explained below.

Both DF and NDF contracts for US dollars (for example) specify a local currency price per US dollar at a specified future date. Under a DF contract, the buyer of the US dollars is contracted to deliver the specified amount of local currency and the seller is contracted to deliver the specified amount of US dollars.

In contrast, under an NDF contract, these specified amounts will be netted out, using the spot exchange rate in some specified market at the time the contract matures; in offshore NDF markets, the net amount is then settled in US dollars. When dealers in offshore financial centres like Singapore and Hong Kong can get ready access to a currency, the forward market in that currency will be a DF market, because DF contracts are generally more convenient than NDF contracts, which must specify exactly how the settlement exchange rate is to be calculated. These settlement rates may contain substantial amounts of 'noise'; in addition, a DF contract can always be settled on a non-delivery basis if this suits both parties, as it often does. However, offshore DF markets are only possible if those contracting to deliver the local currency in the offshore centre are sure of having ready access to it. In practice, this condition is only fulfilled if offshore banks hold substantial amounts of deposits in the domestic currency. Since they must be able to meet withdrawals from such accounts, this condition in turn requires that they must be free to transfer funds to and from their local currency accounts with their corresponding onshore banks.

The currencies that are readily convertible on capital account are therefore those for which substantial offshore deposit markets exist and for which onshore and offshore forward foreign exchange markets are DF markets. These are the countries on lists A and B; the others are on lists C and D.

For countries on list D there is no real offshore forward market, either DF or NDF; however, occasional bilateral deals sometimes occur. An NDF market may fail to emerge either if there is little interest in one, or if – as in the case of Malaysia since September 1998 – despite there being plenty of interest, even offshore banks are reluctant to trade in such a market for fear that the country's central bank would take punitive actions against the onshore branches or subsidiaries of the same banking group.

At least for the countries on lists A, B and C, approximate covered interest parity usually holds onshore: the spread of the onshore domestic currency interest rate over the corresponding US dollar interest rate is usually roughly equal to the premium of the US dollar over the local currency in the onshore forward foreign exchange market.[5] However, substantial deviations from covered interest parity can occur. This happens partly because of transactions costs and the thinness of the markets, and partly because of the risk premia paid by onshore banks in some developing countries, even on US dollar deposits. For countries on lists A and B, a rough approximation to covered interest parity usually holds between offshore interest rates and offshore forward market premia, but because there are not deep interbank markets in baht or rupiah deposits, for example, in offshore financial centres, large deviations from covered interest parity in offshore markets can occur. For countries on list C – and all the more so for those on list D – the question of offshore covered interest parity does not arise: in the absence of significant offshore markets in domestic currency deposits, the offshore domestic currency interest rate can only be derived as the rate implied by adding the premium on the dollar in the offshore NDF market to the corresponding US dollar interest rate.

A second dichotomy exists between countries that restrict domestic currency lending by residents to non-residents and those that do not. The motive for this type of restriction is to hamper speculative attacks by non-residents on the domestic currency: in order to speculate against a weak currency that they generally do not hold in significant amounts, non-residents need to borrow the weak currency, which they can then sell to finance the acquisition of assets denominated in dollars, or some other relatively strong currency. The countries on list A allow residents to lend freely to non-residents in domestic currency, but those on lists B, C and D generally prohibit residents from directly lending to non-residents in local currency. However, unless there are also effective restrictions on indirect lending in the forward and swap markets for foreign exchange, these markets can be used to circumvent restrictions on direct lending. For example, since April 1999, Korean banks have been able to make indirect offshore won loans by using won to buy dollars in the spot market, lending the dollars offshore and selling the future dollar proceeds from these loans for won in the offshore NDF market. The overall effect is exactly like making offshore loans in won: while the dollar transactions net out in both periods, the Korean bank gives up won in the current period and receives won in the future.[6]

Indirect local currency lending to non-residents can also be done through the swap market: rather than using the forward market, as in the previous example, Korean banks could instead make indirect won loans to non-residents by 'swapping' won for dollars in the offshore swap market and then lending the dollar proceeds of the swap offshore. In the 'swap' contract, the two parties exchange amounts of the two currencies whose values are equal in the spot market and the party that delivers dollars in this initial swap simultaneously contracts to buy them back after a specified period at an exchange rate that exceeds the spot value of the dollar by the 'swap premium' for the dollar against the won.[7] The outcome in this example is exactly the same as in the previous one because swapping won for dollars (this example) is equivalent to buying dollars spot and selling them forward (as in the previous example).

Swap contracts do not directly affect either party's net open position in either currency, but they are used by speculators in conjunction with spot exchange market transactions to replenish their liquidity. For example, someone who wishes to speculate on a depreciation of the won can buy dollars in the spot foreign exchange market and swap them for won: the speculation comes in the spot market transaction rather than the swap. The first leg of the swap restores the speculator's initial liquidity in both won and dollars by reversing the spot market operation, while the repurchase agreement ensures that the dollars given up in the first leg can be bought back later at a guaranteed price.

Whenever onshore banks can trade freely in both the onshore and offshore swap or forward foreign exchange markets, the offshore interest rate implied by adding the offshore swap market premium to the US dollar interest rate will be roughly equal to the onshore domestic currency interest rate. On occasion, all the countries on lists B and C have restricted such trades by imposing quantitative restrictions, or bans, on the size of the open positions that onshore banks can take in the offshore forward and swap markets. In several cases, banks were allowed to engage in swap or forward trades with clients that were hedging current account, or approved capital account transactions, but not otherwise. However the tightness of the restrictions in each country has varied substantially over time. As noted above and discussed in more detail in section 3.3, Korea used to impose stringent controls on resident access to the offshore markets and on non-resident access to the onshore ones, but banks have been allowed to arbitrage these markets since April 1999. Indonesia, Korea, Malaysia and Thailand all tightened these restrictions at the onset of the Asian crisis.

Onshore and offshore interest rates on securities denominated in the same domestic currency can differ whenever effective restrictions apply not only to direct lending in the local currency by residents to non-residents, but also to indirect lending via the swap and forward foreign exchange markets. However, since the countries on lists B and C allow non-residents relatively free access to onshore money market instruments, such as certificates of deposit and commercial paper, offshore interest rates cannot be significantly below onshore rates. If they were, non-residents would borrow offshore in domestic currency and buy money market instruments onshore. But because non-residents cannot issue domestic money market instruments, onshore interest rates can be below the offshore yields implied by the premia on the US dollar in the offshore markets. When this happens there is a matching excess of the offshore swap premia on foreign exchange over the corresponding onshore premia.

The offshore–onshore differentials between interest rates, forward rates and swap market premia can be very large when a currency is under strong speculative pressure in offshore markets. In such circumstances, residents of the countries on list B have an incentive to switch their time deposits from onshore to offshore banks, and exporters have an incentive to retain export receipts in the form of offshore domestic currency deposits. However, provided that there are restrictions on the extent to which banks can arbitrage the onshore and offshore markets, large interest rate differentials can persist because of the costs to households and firms of transferring deposits between onshore and offshore accounts. The growth of offshore ringgit deposits that was induced by the excess of offshore ringgit interest rates over the onshore rates was one of the factors that induced Malaysia to tighten exchange controls in September 1998. This is discussed in more detail in section 3.2.

Figure 2.1 shows the spreads for China, Malaysia and Korea of offshore local currency one-year interest rates (that is, the rates implied by adding the swap market premia of the dollar over the local currency to dollar interest rates) over onshore local currency one-year interest rates. The series for Malaysia ends in August 1998 because the Malaysian exchange control tightening in September 1998 led to the closure of the offshore forward and swap markets in ringgits. In the absence of controls, onshore and offshore interest rates in the same currency would differ only because of default risks and transactions costs. The liberalisation of Korea's exchange controls in April 1999 removed the restriction on indirect lending in won by domestic banks to non-residents; since then, the spread between offshore and onshore won interest rates has been small. Even larger spreads have been observed on shorter maturity contracts: just before the 1997 devaluation of the baht, the annualised three-month offshore forward market premium for the dollar relative to the baht was about 50 per cent above the corresponding onshore premium.[8] Figure 3.1 in the next chapter shows that in late 1997, the annualised three-month forward premium for the dollar relative to the won was about 55 per cent above the corresponding onshore rate. On occasions, the gap between onshore and offshore rates for the rupiah were almost as large.[9]

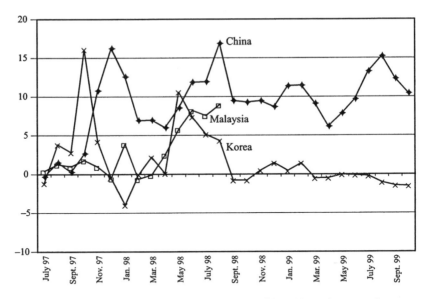

Notes: Offshore interest rates are derived by adding the offshore 12-month swap market premia of the dollar over the relevant currency to 12-month US dollar interest rate (LIBOR). These data were supplied by a private bank. The offshore swap market in Malaysian ringgits ceased operating in September 1998. Onshore interest rates are taken from the CEIC Asian database as follows: China: 12-month time deposits; Malaysia: 12-month fixed deposits; Korea: 12-month monetary stabilization bonds.

Figure 2.1   Spreads of offshore over onshore interest rates (percentage per annum)

The spreads shown in Figure 2.1 indicate the power of exchange controls to insulate domestic interest rates from offshore rates. However, this does not mean that in the absence of the restrictions, onshore rates would equal the offshore rates observed when the restrictions are in place. Since the offshore markets are often quite thin, the rates in a unified market might be much closer to the observed onshore rate than to the observed offshore rate.

2.2   A PORTFOLIO MODEL OF CAPITAL CONTROLS

The three most important capital controls used in Asian countries are restrictions on offshore investment by residents, on investments (or on repatriation of investments) in onshore stock and bond markets by non-residents, and on lending by residents to non-residents in domestic currency. Each of these controls can be analysed using a fairly simple model set out below.

The Workings of the Model

This model contains five markets and three agents. The agents are the domestic private sector, non-residents and 'the authorities', defined as the domestic government and central bank. The five markets are those for tradable goods in the current period, tradable goods in the future, bonds (interest-bearing-securities denominated in domestic currency), domestic equity shares (claims to given stocks of fixed capital, that yield tradable goods in the future at a stochastic rate) and non-interest-bearing domestic base money, which is held for its liquidity services.[10]

To simplify the model it is assumed that non-residents do not hold domestic money and that the government does not hold equity. The private sector holds some of each asset and its asset holdings are defined after consolidating the balance sheets of households, banks and other corporations.

A bond is a claim to one unit of domestic money next period. By definition its price today is $1/(1 + r)$, where r is the domestic interest rate. The sum of the net bond holdings by all three sectors must be zero, because one sector's financial assets are another sector's financial liabilities. The future purchasing power of money, which is a liability of the authorities and an asset of the private sector, is a stochastic variable. Even if the authorities state that the exchange rate and hence the purchasing power of money will remain fixed, this promise may not be entirely credible. The various agents may have different subjective estimates of the probability of devaluation, or revaluation, of any particular amount, but these estimates are all exogenous to the model. Domestic bonds and foreign exchange are therefore not perfect substitutes. The opening stocks of money and bonds are given exogenously by past decisions.

The balance sheets below show the assets and liabilities of the three sectors.

Assets of the authorities	*Liabilities of the authorities*
Official reserves of net foreign currency assets	Net wealth
Domestic currency-denominated securities	Base money (that is, domestic currency plus commercial banks' deposits at the central bank)
Assets of the domestic private sector	*Liabilities of the domestic private sector*
Net foreign currency assets	Net wealth
Domestic currency-denominated securities	
Base money	
Domestic shares	
Assets of non-residents	*Liabilities of non-residents*
Stock of tradable goods and other physical assets located abroad, minus the net foreign currency assets of the domestic authorities and private sector	Net wealth
Domestic currency-denominated securities	
Domestic shares	

The initial proportions in which the stock of domestic capital is divided between the private sector and non-residents are predetermined, but these proportions can be varied by the asset trading on which the model focuses. The share price, q, in units of domestic currency per unit of physical capital is one of the key endogenous variables.[11]

While the model set out here has been made static for simplicity, the price changes that it predicts indicate the resource movements that would occur in a more complete inter-temporal model. In such a model, an increase in q would tend to increase domestic investment by switching resources away from the production of tradable goods towards the production of non-tradable domestic capital. The reduced yield on shares due to a rise in q would also tend to reduce domestic savings and raise consumption. Other things equal, all these effects would increase an initial current account deficit, or reduce an initial current account surplus.

Since the world economy is large compared to the domestic economy, the world real interest rate is assumed to be exogenous at r^*. The foreign currency is the dollar and the price of the tradable good is assumed to be one dollar per unit in both the present period and the future period. Purchasing power parity makes the current exchange rate in domestic currency per dollar, denoted e, identical to the current domestic price of the traded good. Similarly, the future exchange rate will be equal to the future domestic price of the traded good. Because the foreign price level and world interest rate are both assumed to be exogenous, the five markets listed above can be aggregated into four: foreign exchange (which includes current and future tradable goods, whose foreign currency prices are exogenous), bonds, shares and money. With domestic money as numeraire, equilibrium in these four markets determines three relative prices: the price of shares, q, the current price of foreign exchange, e, and the price of domestic bonds, $1/(1 + r)$.

The model can be used to analyse either fixed or flexible exchange rate regimes. In the version below, the authorities are assumed to accommodate any excess supply or demand for foreign exchange in the current period at a fixed exchange rate. The conditions for equilibrium in the equity, bond and money markets are illustrated in Figure 2.2. Since the fixed exchange rate policy ensures that there is never a disequilibrium in the foreign exchange market, it follows that equilibrium in any two of the three markets represented in Figure 2.2 ensures equilibrium in the third.[12] The conditions for equilibrium in these markets determine the price of shares, q, and the domestic interest rate, r.

The domestic nominal interest rate, r, is on the vertical axis of Figure 2.2 and the price of domestic shares, q, is on the horizontal axis. The ES curve shows the combinations of these two variables that are compatible with equilibrium in the share market. The ES curve is downward-sloping because the supply of capital is fixed and the demand for it depends positively on the return that it yields, which is proportional to $1/q$, and negatively on the return to holding bonds. The LM curve shows the combinations of q and r that are compatible

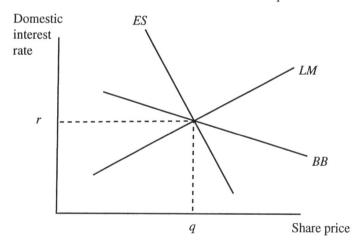

Figure 2.2   Portfolio equilibrium without capital controls

with money market equilibrium when the money supply is exogenously given. Moving away from the origin along the LM curve, the yield on bonds rises and the yield on shares falls by enough to leave the demand for money unchanged. The BB curve shows the combinations of q and r at which the total net bond liabilities of non-residents and the private sector are equal to some exogenously given net holdings of bonds by the authorities. Given that the demand for bonds depends positively on the return on bonds and negatively on the return on shares, the BB curve is downward-sloping, but it must be flatter than the ES curve.[13]

The monetary authorities' holdings of domestic currency bonds are referred to as 'domestic credit'. The balance sheet set out above for 'the authorities' combines the 'monetary authorities', which might be a central bank or a currency board, with the central government; but since the division of assets and liabilities between the central government and the central bank is largely arbitrary, domestic credit in this model corresponds to the authorities' holdings of domestic currency bonds, and 'net domestic credit' (NDC) is domestic credit minus the authorities' net wealth. The balance sheet identity for the authorities therefore demonstrates that base money is equal to the sum of NDC and official foreign currency reserves – often referred to as 'net foreign assets' (NFA).

To keep the exchange rate fixed, the authorities must allow their foreign exchange holdings to vary passively to accommodate changes in supply and demand for foreign exchange by the other two sectors. Therefore they cannot independently fix both the money supply and NDC. Under a currency board system, domestic credit would be exogenous and the model could be most conveniently analysed by focusing on equilibria in the bond and share markets. However, most central banks that operate fixed or managed exchange rate systems vary NDC to sterilise at least part of the effects of balance of payments surpluses or deficits on the supply of base money. Under complete sterilisation, the supply of base money is exogenous and it is convenient to focus on equilibrium in the money market and the share market.

Since domestic consumption and investment decisions are treated as being predetermined, the current account surplus is exogenous and changes in the capital account surplus are equal to changes in the overall surplus of the balance of payments, which is equal to the authorities' net acquisition of foreign exchange reserves. This in turn is equal to non-residents' net acquisition of domestic bonds and shares, minus the private sector's net acquisition of foreign exchange.[14]

In analysing capital controls, it is important to know the relative magnitudes of the elasticities of the demands for shares and bonds of non-residents and the domestic private sector with respect to changes in domestic interest rates and share prices. It is assumed below that non-resident demand for domestic bonds depends only on the domestic and world interest rates, and that non-resident demand for domestic shares depends only on the domestic share price and the world interest rate. These simplifying assumptions are clearly too extreme: presumably there are some cross price effects between non-resident demands for domestic shares and bonds. However, these assumptions greatly simplify the analysis and probably give the correct qualitative effects, since non-resident investors often specialise in different domestic markets.

Changes in the World Interest Rate

For any given setting of the various possible capital controls, a rise in the world interest rate will reduce the demand for shares and therefore shift the ES schedule to the left. It may slightly reduce the demand for money, and therefore shift the LM curve to the right. Except perhaps in economies, such as Hong Kong and Argentina, in which there is strong currency substitutability between foreign exchange and domestic money, money is presumably a closer substitute for domestic bonds than for foreign exchange. To simplify the model, this feature can be exaggerated by assuming that the demand for money does not directly depend on the world interest rate. In this case, a rise in the world interest rate does not affect the position of the LM curve if the authorities sterilise the effects of the balance of payments on the money supply. The domestic interest rate therefore falls, while share prices rise. As a result there is a capital outflow as both non-residents and the private sector switch from bonds and shares to foreign exchange.

The somewhat surprising result that the domestic interest rate moves in the opposite direction to the world interest rate is entirely attributable to the assumption that the authorities completely sterilise the monetary effects of net capital flows. Because there is a net capital outflow, the authorities must expand NDC to keep the money supply constant. If, instead of sterilising the monetary effects of net capital flows, the authorities adopt the currency board rule of holding NDC constant and allowing the money supply to change by the same amount as foreign exchange reserves, the effect of a rise in world interest rates would be to raise domestic interest rates.[15] In practice, central banks almost invariably sterilise most, but usually not quite all, of the monetary effects of capital flows; partial sterilisation also occurs even in countries which nominally operate currency board systems, but to a much smaller extent than in countries with central banks.[16]

Regardless of whether the authorities hold NDC constant, or hold the money supply constant, a rise in world interest rates reduces q and causes a net capital outflow. A fall in q implies a depreciation of the real exchange rate.[17] The conjunction of a capital outflow with a real depreciation in response to an external exogenous shock is a standard prediction of most models of the balance of payments.

Monetary Policy

An increase in the money supply with the world interest rate held constant shifts the LM curve to the right, without affecting the ES curve. In response to the rise in share prices and the fall in domestic interest rates, non-residents will reduce their holdings of both shares and bonds. In addition, the private sector will increase its holdings of foreign exchange. All these portfolio reallocations will contribute to a net capital outflow. The authorities' holdings of foreign exchange reserves will therefore be unambiguously reduced.

In contrast to the case in which the exogenous cause of the capital outflow is a rise in world interest rates, a capital outflow caused by a domestic monetary expansion will therefore be associated with an appreciation of the real exchange rate. If this result seems surprising, it is because it is often implicitly assumed that changes in capital flows are caused by changes in the world supply of capital rather than by changes in domestic monetary policy. The fact that monetary expansion causes a capital outflow is very well known; the fact that with a fixed exchange rate it also causes real appreciation is just the obverse of the fact that depreciation of the nominal exchange rate, combined with a contraction of NDC, is at least a temporary way of artificially boosting the competitiveness of the tradable goods sectors.

Capital Account Convertibility

Under the restrictive assumption that both bonds and shares are perfect substitutes for foreign assets, the domestic interest rate would have to equal the world interest rate plus the expected rate of depreciation of the domestic currency, and the price of shares would have to be such that the expected real return on shares was also equal to the world real interest rate. The BB curve would be horizontal at the world interest rate and the ES curve would be vertical at the share price which made the return on shares equal to the world interest rate. Unless they imposed capital controls, the authorities would have to allow the money supply to adjust passively to whatever amount was demanded by the private sector when the returns on domestic assets were equal to the world interest rate. If the authorities varied NDC, their own foreign exchange reserves would change by an equal and opposite amount, leaving the money supply unaffected. To regain control of the money supply, the authorities would have to restrict all forms of capital account convertibility. In particular, they would have to:

1. ration the private sector's holdings of foreign exchange;
2. ration the holdings of domestic shares by non-residents;
3. ration the holdings of domestic bonds by non-residents.

Since non-residents who wish to buy or sell domestic shares or bonds need to be able make payments into and out of onshore bank accounts denominated in domestic currency, the authorities can implement restrictions (2) and (3) by restricting convertibility of non-resident accounts for capital account transactions. Restriction (1) can be implemented by limiting the right of residents to transfer funds to offshore banks for capital account transactions.

In practice, domestic bonds and shares are not perfect substitutes for foreign exchange and the authorities can influence domestic interest rates, share prices and the money supply, while allowing partial convertibility on capital account. The next three subsections analyse the effects of imposing each of the three partial restrictions on capital account convertibility listed in the preceding paragraph.

Restrictions on the Access of Residents to Offshore Asset Markets

The effects of restricting the access of residents to offshore share markets and bond markets are very similar to those of a fall in the world interest rate. Suppose that the restriction takes the form of fixing the aggregate private sector holdings of foreign shares and bonds at some historical level below the one that would otherwise be chosen under current conditions. Such a restriction could be administered, as in the Sterling Area case described in the previous section, by requiring residents who wish to buy foreign securities to buy the necessary foreign exchange only from residents who wish to sell foreign securities.

Let e denote the exchange rate (domestic price of foreign currency) for current account transactions and e' the rate for capital account transactions. If interest and dividend receipts have to be converted at the current account exchange rate, the rate of return on offshore assets bought by the domestic private sector is $er*/e'$, which is less than $r*$ if the restriction on resident access to offshore markets is binding. The higher the premium of the capital account exchange rate, $(e' - e)/e$, the less the demand by residents for offshore assets and the further to the right will be the ES curve. A sufficiently high premium would reduce resident demand for offshore assets by enough to match any reduction in offshore asset holdings that the authorities might impose.

If the authorities hold the money supply constant, the rightward shift in the ES curve due to restricting the access of residents to offshore markets would raise domestic interest rates and share prices. Regardless of whether the authorities control NDC or the money supply, a restriction on resident access to offshore markets would reduce the capital account deficit.[18]

In the above analysis, as in the case of the Sterling Area restrictions on access to dollar assets, the relative prices to residents of all foreign securities remain equal to their relative prices in offshore markets, even though the capital account exchange rate is not equal to the current account rate. In contrast, many developing countries not only prevent residents buying offshore assets, but also restrict trading among residents in the offshore assets that they already own. The effect of this is to create 'shadow' exchange rate premia – that is, the actual premia at which residents would freely choose the portfolios of foreign assets that they are forced to hold – that may differ for each resident and for each asset.

The important difference between a fall in the world interest rate and a restriction on the access of domestic residents to offshore markets is that the former does not directly affect portfolio diversification, whereas the latter clearly inhibits it. For example, if domestic share prices rise because world interest rates fall, there is no clear presumption whether the private sector will sell domestic shares to non-residents, or buy domestic shares from them; whereas, if domestic share prices rise because the domestic private sector is barred from holding offshore assets at an unchanged world interest rate, there is a clear presumption that the holdings of domestic shares by non-residents will fall, as will the holdings of foreign shares by domestic residents.

The present very simplified model treats all offshore markets as perfect substitutes. In a more sophisticated model that distinguished between offshore money markets, share markets and bond markets, it would be possible to contrast the effects of restricting the access of domestic residents to each offshore market. On the plausible assumption that offshore shares are a relatively close substitute for domestic shares, while offshore bonds are a relatively close substitute for domestic bonds, the main impact of restricting the access of the private sector to offshore share markets would be to boost domestic share prices and induce residents to buy domestic shares from non-residents. Similarly, restricting the private sector's access to offshore bond markets would lead to lower domestic interest rates and induce residents to buy domestic bonds from non-residents.

Restrictions on Non-resident Access to (or Exit from) the Domestic Share Market

Forcing non-residents to hold less shares than they would freely choose shifts the ES curve to the left. Forcing them to hold more shifts it to the right. Given the earlier assumption that non-resident demand for equity does not depend on the domestic interest rate, or is at least relatively insensitive to it, preventing non-residents buying or selling shares makes the ES curve flatter by rotating it in an anticlockwise direction about the point at which non-residents would freely choose to hold the quantity of shares that the regulation forces them to hold. This rotation can be explained by reference to Figure 2.3 which adds an additional quadrant to Figure 2.2. In the new quadrant, non-resident demand for shares is measured vertically downwards as a function of the share price facing non-residents, which is on the horizontal axis. Let $V^N(q/e)$ be non-resident demand for domestic shares as a function of their foreign currency price, q/e. Suppose that starting from an initial equilibrium at A, in which non-residents freely choose to hold an amount of shares equal to $V^N(q_A/e)$, the authorities prevent non-residents from reducing their shareholdings. The new ES curve will coincide with the original schedule, ES_A, in the region above and to the left of A, but will rotate to ES_B in the region below and to the right of A. In this region, the total demand for shares is artificially boosted by the fact that non-residents cannot reduce their shareholdings.

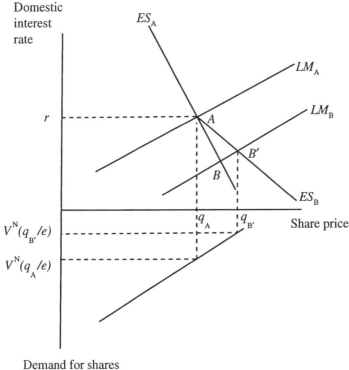

Figure 2.3   Portfolio equilibrium when non-residents are prevented from selling their domestic shares

Now suppose that, with non-residents prevented from reducing their equity holdings below $V^N(q_A/e)$, the authorities expand the money supply, thus shifting the LM curve from LM_A to LM_B. In the absence of the capital control, the new equilibrium would be at B and non-residents would sell shares to residents and repatriate capital by selling the domestic currency proceeds of their share sales to the authorities for foreign exchange at the official rate. However, when non-residents are not allowed to reduce their aggregate shareholdings, the ES schedule rotates from ES_A to ES_B and the new equilibrium is therefore at B'. Share prices rise from q_A to $q_{B'}$.

A given monetary expansion will therefore lower interest rates by less, and raise share prices by more, if non-residents cannot buy or sell shares than if they can trade freely. The increase in NDC, and therefore the reduction in the authorities' foreign exchange reserves needed to achieve a given monetary expansion, will also be smaller if non-residents are prevented from selling their shares.[19]

Define e^* as the shadow exchange rate at which non-residents would freely choose to hold the quantity of shares that they actually hold in situation B', when the share price is $q_{B'}$. By assumption, this is the quantity that they freely held in situation A, when the foreign currency price of shares was q_A/e. To make the foreign currency shadow price of shares in situation B' equal to the actual foreign currency price of shares in A, e^* must satisfy: $q_{B'}/e^* = q_A/e$. Since $q_{B'}$ exceeds q_A, it follows that e^* exceeds e. If non-residents are allowed to trade shares freely with residents in domestic currency, and to trade domestic currency for foreign exchange among each other, so that some non-residents can repatriate their capital by selling the domestic currency to other non-residents who are willing to buy into the domestic share market, an open dual exchange rate system will emerge in which the price of domestic currency will be only 1/e^* units of foreign currency. Of course, such a dual exchange rate system will not emerge openly if such trades are illegal.

Taiwan still restricts foreign access to its domestic share market by limiting the proportion of the shares of any single domestically registered company that can be owned by non-residents and this type of restriction was also used by Indonesia and Korea until the start of the Asian crisis caused them to welcome all capital inflows. When the proportion of a particular company's shares owned by non-residents reached the allowed ceiling, non-residents who wished to buy its shares could only make purchases from a 'foreign board' on which only other non-residents were permitted to sell its shares. When the ceiling was binding, foreign board prices rose above the regular prices at which residents transacted among each other.

If, instead of applying to each stock individually, a ceiling were set on the foreign ownership proportion of all listed stocks, there would be a uniform premium for all stocks of the foreign price over the domestic price. The simplest way of administering such a system would be to allow non-residents to trade freely with residents on the stock market, but require them to buy and sell the resulting local currency on a special exchange market for stock market transactions. The domestic currency would be at a premium on this market, just as dollars for foreign portfolio investment were at a premium over dollars for current account transactions in the Sterling Area system, described above. This is because it makes no difference to market outcomes whether the access of the residents of one country to the stock market of another is restricted by their own government (as in the Sterling Area example) or by the government of the country in which they wish to invest (as in recent Asian examples, described in Chapter 3).

Restrictions on Non-resident Access to the Domestic Bond Market and on Domestic Currency Lending by Residents to Non-residents

The effect of offshore speculative pressure on the domestic currency can be analysed using Figure 2.4. The left panel shows non-resident demand for domestic currency borrowing, measured horizontally to the left from the origin, as a function of the offshore domestic currency interest rate. The initial demand schedule of non-residents for domestic currency loans is D_A. If non-resident speculators come to believe that a devaluation of the domestic currency is more likely than they originally thought, they will try to borrow in domestic currency to finance the acquisition of foreign currency assets and their demand for loans will shift out to D_B. If expectations of the real earnings of capital are unchanged the ES curve will be unaffected, and if residents do not change their estimates of the probability of devaluation the demand for money will not be affected.

Under a currency board system, with NDC held constant, the BB curve will shift outwards from BB_A to BB_B, interest rates will rise, the demand for money will fall, and so will share prices. The new equilibrium will be at B. The fall in the demand for money will exactly equal the capital outflow. This is a stylised approximation to Hong Kong's experience in October 1997, which is described in more detail in section 8.3.

Under a pegged exchange rate system in which the central bank sterilises the effects of the capital flow on the money supply, neither the LM curve nor the ES curve would shift; therefore the BB curve could not shift either. The authorities would have to accommodate the reduced net demand for domestic currency securities by non-residents by expanding NDC. This would lead to a

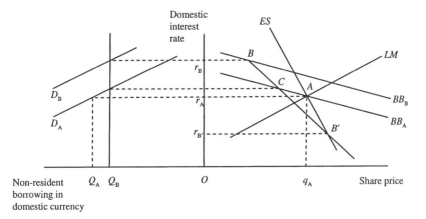

Figure 2.4   *Portfolio equilibrium when there is a quota on domestic currency lending by residents to non-residents*

larger capital outflow, and therefore a larger fall in official reserves, than under the currency board system.[20] If the authorities expanded NDC by supporting the currency in the swap and forward market, and if swap liabilities were excluded from reported official reserves, the authorities could disguise the extent to which they had run down true foreign exchange reserves.

To try to minimise the effects of the kind of speculation described above on the central bank's foreign exchange reserves and domestic interest rates, some governments place restrictions on lending by residents to non-residents in domestic currency. Such restrictions may generate differences between onshore and offshore domestic currency interest rates; but, as explained in the last subsection of section 2.1, whether they actually do so or not depends on whether they are supplemented by controls on indirect lending in local currencies via the swap and forward markets. Restrictions on such indirect lending can be implemented by prohibiting residents from trading in offshore swap and forward markets, and by prohibiting non-residents from trading in the corresponding onshore markets. A less severe form of this control merely limits the size of the net open positions that residents can take in these markets. For example, while non-residents may be banned from the onshore swap and forward markets, and non-bank residents may be banned from trading in the offshore markets, a quota may be set on the size of the open swap and forward positions that onshore banks may take in the offshore markets. In this case, the maximum total direct and indirect lending by residents to non-residents in local currency is whatever amount of the direct lending may be permitted, plus the amount of indirect lending permitted by the quota on the provision of swaps by onshore banks.

The effect of imposing a quantitative limit on lending to non-residents in domestic currency is represented in Figure 2.4. Suppose that the authorities respond to the speculation against the domestic currency by banning direct lending and imposing a quantitative limit on indirect lending via the swap and forward markets, and that the resulting limit on total domestic currency lending to non-residents is OQ_B, which is less than the initial quantity lent, OQ_A. At interest rates above r_B, the constraint is non-binding because, as indicated in the left panel, at such high rates non-resident demand for loans is less than OQ_B, even after the increased expectations of devaluation have shifted the demand curve from D_A to D_B. Therefore, if the authorities hold NDC constant, the new BB curve will coincide with the unconstrained BB_B curve in the region above and to the left of B. However, at lower interest rates, the new curve will lie inside BB_B and at point C the new curve will intersect the original BB_A curve, because at this interest rate the amount that non-residents are allowed to borrow is equal to what they would have chosen to borrow before their expectations of devaluation increased.

If the authorities hold NDC fixed, the new equilibrium will be at B'. The onshore domestic currency interest rate will be $r_{B'}$, whereas the offshore domestic currency interest rate will be r_B. With NDC held constant, there is a one-to-one correspondence between changes in the demand for money and changes in official foreign exchange reserves; the fall in the onshore interest rate from r_A to $r_{B'}$ will expand the demand for money and raise reserves, whereas, in the absence of the restriction on lending offshore, the interest rate would have risen and the demand for money and reserves would both have fallen. If the authorities completely sterilise the monetary effects of capital flows, the equilibrium would remain at point A in Figure 2.4, regardless of whether offshore lending is restricted or not. But whereas in the absence of the restriction the authorities would have had to expand NDC, and therefore deplete their official foreign exchange reserves, the restriction allows them to contract NDC and raise reserves.[21]

2.3 OVERVIEW

Restrictions on capital inflows tend to raise domestic interest rates, and would certainly do so if they were accompanied by subsidies to outflows. Similarly, restrictions on outflows tend to lower domestic interest rates, and would certainly do so if they were accompanied by subsidies to inflows. In practice, inflows and outflows are seldom, if ever, subsidised and may both be restricted. If both inflows and outflows are restricted, the effect is to depress the prices of domestic assets faced by domestic residents, and raise those faced by non-residents; at the same time, the prices of foreign assets faced by domestic residents are increased. The result is a reduction in portfolio diversification.

Outflow restrictions help to bolster government revenue from taxing the earnings of domestically owned capital and from printing money; they also reduce the interest rate on government debt and help check speculation against the domestic currency. In countries in which outflow controls play an important fiscal role, governments try to requisition foreign exchange for their own use, or for 'essential purposes', such as the provision of rationed amounts of certain subsidised foodstuffs, fuels, fertilisers and other inputs. Because foreign exchange transactions are relatively easy to monitor and regulate, exchange controls are widely used in administering systems of quantitative restrictions on both trade and investment. Inflow restrictions are used mainly as a prudential device to moderate the excessive borrowing from abroad that can occur if governments provide safety nets for banks and favoured large corporations.

Under a system of multiple exchange rates and all-embracing exchange controls, the authorities try to close off the routes by which the different rates might be arbitraged by private traders. To do this, non-resident holdings of domestic currency deposits are banned, or at least tightly controlled, and the same is true for resident holdings of foreign currency deposits. The object is to give the central bank a monopoly on national holdings of foreign exchange and prevent residents and non-residents from trading with each other, except through the intermediation of the central bank. To achieve this monopoly middleman position, the authorities must not only impose the necessary restrictions on currency holdings for residents and non-residents, but must also require exporters and borrowers from abroad to be registered and to surrender their foreign exchange receipts within some specified brief time period. Restrictions are also placed on the rights of residents to remit or receive direct payments in foreign currencies, or to hold offshore assets. With such controls in place, the central bank can specify the various rates that it pays for foreign exchange in accordance with the way in which it was generated – for example, by borrowing from a foreign bank, as the result of an FDI project, or by exporting goods of particular types. Similarly, the central bank can set the price that each buyer of foreign exchange is obliged to pay, in accordance with the purpose for which it is to be used.

When countries liberalise their exchange and capital control systems, the all-embracing controls outlined above are usually relaxed bit by bit. Inflow controls are often relaxed first, by licensing inward FDI; subsequently, non-residents may be permitted limited access to the domestic share and bond markets. Sudden surges of portfolio inflows are often restricted by imposing VDRs. Even when other types of outflow are permitted, restrictions are often placed on lending by residents to non-residents in domestic currency. The object of these restrictions is to insulate official reserves and onshore interest rates from the effects of offshore speculation. The time series data in Figure 2.1 confirm that these controls can sometimes generate large differences between onshore and offshore domestic currency interest rates. Of course, this does not imply that in the absence of the restriction on offshore lending in domestic currency, the onshore rate would be equal to the offshore rate observed when the restriction is in place: removing the restriction would lead to an equalisation of the rates somewhere between the two rates observed when it is in place. Since offshore markets are often quite thin, it is probable that the unified rate would often be closer to the onshore rate than the offshore one.

In a crisis, outflows may be restricted by preventing non-residents from reducing their holdings of domestic assets and by preventing residents from buying offshore assets.

Section 2.2 set out a portfolio choice model which was used to analyse the effects on share prices, interest rates and aggregate capital flows of the most important of the policies discussed in section 2.1: restrictions on the freedom of residents to invest offshore, restrictions on non-residents' freedom to enter or leave the domestic share market and restrictions on lending by residents to non-residents in domestic currency.

NOTES

1. The fifth edition of the IMF's *Balance of Payments Manual*, IMF (1993), distinguishes between 'the capital account', which technically now refers only to relatively minor capital transfers, and the 'financial account', which now covers almost everything that previously used to be in the 'capital account'. To conform with these new definitions, what used to be called 'capital flows' would have to be called 'financial flows'. Instead, the present study follows the almost universal practice of using 'capital account' to mean what it always used to mean, that is the sum of what the IMF now calls the 'capital account' and the 'financial account'. Correspondingly, the term 'capital flows' is also used in its traditional sense.

2. Germany and Switzerland used VDRs to try to resist importing inflation from the other industrialised countries under the Bretton Woods fixed exchange rate system. Australia imposed a VDR on capital inflows in the period 1972–83. Many developing countries have also used VDRs. Between April and December 1974, Indonesia imposed a 30 per cent VDR on foreign borrowing by private firms, other than foreign direct investment projects, trade credits and loans for more than 15 years (Arndt, 1974; Bank Indonesia, 1975, pp. 1–2). In the 1990s, VDRs were used by Colombia and Chile. As of October 1999, the framework for operating a VDR is in place in Korea, but the rate is currently zero.

3. Cairncross (1973, p. 60).

4. Evidence that liberalising outflows induces inflows is presented by Bartolini and Drazen (1997) and Labán and Larraín (1997).

5. Suppose that an arbitrageur contracts on 1 January to sell $1 on 31 December at the one-year forward exchange rate of f won/dollar. If he borrows $e/(1 + r_s)$ won on 1 January, where e is the spot exchange rate and r_s is the one-year interest rate on dollar-denominated securities, sells this amount in the spot foreign exchange market on 1 January for $1/(1 + r_s)$ and invests this sum in a dollar-denominated security, he can be sure of having the dollar that must be delivered on 31 December to fulfil the forward contract. On 31 December, the arbitrageur's dollar receipts and payments exactly cancel out; he receives f won from the forward contract, and must repay $e(1 + r_w)/(1 + r_s)$, where r_w is the one-year won interest rate. The condition that such arbitrage round trips just break even is: $f/e = (1 + r_w)/(1 + r_s)$. This is the covered interest parity condition. Provided that both interest rates are small, the won interest rate is approximately equal to $r_s + (f - e)/e$.

6. The covered interest parity condition set out in note 5 can be written as: $1 + r_w = (1 + r_s)f/e$. Won lending (on the left side of this equation), can therefore be replicated (on the right side) by dollar lending, the forward sale of dollars and the spot purchase of dollars.

7. Let the one-year swap premium on dollars be ψ, so that when $1 is swapped for e won on 1 January, the parties contract to reverse the swap at the exchange rate $e(1 + \psi)$ won per dollar on 31 December. If the person that swapped the dollar for e won on 1 January uses the won proceeds of the swap to buy a dollar on 1 January, she ends up with the same won and dollar holdings at the end of 1 January as she had at the beginning of 1 January, but must pay out $e(1 + \psi)$ won to receive $1 in return on 31 December. This is equivalent to a contract written on 1 January to purchase $1 for $e(1 + \psi)$ won on 31 December. To eliminate arbitrage opportunities, it must be the case that $e(1 + \psi) = f$. Using the covered interest parity condition of note 5 now gives: $1 + \psi = (1 + r_w)/(1 + r_s)$, that is, the swap premium must equal the excess, adjusted for compounding, of the won interest rate over the dollar interest rate: $\psi = (r_w - r_s)/(1 + r_s)$.

8. According to data provided by a private bank, the onshore interbank baht three-month interest rate on 18 June 1997 was 14.8 per cent, while the offshore annualised yield on baht implied by combining the premium on three-month forward contracts with LIBOR was 69.8 per cent.

9. On 22 August 1997 the one-month onshore interbank interest rate and the implied offshore annualised one-month yield on the rupiah were 56.9 per cent and 95.8 per cent, respectively. On 10 February 1998, these rates were 36.3 per cent and 75.3 per cent, respectively. The rupiah rates were very variable in 1997–99 and the offshore implied yields were frequently below the onshore interbank interest rates, and occasionally by large amounts. The source for these data is the bank referred to in the previous note.

10.   'Base money' – which is sometimes also called 'reserve money', or 'the monetary base' – is defined as the domestic currency-denominated monetary liabilities of the central bank. These liabilities comprise notes and coins and the deposits of financial institutions at the central bank.

11.   With the exchange rate fixed, q measures the price of non-tradable domestic capital relative to the price of tradable goods. It is an inverse proxy for the 'real exchange rate', which is defined in Chapter 4. An increase in q therefore represents a real appreciation.

12.   The proposition in the main text is a version of Walras's law. The proof is by reduction to absurdity: suppose, in opposition to this proposition, that there is excess demand in just one market, say the market for bonds, and that the other three markets are in equilibrium. What are those who want to add to their bond holdings planning to sell in order to pay for their net bond purchases? They cannot, in aggregate, be planning to reduce their holdings of money, equities or foreign exchange, because if all agents were planning to do this, there would be excess supply in the corresponding market. Therefore, if agents have plans that are consistent with their aggregate balance sheet constraints, the assumption of excess demand in one market alone leads to a contradiction.

13.   In the region vertically above the LM curve there is excess supply of money and shares are in excess supply in the region vertically above the ES curve. This is because a rise in the interest rate is assumed to cause a substitution from both money and shares to bonds. Since equilibrium in two of the three markets implies equilibrium in the third, the BB curve must pass through the point at which the LM and ES curves intersect. If its absolute gradient exceeded that of the ES curve, points on the BB curve would represent points at which the bond market is in equilibrium and either there is excess demand in both the other markets, or there is excess supply in both the other markets. As explained in note 12, such situations of aggregate excess demand, or aggregate excess supply, are inconsistent with the assumption that agents' planned portfolio decisions are consistent with their balance sheets.

14.   To see why, first consolidate the balance sheets of the authorities and the domestic private sector to obtain a balance sheet for all residents which states that their given net wealth is equal to their holdings of foreign currency, shares and domestic bonds. The increases in the foreign currency holdings of the authorities and of the private sector must therefore equal the reductions in their holdings of shares and domestic bonds, which in turn must equal the increases in non-residents' holdings of shares and domestic bonds.

15.   If the authorities' supply of domestic credit is held constant, the net bond holdings of the private sector and non-residents must also stay constant. Therefore the BB curve must shift upwards: at each value of q, r must increase by enough to offset the reduction in the demand for domestic bonds due to the rise in r^*. The main text has explained why a rise in r^* shifts the ES curve to the left. Given the relative gradients of the ES and BB curves, the domestic interest rate is increased both by a leftward shift in the ES curve and by an upward shift in the BB curve.

16.   Table 7.1 presents information on the extent to which a sample of developing countries with central banks and currency boards have engaged in sterilisation.

17.   See note 11.

18.   With money demand and base money held constant, the LM curve does not shift. A rightward shift in the ES curve therefore requires a rightward shift in the BB curve to maintain equilibrium. The authorities must therefore contract domestic credit to hold base money constant. From the identity relating base money to the sum of domestic credit and official foreign exchange reserves, it now follows that reserves must rise. Alternatively, if domestic credit is held constant, the BB curve does not shift and a rightward shift in the ES curve therefore requires a rightward shift in the LM curve to maintain equilibrium; that is, the money supply must expand. With domestic credit held constant, this again means that official reserves must rise.

19.   For the reasons set out in note 13, the BB curve (which is not explicitly shown in Figure 2.3) must be flatter than either ES_A or ES_B, and must therefore shift downwards between A and B'. This shift corresponds to an expansion of domestic credit, that is, to a reduction in the net bond holdings of non-residents and the private sector. Figure 2.3 shows that the downward shift between A and B would be even larger than that between A and B'.

20. The difference between the outcomes under complete sterilisation and under a currency board is due purely to the expansion of domestic credit needed to prevent the contraction of the money supply that would occur under a currency board system. This domestic credit expansion leads to a fall in reserves for the reasons explained in the subsection above on monetary policy.

21. Following the increased expectations of devaluation, the BB curve at the initial level of NDC, but in the absence of any restrictions, is BB_B. To shift this curve back to point A, the authorities must expand domestic credit. In contrast, with the restriction on lending to non-residents in domestic currency in place, the BB curve is BCB'. To shift this curve outwards to point A, the authorities must contract domestic credit.

3. Capital controls and crisis prevention: four case studies

Chapter 2 identified the two main purposes of capital controls as fiscal and 'prudential', broadly interpreted to mean anything that is intended to reduce the frequency and severity of currency and financial crises. The fiscal aspects of capital controls are dealt with in Chapter 4. The first four sections of this chapter survey the capital and exchange controls used in Taiwan, Malaysia, Korea and Chile and the final section assesses their effectiveness as prudential controls.

3.1 THE PARTIAL LIBERALISATION OF TAIWAN'S EXCHANGE AND CAPITAL CONTROLS

Since the late 1980s and 1990s the government of Taiwan has gradually liberalised its controls on capital movements, exchange market transactions and the financial sector. Aside from quantitative restrictions on banks' foreign exchange operations – described below – the banking sector has now been largely deregulated and partially privatised.[1] Planned future reforms include permitting banks to issue medium to long-term bonds and to operate securities services through their subsidiaries.[2] Although Taiwan's exchange controls and capital controls were also substantially liberalised between 1987 and 1997, they were tightened again in May 1998. Their main aim is to prevent a speculative attack on the New Taiwan (NT) dollar.

In 1987 the NT dollar was made freely convertible in a unified foreign exchange market for current account transactions and residents were allowed to invest offshore, although the amounts invested had to be approved by the central bank – the Central Bank of China (CBC). Such approval is still necessary, except that restrictions do not apply to outward and inward capital flows that do not involve conversion of NT dollars by the CBC – for example, the retention overseas of export receipts in foreign currency – and approval is given automatically for payments below a specified ceiling: as of May 1999, companies receive automatic approval for inflows and outflows of up to $50 million in any one year. This limit applies to the aggregate of portfolio investment, FDI and other foreign investment, such as bank lending. The corresponding limit for an individual is $5 million in any one year. Inflows and outflows in excess of these amounts require special approval and FDI projects require the additional approval of the Ministry of Economic Affairs.

In September 1990, the government began to allow approved foreign investors to invest limited amounts in the domestic stock market. Although regulations still prevent more than half the equity in any listed company being owned by non-residents, large foreign institutional investors can apply to become 'Qualified Foreign Institutional Investors' (QFIIs). As of May 1999, the ceiling on any request for inward portfolio investment by a QFII was $600 million in any one year; the amount actually granted may be much less and could be nothing. The CBC may grant approval for further investments in subsequent years. QFIIs can withdraw their investments when they choose, but would have to reapply if they wished to reinvest; since the CBC tries to encourage long-term investors, approval would probably not be given to an investor that had withdrawn funds after a short period. As of late 1998, the CBC had granted approval for QFIIs that amounted to only about 3 per cent of the Taiwanese stock market's total capitalisation.[3]

Inward portfolio investment can also take the form of local companies raising new equity on foreign stock exchanges. The bulk of these issues involve American Depository Receipts (ADRs).[4] Provided that they are undertaking new medium or long-term investments in Taiwan, the CBC allows local companies to convert the foreign exchange raised from ADR issues into NT dollars. Because the access of offshore investors to the Taiwan stock market is rationed, ADRs often trade in the USA at a substantial premium over the prices of the corresponding shares in Taiwan.

The CBC generally grants approval to foreign companies that want to raise equity in Taiwan by issuing Taiwan Depository Receipts, which function in an exactly analogous way to ADRs. The CBC has also approved limited portfolio outflows via the bond market: after obtaining approval from the CBC, some foreign corporations and multilateral institutions, including the Asian Development Bank (ADB) and the European Bank for Reconstruction and Development, have issued bonds in Taiwan denominated in NT dollars. Since the foreign borrowers generally need US dollars, they have typically used cross-currency swaps to convert both the NT dollars obtained and their future NT dollar liabilities into US dollars and future US dollar liabilities.

In July 1995, the CBC began to allow local firms to hedge currency risks related to current account transactions and approved capital account transactions by buying, or selling, DF dollars, or NDF dollars. Since the most effective way of speculating against a currency is to sell it forward, or equivalently, to borrow in it – either directly or in the swap market – to finance the acquisition of foreign currency assets, this reform increased the scope for speculative attacks on the NT dollar. To limit this risk, the CBC reinforced its long-standing bans on direct lending by residents to non-residents in NT dollars by imposing quantitative restrictions on access to the new swap and forward markets.

The DF market is an onshore market in which domestic banks (including local branches of foreign banks) trade with corporate customers. The banks are required by the CBC to check that their customers provide detailed documentation of the underlying current account, or approved capital account, transactions that will provide the currency to be delivered at maturity. Therefore speculators, and especially offshore speculators, whose access to NT dollars is deliberately made as difficult as possible by the CBC, cannot trade in the DF market. Speculative pressure on the NT dollar tends to raise NT dollar interest rates and the premium on the US dollar in the swap and forward markets. The CBC responds to such pressures by easing domestic credit and insulating the onshore markets from the offshore markets in the way analysed in Figure 2.4. In these circumstances, the NT dollar price of forward foreign exchange in the NDF market rises above the onshore price in the DF market.

When the price of NDF US dollars exceeds the price of DF US dollars, the NT dollar interest rate implicit in the NDF price exceeds the onshore interest rate and there are four main channels through which arbitrage could occur, if it were not prohibited:

1. resident banks and corporations could borrow onshore and lend offshore in NT dollars;
2. resident banks could sell NDF US dollars and hedge either by buying DF US dollars, or by borrowing onshore in NT dollars, converting the proceeds and using them to buy US dollar assets;
3. foreign banking groups could instruct their branches in Hong Kong, or Singapore, to sell NDF US dollars and hedge by instructing their Taiwanese branches to buy DF US dollars;
4. exporters that were planning to sell US dollars forward in the DF market could switch to the NDF market, and importers that would otherwise have bought US dollars forward in the NDF market could switch to the DF market.

The CBC's foreign exchange controls are designed to allow domestic firms to hedge their commercial risks, while insulating onshore interest rates from the upward pressures that would be created by these four types of arbitrage.

The long-standing ban on direct lending by residents to non-residents in NT dollars prevents (1) from occurring.

Opportunity (2) above is limited by quantitative ceilings on each bank's net open position in NDF contracts. The CBC maintains the fiction that these ceilings are set by the banks' own head offices: during 1998, branch managers of foreign banks in Taipei were invited to 'coffee mornings' at the CBC where they were advised of the appropriate reductions in the limits on foreign exchange exposure that they should 'request' their head offices to set. The ceilings are not made public, but it appears that they were roughly halved in August 1998; in 1999 they were rumoured to be slightly less than $500 million in aggregate, or only 0.6 per cent of Taiwan's official foreign exchange reserves, which were $84 billion in late 1998.

Opportunity (3) is limited by a requirement that each onshore bank must keep its net open foreign exchange position – that is, the absolute value of the difference between its aggregate foreign exchange assets and liabilities – below a quantitative ceiling, which is specified for each bank. Each bank must report its net foreign exchange exposure, including exposure resulting from trades in currency derivatives, to the CBC on a daily basis.

In May 1998, the CBC reduced the scope for opportunity (4) by prohibiting local corporations (other than banks and corporations created by FDI) from using the NDF market. The ban forced exporters wanting to hedge to do so in the DF rather than the NDF market. Since most of the transactions in the NDF market involved local firms, this ban also greatly reduced its size and reduced the scope for arbitrage by domestic companies that were using fake documents to justify buying forward dollars in the DF market for resale in the NDF market. Since the prohibition on NDF trading by local companies is not easy to enforce, some of them – particularly exporters – have presumably been selling foreign exchange forward at the relatively high offshore NDF price.

Although the CBC's regulations drive a wedge between the prices of DF and NDF dollars, arbitrage does ensure that the price of DF dollars is generally fairly close to that predicted by covered interest parity: it generally exceeds the spot market price by a premium equal to the excess of the onshore NT dollar interest rate over the dollar interest rate in world markets. However, onshore covered interest parity does not hold exactly because of transactions costs and because onshore banks have to pay a premium for dollar deposits over the rates paid by major international banks. This arbitrage is possible because onshore banks can borrow from, or lend to, local customers in NT dollars, can buy or sell foreign exchange in the spot market, and can borrow from, or lend to, offshore banks in dollars. Finally, the scope for arbitraging any differences between covered interest parity and the DF rate is not affected by the CBC's quantitative control on each bank's net open position in foreign exchange, because net positions are not affected by arbitrage. Because of these arbitrage opportunities, a rise in the price of DF dollars puts immediate upward pressure on domestic interest rates and on the spot exchange rate: if the price of DF dollars rises at initially unchanged interest rates, banks sell DF dollars and hedge by borrowing NT dollars onshore, selling them in the foreign exchange market, and lending the dollars thus acquired to cover their DF liabilities.

Speculation can and sometimes has created a large forward discount on the NT dollar in the offshore NDF market. In May, June and July 1998, the excess of the one-year NDF price over the DF price was between 5 per cent and 10 per cent. During this period, the annualised premia on six-month and three-month NDF dollars were sometimes substantially higher than those on one-year NDF dollars.[5]

Although the regulations described above prevent offshore speculative pressure on the NT dollar from being immediately and fully translated into an increase in the onshore interest rate and DF price, such speculative pressure does put upward pressure on the onshore DF price and hence on onshore interest rates. This happens partly because not all institutions are always constrained by their quantitative ceilings on open positions in NDF contracts and in foreign exchange, and partly because divergences between the DF and NDF prices increase the incentives for exporters and others to hedge illegally in the NDF market.

3.2   MALAYSIA'S CONTROLS ON INFLOWS AND OUTFLOWS

Malaysia's Inflow and Outflow Controls before September 1998

After relaxing its capital controls in the 1980s, Malaysia partially reintroduced direct controls in an attempt to moderate the large private capital inflows of the early 1990s, which averaged just over 15 per cent of GDP in 1992 and 1993. In January 1994, a ban was introduced on the sale by residents to non-residents of bills and other short-term ringgit securities issued by Malaysian banks, the central bank, or the Malaysian government. In February 1994 this ban was extended to prevent the issuing or reselling by residents to non-residents of privately issued debt securities, including commercial paper. In addition, all swap transactions not related to trade transactions were prohibited, commercial banks were required to deposit the ringgit funds of non-resident foreign banking institutions at the central bank, and ceilings were placed on the extent to which banks could incur foreign liabilities, other than those related to trade and investment.[6]

Private capital inflows declined sharply in the second half of 1994 in response to the combined effects of a rise in dollar interest rates, the new controls, and the effects of the earlier inflows on the Malaysian economy: inter-bank interest rates fell from an average of 8.1 per cent in 1992 to 5.6 per cent in 1994 and the real exchange rate appreciated by about 12 per cent between 1990 and 1993.[7] It is hard to assess the relative importance of the new controls relative to these interest rate and price changes, which would have tended to limit the inflows, even in the absence of the controls.

The authorities lifted the restrictions on sales of Malaysian securities to non-residents in August; then in December 1994, the regulations on borrowing by non-residents and on foreign currency borrowing by residents were also liberalised.

After the onset of the Asian crisis in 1997, Malaysia's exchange and capital controls operated primarily to restrict outflows, rather than inflows. These outflow controls, which have strong similarities with those of Taiwan, have always sought to prevent most forms of capital exports by residents and to stop speculation against the ringgit by residents and non-residents.[8]

Malaysia's rapid growth and its increasing openness to international trade and investment led to the development of an offshore market for ringgit bank deposits in the 1990s that was based mainly in Singapore and to a lesser extent in Hong Kong and London. These deposits were held both by non-residents and by residents and could be used to settle transactions with Malaysian residents by means of crediting or debiting the correspondent accounts of the foreign banks at onshore banks. The central bank, Bank Negara Malaysia (BNM), always disapproved of offshore ringgit deposits and the banks in Malaysia's own offshore financial centre in Labuan were banned from accepting ringgit deposits. However, until the tightening of exchange controls in September 1998, BNM did little else to check the growth of the offshore ringgit market.

Malaysia has generally prohibited direct lending in ringgits to non-residents by onshore banks. The main exceptions to the general prohibition are that, until September 1998, small ringgit loans could be made to correspondent banks and non-resident brokerage firms trading on the Kuala Lumpur Stock Exchange. To be eligible for ringgit loans, the non-resident banks and brokerage firms had to hold external accounts at onshore banks and had to convince BNM that they were using the loans to bridge unforeseen mismatches between payments and receipts. Before September 1998, non-resident brokerage firms and correspondent banks were automatically entitled to borrow up to Rgt. 5 million in aggregate from onshore banks to finance such funding gaps and they could apply for larger amounts. Since September 1998, these ringgit loans have been banned.

Despite the restrictions on direct lending offshore, the lack of restrictions on indirect lending in the swap and forward markets normally prevented large disparities between onshore and offshore ringgit interest rates in the period before Malaysia's initial tightening of exchange controls in August 1997, when BNM restricted indirect borrowing in ringgits by non-residents through the swap market. Non-residents with underlying commercial transactions, such as purchasers of Malaysian exports, were not affected, but non-residents without such underlying transactions were limited to swapping not more than $2 million, per offshore group, for ringgits provided by Malaysian banks.

The ongoing freedom of non-residents to buy ringgit securities onshore continued to mean that offshore ringgit interest rates could never fall substantially below onshore rates; however the August 1997 restriction on indirect lending in the swap and forward markets made the restrictions on lending by residents to non-residents in ringgits effective and made it possible for offshore ringgit interest rates to exceed onshore rates. As the Asian crisis unfolded in 1997 and 1998, speculation against the ringgit drove offshore interest rates on ringgit deposits in Singapore up to levels of between 20 per cent and 40 per cent per year, while onshore ringgit interest rates were about 11 per cent. Onshore dollar interest rates were roughly equal to those offshore because Malaysian residents were allowed to borrow from non-residents in dollars, subject only to reporting requirements and provided that the banks in the Labuan International Financial Centre were given first refusal for the chance to intermediate the loans.[9] The covered interest parity condition between the swap premium and the interest rate spread was approximately fulfilled in both the onshore and offshore markets; in consequence, the excess of offshore ringgit interest rates over those onshore was usually roughly matched by the excess of the offshore swap market premium on the dollar relative to the ringgit over the corresponding onshore premium.

The high offshore ringgit interest rates added to the incentives to get ringgits out of Malaysia by under-invoicing exports, over-invoicing imports and by smuggling currency. However, the size of the offshore market in ringgit deposits remained modest. The *Business Times* of Singapore estimated that, just before this market was effectively closed down by the September 1998 tightening of Malaysia's exchange controls, the total volume of offshore ringgit deposits had reached Rgt. 25 billion, but that most deposits were inter-bank deposits and that when these were netted out, what was left amounted to only Rgt. 1 billion or Rgt. 2 billion.[10] The gross estimate corresponds to about $6 billion, or 9 per cent of broad money (M2); the net estimates correspond to between 0.4 per cent and 0.7 per cent of broad money.

The September 1998 Controls

Unlike the other countries severely affected by the Asian crisis, Malaysia did not ask the IMF for emergency assistance, but it nevertheless initially adopted policies which were similar to those prescribed by the IMF for Thailand, Korea and Indonesia: tight money, a floating exchange rate and relatively free capital mobility, apart from the restrictions on direct and indirect lending by residents to non-residents in ringgits. In August 1998, the government decided to break with these IMF-style policies and to ease monetary policy. On 1 September 1998, it announced that the ringgit was to be pegged at Rgt. 3.80 per dollar and that exchange controls were to be tightened.[11] This tightening took three main forms, set out in more detail in the remainder of this subsection: a partial freeze for one year on the external ringgit accounts of non-residents at onshore banks, a further tightening of the existing restrictions on ringgit-denominated lending by residents to non-residents and a further tightening of the ceilings on the amounts of small capital outflows that could be made without special permission from BNM.

The most important external accounts are the correspondent accounts of offshore banks and the accounts of non-resident insurance companies, mutual funds and other portfolio investors. The partial freeze on external accounts had two separate purposes: to prevent the exit of foreign portfolio investment that had already entered Malaysia and to force the closure of the offshore ringgit deposit market. Foreign portfolio investment was trapped inside Malaysia by the requirement that withdrawals from external accounts could only be used to buy ringgit assets: foreign portfolio investors could sell their Malaysian shares and credit the proceeds to their onshore accounts, but could not remit these proceeds to their offshore accounts. The offshore ringgit deposit market was undermined by making it illegal for onshore banks to transfer funds from the correspondent accounts of offshore banks to resident accounts; once offshore ringgit accounts could no longer be used to make onshore payments, the demand for them largely evaporated. Holders of offshore ringgit deposits were given a one month grace period, from 1 September to 30 September, to transfer these deposits to resident deposits at onshore banks. Thereafter, transfers to resident accounts were not permitted. To reinforce the freeze on external accounts, the government prohibited travellers from taking more than Rgt. 1000 in ringgit notes either into or out of Malaysia, and made it illegal for exporters to accept payment in ringgit: after September 1998, all exports had to be paid for in foreign currency.

The second of the exchange control measures listed above was the tightening of the existing restrictions on ringgit-denominated lending to non-residents. The provision for non-resident banks or brokerage companies to borrow up to Rgt. 5 million from onshore banks was abolished. In addition, the September 1998 regulations prohibited indirect ringgit lending to non-residents by onshore banks in the swap and forward markets.[12] The lack of convertibility of the ringgit removed the preconditions for a DF market and although some bilateral NDF trades have occurred, an NDF market has not grown up to replace the DF market.[13] One reason cited by offshore dealers for the failure of a ringgit NDF market to develop is the fear of antagonising BNM. Another is the lack of underlying demand; the head of currency options at JP Morgan, Singapore, was quoted as saying: 'If a ringgit NDF market is to develop it will be because there are real capital flows underpinning its development. Clearly the recent imposition of capital controls frustrates the development of such a market'.[14]

The third group of measures tightened the limits on capital outflows that could be made without special approval. Before September 1998, residents with no outstanding loan from domestic financial institutions were free to make foreign investments of any size and those with loans from domestic financial institutions were allowed to invest up to Rgt. 10 million per year per corporate group. After September 1998, a limit of Rgt. 10 000 per year per corporate group was imposed, regardless of whether the investor had borrowed domestically or not. Beyond this limit, foreign investments required the approval of BNM.

It seems unlikely that either the second or third of the three groups of exchange control measures described above had a large effect in stemming capital outflows or preventing speculative attacks on the ringgit. The abolition of the right of onshore banks to lend up to Rgt. 5 million to offshore banks and brokerage companies was a relatively minor change, because it would have taken so many transactions at these levels to have significantly dented BNM's foreign exchange reserves, which stood at $21 billion at the end of September 1998. The same is true of the closure of the offshore DF foreign exchange market. The original imposition of the $2 million limit on offer-side ringgit swaps in August 1997, up to which time no limit had existed, was far more important than the reduction in the limit from $2 million to zero. The reason is that $2 million is a trivially small limit relative to the volume of trading in such markets. The lowering of the ceilings on permitted capital outflows were also of minor importance, because other devices, such as under-invoicing exports, could easily be used for the same purpose on a much larger scale: under-invoicing annual exports by just 3 per cent would finance as much capital flight as could have been undertaken by 1000 corporate groups at the previous limit of Rgt. 10 million per year each.

The September 1998 exchange controls forced the closure of the offshore ringgit deposit market, but did not bring the offshore ringgit deposits back to Malaysia. Following the announcement of the Malaysian measures in September 1998, the Singapore banks agreed to convert ringgit deposits to dollars at Rgt. 4 per dollar, which involved a discount of only about 5 per cent relative to the official exchange rate. Anecdotal evidence suggests that most of the offshore depositors chose to convert their deposits to dollars rather than repatriate them. The unwinding of the market therefore apparently did not involve the return of flight capital to Malaysia. Those speculating on the devaluation of the ringgit – that is, the speculators to whom the Singapore banks had made indirect ringgit loans in the swap and forward markets – closed out their oversold forward market positions in ringgits, while the Singapore banks closed out their matching overbought forward market positions in ringgits and converted their ringgit deposit liabilities to dollar deposit liabilities. After conversion, those who formerly held ringgit deposits in Singapore ended up holding dollar assets equal in value to the dollar assets formerly held by the speculators, who paid off the ringgit loans that had been financing their holdings of these dollar assets.

Whether the small net effect on BNM's foreign exchange reserves of the closure of the offshore ringgit market was positive or negative depends on whether the proportion of offshore deposits repatriated was greater or less than the proportion of their ringgit deposit liabilities that the Singapore banks held in correspondent accounts at banks in Malaysia.[15] There is certainly no indication of large-scale repatriation of deposits in the official Malaysian money supply figures, which would have been boosted by the return of offshore deposits, had it occurred: despite the government's moves to loosen monetary policy, broad money (M2) rose during September 1998 by only about Rgt. 450 million, or 0.2 per cent. Whether it was positive or negative, the net capital flow due to the closure of the offshore ringgit deposit market appears to have been very small.

Neither of the two effects of controls so far discussed appears to have been quantitatively important. The remaining effect was the ban on the repatriation of foreign portfolio capital that resulted from the requirement that, for 12 months from September 1998, external accounts could only be used to purchase ringgit assets. The actual amounts in the external accounts were only about Rgt. 9 billion, but in the absence of the new restriction, non-resident portfolio investors could have sold securities to residents (if residents had been willing to offer an acceptable price), credited the proceeds to their external accounts and then used them to buy dollars and thus repatriate their capital.

This control was analysed in section 2.2 using Figure 2.3. A binding restriction on the exit of non-residents from the domestic share market prevents a leftward shift in the ES curve and therefore prevents a capital outflow and a fall in share prices. The practical importance of this restriction depends on the extent to which non-residents would actually have repatriated their portfolio capital. In late August and early September 1998, when the Malaysian government decided to ease monetary policy, revalue the exchange rate and impose controls, the Asian crisis appeared to be in full swing and world interest rates were high. Had they remained high and had Malaysia not tightened outflow controls, it might well have been faced with large capital outflows as a result of its easing of monetary policy and the revaluation of the ringgit from about Rgt. 4.20 to Rgt. 3.80 per dollar. However, in September and October 1998, there was a partial restoration of investor confidence in all the Asian countries. In part, the restoration of capital inflows to Asia was probably due to the realisation by foreign and domestic investors that the slump in Asian asset prices had been excessive and offered opportunities for high returns. In part also, the return of capital to Asia was boosted by a reduction in the US discount rate from 5 per cent to 4.5 per cent in the last quarter of 1998 and by the strengthening of the yen.[16] Given that portfolio and other capital was beginning to flow back into the other Asian countries, it seems likely – at least with hindsight – that Malaysia's controls did more to discourage inflows, than to limit outflows.

The view that Malaysia's controls were irrelevant to its macroeconomic performance in 1998–99 is supported by the fact that this performance has been quite similar to that of the other countries most affected by the Asian crisis. Nominal interest rates in Malaysia fell from 10.1 per cent in August 1998 to 7.7 per cent in September 1998, to 6.5 per cent in December and to 3.2 per cent in August 1999. However, because of the return of confidence in the Asian countries, interest rates fell over this period in all the countries affected by the Asian crisis and there is little or no evidence that onshore interest rates fell by more in Malaysia than in the other countries.[17]

The pegging of the ringgit in September 1998 at Rgt. 3.8 per dollar caused it to strengthen by between 6 per cent and 13 per cent between August and September relative to the won, the baht and the Philippines peso. However, the strengthening of these other currencies relative to the dollar in the next four months, meant that by January 1999, they had all strengthened relative to the ringgit over the period since August 1998. However, the ringgit then strengthened against the won, the baht and the peso, so that by August 1999 its value in terms of each of these three currencies was within plus or minus 2 per cent of the corresponding value in August 1998, just before the imposition of the Malaysian controls. In contrast, the rupiah continued to strengthen relative to the ringgit in the first half of 1999, and by August 1999 the rupiah value of the ringgit had fallen by 25 per cent over the preceding 12 months.

Lags in the effects of policy on growth and the influence of other factors make it hard to assess the effect of Malaysia's exchange controls on its growth performance. Preliminary indications are that this effect, whether positive or negative, was not large. The last quarter before Malaysia's tightening of exchange controls was the third quarter of 1998. Between this quarter and the third quarter of 1999, real GDP grew by 12.3 per cent in Korea, 8.1 per cent in Malaysia, 3.3 per cent in the Philippines, 7.7 per cent in Thailand and 0.5 per cent in Indonesia.

In 1999, Malaysia replaced the freeze on external accounts by a graduated levy. The form and coverage of this levy changed during the year until by September 1999, it amounted to a tax at 10 per cent on the remission abroad of profits earned on new portfolio investments. Earnings from FDI, trade credits and bank lending are not subject to this levy, which applies only to remittances abroad from external accounts. It appears hard to rationalise the levy for two reasons: first, in the aftermath of the Asian crisis, the affected countries need to attract, not repel, capital inflows. After all, the original purpose of Malaysia's controls was to reduce outflows. Second, if inflows are to be discouraged, the rationale is presumably to guard against the moral hazard created by government guarantees of bank deposits. From this perspective, a tax on portfolio inflows that exempts bank lending is counterproductive both because portfolio investment is not guaranteed by the government, whereas governments have often provided *ex post* bail-outs for foreign bank lenders, and because, when an adverse shock occurs, foreign portfolio investors automatically share in losses, whereas foreign bank lenders only share in losses in those crisis situations in which borrowers default on their contracted debt repayments.

3.3   KOREA

Partial Liberalisation of Controls before 1997

Korea's capital and exchange controls have been substantially liberalised since the early 1980s. Three factors have strongly influenced this process: commitments to the OECD and the IMF, the extent to which the exchange rate was allowed to float and the state of the balance of payments.

Both before and after Korea's entry to the OECD in 1996, the liberalisation of capital controls was prodded forward by the government's desire to conform with the OECD's Code of Liberalisation of Capital Movements. In 1998–99, liberalisation was also strongly influenced by the commitments made to the IMF in exchange for the emergency loan package of December 1997.

Korea's exchange rate system moved slowly towards a floating rate system over a long period, which began in January 1980, when the dollar value of the won was reduced by 16 per cent and the rigid peg to the dollar was replaced by a policy of loosely pegging the won to a basket of currencies in which the dollar and yen were believed to have the main weights, though these weights were never disclosed.[18] Over the next decade, the won's dollar valued was allowed to fall by a further 15 per cent, and its yen value by a further 49 per cent. These movements understate the flexibility of the exchange rate in the 1980s, because the won depreciated by about one-third against the dollar in the early 1980s and then appreciated sharply in the late 1980s. In 1990, exchange rate policy became more flexible still with the adoption of a system that allowed the won to float each day within a band on either side of its average value in terms of a basket of currencies on the preceding day. The band was initially ± 0.4 per cent of the average rate on the previous day, but was widened in four steps to ± 2.25 per cent on the eve of the Asian crisis.

While the overall trend towards liberalisation of capital and exchange controls has both influenced and been influenced by Korea's international commitments and its exchange rate regime, the timing and choice of liberalisation measures has been strongly influenced by the state of the balance of payments. When the current account has been in deficit, inflow controls have been eased and outflow controls left unchanged or tightened; when the current account has been in surplus, outflow controls have been eased. Thus the current account deficits of the early 1980s prompted the government to restrict capital outflows and ease controls on inflows by allowing non-residents to invest in certain special funds that held stocks listed in the Korean stock market and by allowing approved resident companies to raise capital offshore by issuing convertible bonds, bonds with warrants and depository receipts.[19] When the current account moved into surplus in the late 1980s, the government made the won convertible on current account transactions, removed the ban on the purchase of foreign real estate by businesses, granted automatic approval for all offshore investments below $1 million and restricted foreign borrowing by domestic firms.

The large current account deficits, and small overall deficits, of the early 1990s led to the liberalisation of FDI and portfolio inflows: the ceilings on the size of FDI projects that received automatic approval were raised, the number of sectors that were open to FDI was increased and tax incentives for FDI projects were raised. In 1992 non-residents were allowed to invest directly in the Korean stock market, provided that the non-resident share of any listed company did not exceed 10 per cent. This ceiling was raised in stages to 15 per cent in 1995. These measures were followed by very large capital inflows and such a large overall balance of payments surplus in the mid-1990s that, despite the current account deficit, outflow controls were eased by allowing Korean pension funds and investment and finance companies to make offshore portfolio investments and by raising the ceilings on permitted offshore portfolio investment by domestic securities companies, trust companies and insurance companies.[20]

Korea's Controls and the 1997–98 Crisis

Although Korea still had some exchange and capital controls in place in 1997, they were unable to protect the exchange rate and financial system from speculative attack. In 1997, as in 2000, the won was not fully convertible on capital account. Even after the liberalisation of exchange controls in April 1999, residents cannot take more than $10 000 out of the country at a time. Residents can hold deposits denominated in dollars at foreign exchange banks onshore, but these so-called 'dollar deposits' are really dollar-indexed won deposits, since they cannot be used to transfer funds to offshore accounts. Differences between onshore interest rates on 'dollar' accounts and offshore dollar interest rates do not therefore create legal opportunities for arbitrage.

Controls on lending by residents to non-residents in won limit the borrowing of each non-resident banking group to not more than 100 billion won from all domestic banks, in aggregate. In 1997, this control was reinforced by controls (which have subsequently been relaxed) on indirect lending: domestic banks were not allowed to trade in the offshore NDF market and other trades in the onshore DF market were limited by the 'real demand principle', that is, banks could only trade in the onshore DF market with firms that were hedging current account, or approved capital account transactions.

The controls on lending by residents to non-residents in won created the kinds of differentials between onshore and offshore interest rates illustrated in Figure 2.1 and analysed in the last subsection of section 2.2. The won price of offshore NDF dollars was never far below the onshore price of DF dollars and was sometimes far above the DF price, implying that offshore won interest rates were never much below, and were sometimes far above the onshore won interest rates.[21] Figure 3.1 shows that for most of the 13 months from August 1997 to August 1998, the annualised excess of the three-month NDF dollar premium over the three-month DF dollar premium was more than 10 per cent; in October 1997 this excess was a massive 55 per cent and in December 1997 it was 29 per cent.[22] Figure 3.1 also shows that the onshore dollar interest rates implied by the DF swap premium were usually above the corresponding offshore rates, and in November 1997 this country-specific risk premium rose to 5 percent.[23]

In July 1998, in partial fulfilment of its commitments to the IMF, the government abolished the former restrictions on the maximum maturities of trade credits and on most foreign exchange transactions by foreign investors, except those related to won deposit accounts and to direct and indirect lending in won to non-residents. In April 1999, ceilings on the value of permitted outward FDI were removed and outward FDI was permitted in real estate and in services

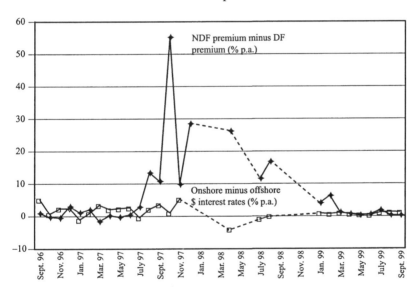

Note: All the data refer to three-month contracts and are expressed at annualised percentage rates. In deriving the series 'Onshore minus offshore $ interest rates', the onshore dollar rate was estimated as the excess of the interest rate on won certificates of deposit over the onshore DF premium on the dollar. The offshore dollar interest rate is LIBOR. The data were supplied by the Bank of Korea.

Figure 3.1   Excess of NDF (offshore) dollar premium over DF (onshore) dollar premium and the onshore–offshore US dollar interest rate spread in Korea

sectors. In addition, domestic banks were allowed to trade in the offshore NDF market and domestic firms were exempted from the 'real demand principle' in the forward foreign exchange market – that is, they were allowed to buy and sell foreign exchange for speculative purposes, even if they did not have underlying current account or approved capital account transactions. The reforms removed the control on indirect lending in won to non-residents. Since then, as Figure 3.1 shows, the divergences between the NDF and DF rates have been relatively small by past standards. The government has announced plans for the introduction of full capital account convertibility in January 2001.

The balance of payments data in Table 3.1 help explain why Korea's exchange and capital controls were unable to prevent the 1997–98 crisis. In 1996, Korea's current account deficit of $23 billion was financed by a net capital inflow of $23 billion. However, in 1997, there was an overall balance of payments deficit of $23 billion: although the current account deficit shrank to $8 billion, there was a net capital outflow of $10 billion. In addition, 'errors and omissions' contributed a further $5 billion to the overall deficit.[24] The net outflow of FDI barely changed between 1996 and 1997, while the net inflow of portfolio investment was almost unchanged, as was the gross outflow of 'other investment assets'. In an accounting sense, the $33 billion turnaround in the capital account between 1996 and 1997 was the result of a $33 billion turnaround in 'other investment liabilities', which measures the net repayments by residents to non-

Table 3.1   Korea's balance of payments, 1996–97

	1996 $billion	1997 $billion	Change $billion
Surplus on:			
Current account	−23.0	−8.2	14.8
Capital and financial accounts	23.3	−9.8	−33.1
Errors and omissions	1.1	−5.0	−6.1
Overall balance	1.4	−23.0	−24.4
Memo items:			
Net inflow of FDI	−2.3	−1.6	0.7
Portfolio investment assets	−6.0	2.0	8.0
Portfolio investment liabilities	21.2	12.3	−8.9
Other investment assets	−13.5	−13.6	−0.1
Other investment liabilities	24.6	−8.3	−32.9
Surplus on financial account	23.9	−9.2	−33.1

Source: IMF, *International Financial Statistics* CD-ROM.

residents of bank loans, trade credits and other liabilities, plus the net withdrawals of deposits by non-residents from domestic banks. This $33 billion turnaround was not prevented by Korea's exchange controls because they did not restrict the right of non-residents to withdraw their deposits from onshore banks, nor to demand repayment of outstanding short-term loans, rather than to roll them over.

Other than by freezing non-resident bank accounts and preventing Korean firms meeting their contracted debt service payments, the Bank of Korea (BOK) could only have prevented the erosion of its foreign exchange reserves during 1997 by severely tightening monetary policy. It chose not to do so because of the weak state of the banks and the extreme indebtedness of the large business conglomerates. Instead, the BOK largely sterilised the monetary effects of the balance of payments deficit: money market interest rates, which had been between 14 per cent and 15 per cent in late 1996, were still only 14 per cent in November 1997, although they did rise to 22 per cent in December. Base money was allowed to contract by 12 per cent during 1997, but this was much less than the fall in the true net foreign exchange reserves of the BOK. Between the end of December 1996 and the end of December 1997, the BOK's foreign exchange reserves, as officially reported, fell from $34.0 billion to $20.4 billion; but $11.5 billion of the latter amount consisted of loans to offshore branches of Korean banks that could not be readily recalled by the BOK without threatening the survival of the banks to which they had been lent. This left only $8.9 billion in the form of assets in short-term foreign money markets that were 'usable'. Since the BOK had net liabilities of $8 billion in the forward and swap markets, its usable reserves at the end of December 1997, net of its short-term dollar liabilities, were less than $1 billion.[25] It is not surprising that a panic developed as markets began to realise the extent to which the BOK's official reserves overstated its ability to defend the won.

3.4   VDR RESTRICTIONS ON CAPITAL INFLOWS: CHILE

Before the relaxation of its capital inflow controls in 1978–82, Chile imposed quantitative limits on the amounts which banks could borrow from abroad. These controls were relaxed in three steps in December 1978, June 1979 and April 1980.[26] Besides the controls on bank-intermediated borrowing from abroad, there was also a ban on foreign borrowing, other than trade credits, for periods of less than two years. Although loans for longer than two years were not banned, they were subject to interest rate ceilings and, until May 1979, foreign currency deposits equal to 25 per cent of gross foreign borrowings had to be placed in non-interest bearing deposits at the central bank. In May 1979, the required deposit proportion was reduced to 15 per cent for amounts bor-

rowed for periods of three to four years and to 10 per cent for amounts borrowed for four to five and a half years. No deposits were required for amounts
borrowed for more than five and a half years, and loans for less than two years
continued to be banned.[27] In June 1980, the deposit proportion on loans for two
to three years was reduced from 25 per cent to 15 per cent. In May 1982, in an
unsuccessful attempt to offset the capital outflows that preceded the devaluation of June 1982, the ban on borrowing for less than two years was replaced by
a 20 per cent deposit requirement. The deposit proportions on two to four year
loans and four to five and a half year loans remained at 15 per cent and 10 per
cent respectively. In July 1982, a uniform deposit requirement of 5 per cent was
set on all loans for less than 70 months.

In the aftermath of the 1982 crisis, Chile partially reimposed the outflow
controls that had been relaxed in the late 1970s and early 1980s. In the 1990s, it
gradually removed almost all controls over outflows; however, in June 1991, in
response to large inflows of capital, it set a 20 per cent non-interest bearing
deposit requirement on foreign borrowing.[28] This deposit requirement applied
to most capital inflows other than FDI, some portfolio equity investments in the
form of ADRs and suppliers' credits on imports and payments for exports made
in advance. Although FDI has never been subject to the deposit requirements
applied to most other types of capital inflow, FDI projects for periods of less
than one year are not permitted. In the case of both foreign currency deposits at
commercial banks and external lines of credit, including lines of credit used for
trade finance, the deposit requirement was applied to the average monthly
balance.[29] Therefore the tax burden on three or six-month deposits and credit
lines was no higher than on annual deposits and credit lines. In the case of loans
and bonds with a maturity of more than a year, the zero interest deposit was
returned after one year. Although the proportion of inflows that had to be
deposited was the same for all inflows to which it applied, the deposit requirement
was variable in the sense that the implicit tax rate on foreign borrowing varied
inversely with the maturity of the loan.

In May 1992, the deposit proportion was raised from 20 to 30 per cent of the
gross amount borrowed. From 1994 onwards, the deposits had to be made solely
in US dollars.[30] In July 1998 the deposit proportion was reduced to 20 per cent
in an attempt to attract capital inflows, which had fallen off as a result of the
financial crises in Asia and Brazil. In September 1998 the rate of the VDR was
reduced from 20 per cent to zero; however, the government subsequently
indicated that it might eventually reintroduce the control.[31]

For a given interest rate received by foreign lenders, a 30 per cent deposit
requirement raises the interest rate effectively paid by borrowers by a factor of
10/7 on loans with a maturity of one year. This happens because borrowers
must pay foreign lenders interest on $100 in order to get the use of $70, since
the remaining $30 is deposited at the central bank. At a world interest rate of

7 per cent, the tax therefore adds 3 percentage points to the cost of borrowing. In the case of a loan for less than one year, the effect of a requirement to place a deposit for a full year would make the implicit tax higher than for a one year loan. However, since the zero interest deposits required on lines of credit and bank deposits were calculated as 30 per cent of the average amount borrowed, this additional burden could be avoided by using a line of credit, or placing the amount lent on deposit at a Chilean bank, which could then make the short-term loan.

The tax burden is lower on loans for longer than one year. With the world interest rate at 7 per cent, a Chilean resident who borrowed abroad for five years would need to pay interest at 10 per cent for the first year, but only at 7 per cent for the next four years. In this example, the average cost of funds to the borrower turns out to be only about 0.5 percentage points above the world interest rate: the average annual interest rate facing the borrower would be 7.5 per cent, over five years, rather than the 7 per cent received by the foreign lender.[32]

Offshore transactions in derivatives can be used to convert what appears to domestic regulators to be a long-term onshore loan into what is really a short-term loan that can be rolled over at the discretion of the lender. For large borrowers with easy access to offshore markets in derivatives, the effective tax rate on a one-year loan may well have been closer to the low rate of 0.5 percentage points per year calculated above for the case of a five-year loan, than to the 3 percentage points per year that would have been paid on a one-year loan by a borrower who made no attempt to evade the tax. The camouflaging of short-term loans as long-term loans would of course increase the measured proportion of long-term loans in total capital flows, without necessarily affecting the true proportion. This provides a plausible rationalisation for research findings that the introduction of Chile's VDR was associated with a reduction in the measured proportion of short-term loans, but with little change in total capital inflows.[33]

Chile's VDR was intended to insulate it against 'dangerously large' capital inflows. However, the 30 per cent deposit rate chosen appears to have been too small for this purpose, since the effect of the control on domestic interest rates is small relative to the fluctuations over time in world interest rates. Suppose that a defender of the VDR claims that for a given state of the Chilean economy, and with world interest rates at 5 per cent, capital inflows would be 'dangerously large' in the absence of the control, but could be reduced to a 'safe' level by raising the domestic cost of borrowing to, say, 6.5 per cent. The 30 per cent VDR gives a margin of safety because, at least in the case of one-year loans, it raises the domestic cost of borrowing to 7.1 per cent. But the same margin of safety would occur without the need for any VDR if world interest rates rose to 7.1 per cent, and the 30 per cent VDR would be inadequate if world interest rates fall below 4.55 per cent, because at this level the domestic cost of borrowing, even with the VDR in place is 6.5 per cent, which is 'dangerously low' according to the illustrative assumption above. In the period during which the Chilean deposit requirement was held constant at 30 per cent, the interest rate on one-year dollar deposits varied between 3.2 per cent and 7.6 per cent.[34] On the illustrative assumption above, the VDR was often either inadequate or unnecessary. The illustrative assumption could be changed: for example, by assuming that a domestic cost of borrowing above 4.6 per cent (that is, 3.2/0.7) would prevent 'dangerously large' capital flows, a defender of the VDR could argue that it was never inadequate, but would then have to acknowledge that it had been unnecessary ever since mid-1994, when dollar interest rates rose above 4.6 per cent; alternatively, by setting the 'safe' level at 10.9 per cent (that is, 7.6/0.7) a defender of the VDR could argue that it was never unnecessary, but would have to admit that it was almost always inadequate.

Any attempted rationalisation of Chile's 30 per cent deposit requirement as a prudential device for preventing financial and currency crises faces the difficulty that, since the interest rate raising effect of a 30 per cent deposit requirement is quite small relative to fluctuations in world interest rates, the requirement would have to be adjusted more often and by larger amounts than happened in Chile to prevent it often being either unnecessary or inadequate. Since the interest rate-raising effects of the requirement on five-year loans are much smaller than those on one-year loans, this criticism becomes very much stronger if the calculations are done using five-year loans, rather than one-year loans.

3.5   OVERVIEW

Taiwan

Taiwan liberalised but did not remove its exchange controls before the Asian crisis and it managed to avoid the worst of the crisis. However, it is unlikely that its exchange and capital controls were a major factor in this achievement. Taiwan's most important exchange control is its restriction on direct and indirect lending in local currency to non-residents. Similar controls did not save Korea, Thailand, Indonesia and Malaysia even though they produced larger divergences between onshore and offshore local currency interest rates than those observed in Taiwan's case.[35] This suggests that other factors played a larger part in Taiwan's resilience to the crisis. Chief among these other factors were Taiwan's small foreign debts, its very large foreign exchange reserves (which, at $84 billion in late 1998, were the fourth highest in the world after China, Japan and Hong Kong), the fact that its main export markets – China and the USA – were not affected by the crisis, and its relatively effective bankruptcy procedures, which both discourage excessive risk-taking and promote the rapid resolution of bad debts when problems nevertheless occur.[36] In addition, Taiwan's banks had higher capital adequacy ratios before the crisis than those of Indonesia, Korea or Malaysia, and the large share of deposits held at state banks probably helped to avert the risk of a banking panic, although at a high cost in terms of efficiency.

Malaysia

It was argued in section 3.2 that the outflow controls imposed by Malaysia in September 1998 did more to discourage inflows than to limit outflows because they were imposed just as capital was about to start flowing back to the Asian crisis countries. If the return in investor confidence in Asia, and the falls in world interest rates, could have been anticipated in early September 1998, it would have been impossible to make a good case for Malaysia's controls: the moves to restrict outflows which disrupted markets, antagonised foreign investors and damaged Malaysia's long-term reputation as a location for foreign businesses free from excessive bureaucratic controls were implemented just at the moment when capital outflows were turning to inflows. In return for their obvious disadvantages, the controls were supposed to produce substantial macroeconomic benefits. In fact, Malaysia's performance in 1998–99 – in terms of its short-term interest rate, exchange rate and real GDP growth – has not been markedly better, nor markedly worse, than that of the average of the other countries most affected by the Asian crisis. However, since the return in confidence could not have been easily anticipated, a theoretical case can be made for the controls: they might have served a useful macroeconomic purpose if world interest rates had remained high and if investor confidence in Asia had not recovered. At the very least it seems fair to concede that the controls did not cause significant short-run macroeconomic damage. Whether, and to what extent, they may discourage future inward investment, or add to the readiness of investors to panic at the first hint of a new crisis, is hard to know. These future costs may well be borne in part by other emerging market economies and not only by Malaysia.

Korea

Despite their ability to create the very large divergences shown in Figure 3.1 between onshore and offshore won interest rates, exchange controls were unable to save Korea from being one of the countries most severely affected by the Asian crisis. The basic reasons are that no outflow controls could have generated the continuing inflows that were needed to finance the 1997 current account deficit, and Korea's actual outflow controls could not prevent a $23 billion outflow of 'other investment liabilities', in the form of the repayment of loans and trade credits and the withdrawal of onshore deposits by non-residents.

Even the imposition of controls like those introduced by Malaysia in September 1998 would not have prevented Korean residents repaying short-term bank loans, although it would have prevented non-residents withdrawing their deposits from Korean banks. For the government to have introduced controls to stop Korean firms repaying contracted foreign debts would have been enormously damaging to Korea's reputation and is not something envisaged by any of the control systems analysed in this chapter.

Chile

Section 3.4 showed that, relative to fluctuations in world interest rates, the effects on domestic interest rates of Chile's VDR have been small. Chile's country-specific risk premium has also fluctuated by large amounts relative to the tax implicit in the VDR. It is therefore implausible to suggest that Chile's success in avoiding a banking or currency crisis in the 1990s can be attributed primarily to its deposit requirement on capital inflows: the control presumably somewhat modified capital inflows, but, as a crisis prevention measure, it must often have been either inadequate or excessive. Many other emerging countries have also avoided crises in the 1990s. Among the possible reasons for Chile's success in doing so are its tightening of prudential controls in 1986, its relatively open banking sector (in which foreign banks accounted for 21.4 per cent of total assets in 1995) and the fact that it sterilised the monetary effects of balance of payments surpluses and deficits to a much smaller extent than most other countries with exchange rates pegged by central banks.[37]

Further evidence that Chile's VDR was probably not an important reason for its avoidance of a currency or banking crisis in the 1990s is provided by Edwards (1998), who shows that the controls used by Chile in the period preceding its 1982 crisis were similar to those which it used after 1991. In fact, the controls in the 1976–82 period were more restrictive than those in the 1991–98 period: in the earlier period, foreign loans for periods of less than two years were prohibited and the implied taxes on those that were not banned were substantially higher, on average, than those in the 1990s. For three-year loans, the ratio of the implicit tax in the earlier period to that in the later period was 1.46, while for five-year loans this ratio was 1.49.[38]

Between December 1978 and April 1980, Chile relaxed the quantitative restrictions that limited what banks could borrow. Following the relaxation of these restrictions, capital inflows grew very rapidly. However, although the quantitative restrictions that applied specifically to foreign borrowing by banks were removed, the general ban on short-term borrowing and the requirement that all those who borrowed from abroad had to place non-interest-bearing deposits at the central bank remained in place during the period of rapid inflows from 1976 to 1981. These inflow controls were not removed until 1982 when the problem confronting the authorities was outflows, not inflows. In summary, the deposit requirement of the period 1991–98 can hardly have been a very reliable safety device, because Chile retained a similar, but more stringent, set of capital controls throughout the whole of the 1976–81 period of rapid inflows, but still did not manage to avoid the debacle of 1982.

Conclusion

The most frequent defence of capital controls is based on the assumption that they are an effective way of preventing currency and financial crises.[39] The case studies reviewed in this chapter show that, at least in the case of mild to moderate exchange controls, this assumption does not hold. Even though they sometimes created very large differentials between onshore and offshore domestic currency interest rates, the restrictions on speculation in the swap and forward markets operated by Korea were unable to prevent the 1997 crisis. Taiwan operated similar controls and avoided the crisis, but this was probably mainly for other reasons. Fluctuations in world interest rates have been so large, relative to the interest rate raising effects of Chile's inflow controls, that it is implausible to argue that they have been responsible for Chile's success in avoiding the emerging markets' crises of the 1990s. Besides, even more restrictive controls had not managed to prevent the Chilean crisis of 1982.

Countries such as China and Vietnam operated much more restrictive controls than those of the four countries surveyed here, and very restrictive controls presumably can prevent most speculative crises, provided that the government does not persistently try to finance spending by excessive credit creation. However, very restrictive controls are not compatible with the development of the kind of sophisticated financial sector that is needed by a country that aspires to a level of development comparable to that of Korea or Taiwan.

NOTES

1. Tang (1995), Casserley and Gibb (1999).
2. Chiu (1999).
3. *The Economist*, 7 November 1998.
4. To facilitate the acquisition of equity in local companies by US portfolio investors, the local company places share certificates with the local branch of a US bank, and, subject to regulatory approval in the USA, the receipts for these shares can then be listed on a US stock exchange. The US bank converts the dividends into US dollars so that the US purchaser of the ADR avoids the inconvenience of having to deal in foreign exchange.
5. Information supplied by an onshore Taiwanese bank.
6. See International Monetary Fund (1995, pp. 308–9), and Quirk, Evans *et al.* (1995, p. 43).
7. The real exchange rate was estimated as the ratio of wholesale prices in Malaysia to a trade-weighted average of the consumer prices in its 17 principal trading partners using the formula in note 16 of Chapter 4. All price indices were converted to dollars using market exchange rates.
8. Malaysia's exchange controls are set out in Bank Negara Malaysia (1994).

9. To strengthen its political support in the province of Sabah by drawing business away from Singapore, the Mahathir government set up Malaysia's own offshore financial centre on the island of Labuan in the late 1980s by giving banks there a monopoly on the right to intermediate foreign currency lending to Malaysian residents.

10. *Business Times* (Singapore), 3 September 1998.

11. Bank Negara Malaysia (1998a).

12. Bank Negara Malaysia (1998b, p. 71).

13. *Asia Risk*, October 1998, states that offers by two offshore banks in September 1998 to buy NDF ringgits one year forward at Rgt. 5.5 per dollar were 'snapped up'. With the spot rate at Rgt. 3.8 per dollar and the one-year interest rate on dollars (LIBOR) at 5.3 per cent in September 1998, the implied annual ringgit interest rate is 37 per cent. However, 'the two banks then stepped away from the market'.

14. *Asia Risk*, October 1998, p. 6.

15. Suppose that the Singapore banks held deposits at correspondent banks in Malaysia equal to 5 per cent of their ringgit deposit liabilities and lent the remaining 95 per cent in the swap and forward markets. If more than 95 per cent of offshore ringgit deposits were converted to foreign currencies and held offshore after September 1998, and less than 5 per cent repatriated, then the capital outflow from Malaysia due to the Singapore banks' reduced demand for onshore deposits would have exceeded the inflow due to repatriation by their customers. If less than 95 per cent of deposits were converted, there would have been a net capital inflow as a result of the closure of the offshore ringgit deposit market.

16. The three-month call rate in Japan fell from 0.9 per cent in August 1998 to 0.6 per cent in December and to 0.4 per cent in March 1999. The yen strengthened from 145 per dollar in August 1998 to 135 in September and to 118 in December 1998.

17. In August 1998 the short-term annualised interest rate in Malaysia was about 31 percentage points below that in Indonesia, 7 percentage points below that in the Philippines, 3 percentage points below that in Thailand and 1 percentage point below that in Korea. By December 1998, the spreads for Korea and Indonesia were roughly unchanged; Thailand's spread relative to Malaysia had narrowed by 2 percentage points, but the Philippines' spread had increased by 2 percentage points. By March 1999, the interest rate spreads in the other four countries, relative to Malaysia, had all narrowed relative to August 1998. By August 1999, the spreads relative to Malaysia for Indonesia, Thailand and the Philippines had all narrowed since August 1998; only in Korea had the spread relative to Malaysia widened over this period. These spreads are calculated as $1 + s = (1 + r)/(1 + r_R)$, where s is the spread relative to the ringgit for the country whose interest rate is r, and r_R is the ringgit interest rate. All estimates refer to annualised three-month money market interest rates in the Asian database marketed by CEIC Ltd., Hong Kong. The Thai rates are calculated as a weighted average for three commercial banks.

18. Rhee and Song (1999, p. 72).

19. Park and Song (1998, p. 91).

20. Johnson *et al.* (1997, pp. 28, 81–2).

21. As explained in section 2.2, the differentials between the offshore NDF and onshore DF exchange rates would equal the excess of the implied offshore won interest rate over the onshore rate if covered interest parity held onshore and if the onshore and offshore dollar interest rates were equal. In fact, onshore dollar rates were usually above offshore dollar interest rates, because of the greater riskiness of onshore banks.

22. The data on annualised three-month premia were supplied by the Bank of Korea. The series in the Figure 3.1 was derived as $100[(p_{NDF}/p_{DF})^4 - 1]$, where p_{NDF} and p_{DF} are three-month forward won prices of dollars in the NDF and DF markets. The price differential is raised to the power 4 to express the three-month forward rates at an annual rate. The annualised differentials on three-month won contracts were often much higher than the differentials on one-year won contracts shown in Figure 2.1.

23. The spread of the onshore dollar rate over the offshore rate actually rose to 45 per cent on 31 December 1997. This observation is not shown in Figure 3.1 because, according to an official of the Bank of Korea, it resulted from an unrepresentative one-day-only scramble by domestic banks for onshore dollars for 'window dressing' purposes, to meet prudential restrictions on their net open positions, as measured by their end of year balance sheets.

24. 'Errors and omissions' reflect discrepancies between changes in official reserves and recorded flows of trade, factor payments and capital. It is often assumed that errors and omissions reflect unrecorded capital flows. This assumption may sometimes be correct, but it neglects the fact that errors and omissions measure discrepancies between official estimates of flows and changes in reserves, rather than discrepancies between official estimates and the truth. For example, if $1 million of unrecorded export smuggling were used to finance $1 million of unrecorded capital flight, there would be no measured exports, no measured capital movements, no change in official reserves and therefore no errors and omissions.
25. The data on net swap liabilities, and on usable and total reserves were provided by the Bank of Korea.
26. Edwards and Edwards (1991, pp. 38, 55–6).
27. For details of Chile's controls see International Monetary Fund, *Exchange Arrangements and Exchange Rate Restrictions*, various issues.
28. Massad (1998, pp. 40–2).
29. See Le Fort and Budnevich (1998, pp. 54 and 60).
30. Johnson *et al.* (1997, p. 18).
31. *Financial Times*, 13 April 1999.
32. The average implicit dollar interest rate, r, on a loan for N years facing a borrower, who must place a fraction α of the principal in a zero interest account for one year, when the world dollar interest rate is r^*, was found by searching for solutions to the equation:
$$0 = [1 - \alpha] + [\alpha e^{-r}] - [e^{-rN}] - [r^*(1 - e^{-rN})/r].$$
The first term in square brackets is the principal immediately received, per dollar borrowed; the second term is the present value, at interest rate r, of the deposit which is returned by the central bank to the borrower after one year; the third term is the present value of the repayment to the foreign lender after N years; the fourth term is the present value of the stream of interest payments over N years.
33. Quirk, Evans *et al.* (1995, pp. 39–40) found little evidence that the controls had much effect, if any, either on domestic interest rates or on the magnitude of capital flows.
34. The interest rates quoted refer to one-year LIBOR. The source is IMF, *International Financial Statistics* CD-ROM.
35. The divergences between onshore and offshore ringgit interest rates in 1997–98 are reported in section 3.2. Those for the rupiah, baht and won are reported at the end of section 2.1.
36. *The Economist*, 'The Flexible Tiger', 3 January, 1998 and 'The Survivor's Tale', 7 November 1998.
37. See the estimated sterilisation coefficients in Table 7.1.
38. Between June 1980 and May 1982 the deposit requirements were 15 per cent of borrowings for two to four years and 10 per cent of borrowings for four to five and a half years. As noted in section 3.4, even higher requirements applied before June 1980. At an illustrative annual world interest rate of 7 per cent, deposit requirements of 15 and 10 per cent, which must be maintained for the duration of the loan, raise the domestic cost of capital by 1.235 percentage points and 0.778 percentage points, respectively. At the same illustrative interest rate, a 30 per cent deposit requirement that is returned after one year raises the annual interest rates on three and five-year loans by 0.847 and 0.522 percentage points, respectively. These amounts are calculated using the formula in note 32.
39. Rodrik (1998).

4. First and second-best arguments for capital controls

In 'second-best' situations, some policies that have been badly set must be taken as given. In such situations, the effects of capital account liberalisation include not only the beneficial direct effects listed in section 1.1, but also indirect effects, which depend on how the relaxation of controls interacts with existing market failures. These indirect effects may be large or small, beneficial or harmful. They will be beneficial if they result either in a reduction of activity in markets in which it is initially too high, or in an increase of activity in those in which it is initially too low. In the opposite cases, the indirect effects will be harmful. Second-best justifications for controls are those that claim that these indirect effects are both harmful and so large that they outweigh the direct effects of relaxing controls, which are beneficial, provided that 'first-best' justifications, defined as those that do not depend on assuming that some unalterable policies have been badly set, would at most justify milder controls than those initially in place.

Sections 4.1 and 4.2 deal with first-best justifications for taxing capital inflows. Because of the risk of sovereign default, even countries that are too small to affect world interest rates can affect the interest rates charged on their own foreign borrowing. The resulting case for a tax to restrict foreign borrowing is set out in section 4.1. Section 4.2 deals with the appropriate tax treatment of the domestic income from foreign capital and the foreign income of domestic residents.

Section 4.3 discusses the second-best case for exchange and capital controls in countries in which a large government budget deficit is financed by printing money. Sections 4.4 discusses the second-best arguments for restricting capital flows when trade restrictions must be taken as given in the short term. Section 4.5 summarises and criticises the arguments for encouraging foreign direct investment but restricting short-term capital inflows. The last section gives an overview.

4.1   SOVEREIGN DEFAULT RISK AND TAXES ON CAPITAL INFLOWS

This section deals with two cases for restricting capital inflows which are quite distinct, but are nevertheless related by the fact that in both cases domestic interest rates depend on the amount borrowed by the capital-importing country. The first is the 'true monopsony case' in which the home country is large enough to affect the world interest rate and is therefore in a situation like that of a 'monopsonist', that is, a buyer who, acting alone, can influence the market price paid by varying the quantity bought. It is in the self-interest of such a country to impose a tax on capital inflows (or, equivalently, a tax on interest payments abroad) since by restricting the amount that it borrows it can reduce the average interest rate that its residents pay on their foreign borrowings. It is well known that in this case, the optimal tax on interest payments abroad, expressed as a fraction of the world interest rate, is the reciprocal of the interest elasticity of supply of world lending to the domestic country.[1]

The second case, which is referred to here as the 'sovereign default risk case', is due to Harberger (1980) and Aizenman (1989). It is based on the increased probability of sovereign default due to increased foreign borrowing. Countries that default, or partially default, on their foreign debts may suffer penalties, such as the seizure of property and the disruption of trade, and will also suffer a loss of reputation and at least temporary exclusion from further international borrowing. Nevertheless, if their debts are sufficiently large, it may be less costly to incur such penalties than to repay in full. Because lenders can anticipate the risk of default, they must be compensated for it; therefore the 'contract interest rate' – that is, the interest rate written into loan contracts between residents of the risky country and foreign lenders – will exceed the risk-free world interest rate by a country-specific risk premium.[2] Since the probability of default rises with the amount borrowed, the country-specific risk premium and the contract interest rate will both be increasing functions of the amount borrowed, even if the country is too small to affect the world interest rate.

Although the true monopsony case for restricting capital flows is of no practical importance for small countries that cannot affect world interest rates, the sovereign default risk case provides a closely analogous argument for taxing capital inflows even in the case of a country that is too small to affect the world interest rate. Despite the significant differences between the true monopsony and sovereign default risk cases – in the former there is no possibility of default, while in the latter the capital-importing country has no monopsony power – the optimal proportional rate of tax on interest payments abroad in this latter case is also given by the reciprocal of the elasticity of supply of foreign loans with respect to the contract interest rate.

The intuition behind the surprising coincidence between the optimal tax formulas in these two quite different cases can be explained as follows. When sovereign risk is important, borrowing by one resident has two external effects on other residents: it raises the contract interest rates paid by all borrowers in the absence of default and it increases the probability of national default. If the government of the borrowing country makes default decisions optimally from the perspective of its own citizens, small changes in the circumstances under which default occurs do not have a first-order effect on welfare, so that the second externality becomes irrelevant: increased borrowing raises the probability that domestic residents will incur the penalties of national default, but the other side of the same coin is that it also raises the probability that domestic residents will avoid having to repay all their foreign debts. If the government makes default decisions optimally from the point of view of its own citizens – balancing the costs of incurring default penalties against the benefits to domestic residents of not having to repay their borrowings in full – these costs and benefits exactly cancel out. This leaves only the first externality, which is formally equivalent to the sole external effect in the true monopsony case.

Harberger (1985, p. 256) derived essentially the same formula for the optimal tax on foreign borrowing under the assumption that lenders believe that default is possible, but that borrowers believe either that they will have to repay in full or that they will gain nothing from default if it occurs. Harberger pointed out that if the schedule relating the amount borrowed to the contract interest rate is approximately linear, then the optimal tax rate is approximately equal to the country risk premium, as measured by the excess of the country's contract interest rate over the interest rate charged to the world's most secure borrowers.[3] This proposition implicitly assumes that the optimal tax on capital inflows is in place when the country risk premium is measured; the optimal tax will be somewhat less than the risk premium observed when no tax is in place, because imposing the tax will reduce foreign borrowing, and will therefore also reduce the risk premium.[4]

In periods when a country experiences large capital inflows and the Harberger–Aizenman tax can be justified as a way of limiting the risk of sovereign default, the country-specific risk premium in developing countries is typically of the order of 1 percentage point per year.[5] Most developing countries already tax capital inflows much more heavily than this. In crisis periods, country risk premia are often very large, but in these periods a tax on inflows would be counterproductive because governments are anxious to attract whatever capital inflows they can: governments that have restricted inflows in good times have usually eased or removed their restrictions in periods when inflows have dried up, or turned to outflows.[6] In the Harberger–Aizenman model, capital inflows should always be taxed because they always increase the risk of sovereign default. Their model ignores the fact that any capital inflows that can be attracted in a crisis period can *reduce* the probability of default by making it possible for official and private debtors to roll over their debts. It would therefore be counterproductive to tax inflows in crisis periods. But these are the only periods in which a tax on inflows at a rate equal to the country-specific risk premium would ever exceed the taxes already imposed in developing countries, other than tax havens, on the domestic earnings of foreign capital.

4.2 WITHHOLDING TAXES, CORPORATE TAXES AND THE CASE FOR FREE TRADE IN CAPITAL

The almost universal practice of taxing the domestic earnings of imported capital seldom attracts the criticisms that are widely applied to tariffs and export taxes. However, taxing the earnings of imported foreign capital is not qualitatively different from taxing imports of foreign goods. Subject to the argument for taxing capital inflows based on sovereign default risk, which was summarised in the preceding section, and subject also to two additional qualifications set out below, the basic case for free international capital flows is the same as the case for free trade: if a country is too small to affect the prices of exports and imports, including the exports and imports of capital, then taxes on such transactions merely distort the behaviour of domestic firms and households by creating divergences between domestic prices and interest rates and the fixed terms on which the home country can trade with, or borrow from, the rest of the world.

The Case for Taxing Income Earned by Capital Imported from Countries with Foreign Tax Credit (FTC) Systems

The first qualification to the case against taxing the earnings of foreign capital is that if a substantial part of the capital borrowed from abroad comes from countries that operate FTC systems, then even for a country that is too small to affect world interest rates, a nationalistic case can be made for taxing the earnings of foreign capital at a rate set slightly below the corporate tax rates in the foreign countries from which most capital is borrowed. The reason is that if capital is imported from a country that operates an FTC regime, a tax in the capital-importing country on the dividends and underlying profits earned by domestically employed foreign capital would merely divert tax revenue from the government of the capital-exporting country to the government of the capital-importing country. It would not affect the after-all-tax return to foreign private lenders, provided that the rate was low enough to allow these lenders to obtain full credits in their own countries for all payments of the tax in the capital-importing country. Such taxes would therefore have no effect on the volume of international capital flows.

However, if most capital is imported from countries that operate foreign tax deduction (FTD) systems – in which the base for tax in the capital-exporting country is gross earnings net of taxes in the capital-importing country – then a small country that imposes domestic corporate and withholding taxes on the earnings of imported capital raises the interest rate facing domestic borrowers above the marginal cost of capital to the country. For example, if the pre-tax rate of return in a large capital-exporting country is fixed at 6 per cent, and if that country operates an FTD system, then the cost of capital to the capital-importing country is also 6 per cent. However, if the capital-importing country taxes the earnings of imported capital at, say, 25 per cent, the pre-tax interest rate and the rate of return on capital in the capital-importing country will both be 8 per cent, because only at this rate will foreign investors receive a return, net of taxes in the importing country – and therefore pre-tax in the exporting country – of 6 per cent. In this case, taxing the earnings of foreign capital is inefficient because it causes domestic investors to face an interest rate of 8 per cent when the cost of capital to the country is only 6 per cent. The inefficiencies caused in this case are exactly analogous to those caused by imposing a tariff on imports of widgets of $2 per widget, when the world price of widgets is $6. Taxing imports of capital, like taxing imports of widgets, is generally a less efficient way of raising revenue than taxing the consumption of residents.

The possibility of transferring revenue from foreign countries to the home country, without affecting the level of capital imports, also disappears if the foreign capital exporter operates a foreign tax exemption (FTE) system, meaning that it does not levy any tax on the income its residents earn from capital employed in foreign countries, if that income has already been taxed in the foreign country. Many countries operate conditional FTE systems in which tax exempt status is denied to income earned in tax havens, but granted to income earned in specified countries, including some that have slightly lower corporate tax rates than the rate in the capital-exporting country. In these cases, the differences between FTE and FTC systems are small: an FTC system is equivalent to a conditional FTE system, in which tax exempt status is granted only to income earned in countries with corporate taxes at higher rates than the rate in the capital-exporting country. Other things equal, it is in the self-interest of capital-importing countries to reduce tax rates to the point at which any further reduction would jeopardise their right to tax exempt treatment from the main capital-exporting countries that operate conditional FTE systems.

Because countries with FTC systems do not all have the same tax rates, and because some capital will generally be imported from countries with FTD or FTE systems, the optimal tax treatment of earnings from imported foreign capital is not clear-cut. The analysis of the optimal tax treatment of earnings from imported foreign capital is further complicated by two factors. First, one of the effects of a corporate tax 'imputation' system – as described in the next subsection – is to convert a regime that is nominally an FTC or FTE regime, into one that is closer in reality to an FTD regime. Second, the fact that capital-exporting countries generally only tax the income earned by their subsidiaries in capital-importing countries when dividends are remitted, rather than as profits accrue, converts what is nominally an FTC or FTD regime into one that is closer in reality to an FTE regime.

Imputation[7]

The 'classical' income tax system taxes the income of 'persons'. Because of the legal fiction that corporations are 'persons', it therefore taxes the profits earned by corporations at the corporate tax rate, and then taxes the dividends paid out of post-corporate tax profits at the marginal tax rates of the individual share-holders. Income from corporate equity is therefore taxed twice. 'Imputation' is designed to avoid the inefficient bias of the classical system against corporate equity income. Under an imputation system, domestic residents are taxed on their dividends 'grossed up' for corporate tax, but receive imputed tax credits equal to the corporate tax paid on their behalf by the corporations that have paid them dividends; in effect, they are taxed on their total gross earnings from all sources, including pre-corporate tax income from capital.[8] Imputation converts a corporate tax into a withholding tax for taxpayers whose marginal tax rates exceed the corporate tax rate, and into a final tax for those with lower marginal rates.

If a capital-exporting country uses both imputation and an FTC system, the dividends earned by a foreign subsidiary or branch that operates in a country whose corporate tax rate is at least as high as the rate of the exporting country will not be subject to corporate tax in the exporting country. But if these profits are fully distributed as dividends, the foreign tax credits will be lost: because no corporate tax has been paid in the capital-exporting country, individual shareholders in that country will not receive any imputed corporate tax credits. In the case of full distribution of after-tax profits by both the subsidiary (or branch) and the parent, the gross dividends of the shareholders of the parent company will equal the after-foreign tax profits of the subsidiary (or branch); these shareholders will therefore end up with the same dividends, net of all taxes, as they would have received if the capital-exporting country operated an FTD system.

To avoid the effective denial of credits for foreign taxes under imputation, it would be necessary for the capital-exporting country to allow its domestic parent companies to 'gross-up' the dividends paid to their domestic shareholders out of the profits of their foreign subsidiaries and branches for all foreign taxes paid, and to allow the shareholders to claim domestic income tax credits for these foreign corporate taxes. Since actual FTC systems are never so generous as this, credits for foreign taxes paid by subsidiaries and branches are partially or wholly lost under full distribution of earnings, except in the case of shareholders who do not have to pay income tax.

Taxation of Dividends, Not True Economic Income

Most, if not all, countries tax the income earned by the foreign subsidiaries of domestic parent corporations only when the parents receive dividends from their subsidiaries. This ability to avoid paying domestic tax on foreign income as it accrues has the effect of partially exempting tax on foreign income, regardless of whether the nominal system is an FTC or an FTD system.[9] The longer the period for which tax is delayed – and the parent company can determine the length of the delay – the closer is the actual system to an FTE system.

Although the factors discussed in this subsection and the previous one complicate the analysis, they simplify the policy conclusions: the closer foreign tax regimes are to either FTD or FTE regimes, the lower is the rate of the optimal domestic tax on imported foreign capital.

Intellectual Property Rights[10]

The second qualification to the case for not taxing the domestic earnings of imported capital arises when a high proportion of FDI is associated with the transmission of technologies over which the foreign owners have intellectual property rights or firm-specific advantages. Whereas a small country can buy as much or as little steel as it chooses at the going world price, this is not the case for products that are protected by intellectual property rights. The copyrights, trademarks and patents needed to provide incentives for innovation also give innovators a temporary monopoly in the right to use the technologies and ideas that they have developed. In addition, intellectual property rights are reinforced by the natural entry barriers arising from the costs of learning to use new technologies. The supply of such products to small countries is therefore not perfectly elastic and some low rate of tax on the earnings of imported capital can be rationalised as a way of extracting for the home country some of the monopoly profits that would otherwise accrue entirely to the foreign owners of the imported technologies.

4.3   CAPITAL ACCOUNT LIBERALISATION AND SEIGNIORAGE

Particularly in economies with relatively unsophisticated tax systems, capital controls and currency restrictions may play a role in financing government spending. These effects can be illustrated using Figure 4.1. The curve through *A* shows the relationship between the nominal interest rate and the revenue saving to the government from being able to issue domestic 'base money', rather than having to issue interest-bearing government bonds.[11]

The revenue from issuing money is often referred to as 'seigniorage', by analogy to the fees which used to be charged by governments for the right to mint precious metals into coins. The gross annual revenue from seigniorage is the amount of interest which the government would have to pay if base money had to be replaced by interest-bearing government bonds.[12] This revenue is

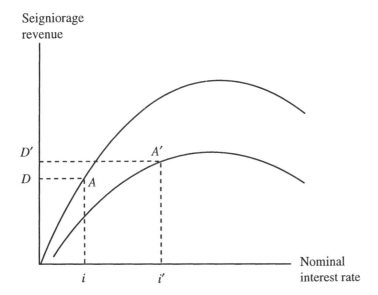

Figure 4.1   Seigniorage and inflation

equal to the real value of the base money held, which is the base of the tax, times the nominal annual interest rate, which is the rate of the seigniorage tax and measures the difference between what holders of base money pay per period for using it, and the cost to the government of issuing it, which (aside from administrative costs) is nothing. The net on-budget revenue from seigniorage is the amount remitted to the treasury by the central bank. This is usually substantially less than the gross revenue, because central banks typically spend a considerable amount on themselves, or in providing off-budget subsidised credits to favoured borrowers.

A convenient simplifying assumption in discussing the revenue from seigniorage is that the nominal interest rate is equal to the rate of inflation plus an exogenous real interest rate. As the inflation rate rises, the nominal interest rate rises but the real value of holdings of base money declines. The amount of seigniorage revenue obtained at any given value of the nominal interest rate depends on the relationship between the nominal interest rate and the demand for real base money; in deriving the curve depicted in Figure 4.1, it is assumed that the first effect is dominant at low rates of inflation, but that beyond some very high rate of inflation, the second effect becomes dominant. This is consistent with the empirical evidence that the revenue from seigniorage continues to increase with the rate of inflation up to very high rates.[13]

Relaxing controls on capital outflows can raise inflation in a country with a repressed financial system if the government uses money creation as an endogenous residual to cover the deficit between spending and the revenue from grants, explicit taxes and the profits of state owned enterprises. If the budget deficit, D, and the real interest rate, r^*, are assumed to be exogenous, then Figure 4.1 implies that the rate of inflation will normally be $\pi = i - r^*$, where i is the lower of the two nominal interest rates at which the revenue from seigniorage is D. Only in an unstable hyperinflationary equilibrium would the nominal interest rate exceed the rate at which the revenue from seigniorage is maximised.

The relevance of all this to capital controls is that they can affect both the budget deficit and the position of the revenue curve in Figure 4.1. They can affect the position of the revenue curve because they help bolster the demand for domestic money by prohibiting residents from holding foreign currency deposits. In financially repressed economies, the revenue from seigniorage can be increased by using high reserve requirements to force banks to hold more base money than they otherwise would.[14] Capital controls can be used to prevent this tax being undermined by competition from offshore banks that are not subject to the high reserve requirements. If the loans and deposits of residents are intermediated by offshore banks, or if foreign currencies are substituted for domestic money, the seigniorage revenue curve in Figure 4.1 will shift downwards and the rate of inflation needed to finance a given deficit will increase.

Relaxing controls on capital outflows may also raise the government's budget deficit by raising the interest cost of the government's debts. If relaxing capital controls raised the budget deficit from D to D' and caused the revenue curve to shift downwards from the curve through A to the one through A', and if no other fiscal reform were undertaken, the nominal interest rate would rise from i to i'. At any given real interest rate, the rate of inflation would rise by the same amount as the nominal interest rate.

McKinnon (1991, p. 105) cites two instances to illustrate these dangers. The first example is Israel's relaxation of exchange and currency controls in 1977 and its subsequent sharp acceleration in inflation. The second example is Argentina's relaxation of capital controls in 1977–78 and of financial controls in 1979–80; this was followed by the breakdown of the managed rate of devaluation of the peso in 1981, and by Argentina's subsequent slide into hyperinflation.

Table 4.1 shows the gross revenue from seigniorage as a percentage of government on-budget current revenue for seven developing countries in the period 1981–95.[15] In the 1980s, when inflation and nominal interest rates in the Latin American countries sometimes exceeded 100 per cent per year, the ratio of the gross revenue from seigniorage to total government on-budget current

Table 4.1   Seigniorage revenue as percentage of on-budget current government revenue

	Indonesia	Malaysia	Thailand	Korea	Argentina	Chile	Mexico
1981–85	3.3	4.3	5.7	3.5	336.7	42.6	54.7
1986–90	6.2	2.6	3.6	4.2	191.4	45.3	28.3
1991–95	5.3	4.5	3.7	4.1	5.2	19.2	5.9
Memo: Interest rate (% p.a.)							
1981–85	10.6	9.2	10.4	10.4	263.9	41.8	52.2
1986–90	17.9	4.9	6.7	10.0	243.8	24.7	62.6
1991–95	27.5	6.9	7.4	9.1	13.0	12.3	20.5

Notes: Seigniorage revenue is estimated as the nominal interest rate multiplied by base money. Base (or 'reserve') money and nominal interest rates are derived from IMF, *International Financial Statistics* CD-ROM. Ideally, the interest rate should be the average interest rate on all government securities; the rates actually used were those on six-month time deposits. Current government revenue is derived from World Bank, *World Tables*.

revenue sometimes also exceeded 100 per cent. In Mexico in the early 1990s, and in Argentina since its adoption of a currency board in 1991, the corresponding proportion has been below 6 per cent. However, the jump in interest rates in Mexico in 1995 brought the ratio for that year to 12 per cent. Since Table 4.1 excludes the periods of high interest rates in 1997–98, seigniorage was small in the four Asian countries shown. For these countries, the ratio of the gross revenue from seigniorage to total government current revenue ranged between 2.6 per cent and 6.2 per cent.

The table therefore confirms that in well-managed economies, even the gross revenue from seigniorage is small compared to total on-budget current revenue; but the data for the Latin American countries in the 1980s show that seigniorage can be important in economies with rapid inflation and was actually more than three times as large as all on-budget current revenue in Argentina in the early 1980s.

4.4   TRADE RESTRICTIONS AS A SECOND-BEST GROUND FOR RESTRICTING CAPITAL INFLOWS

Alternative Concepts of Competitiveness and 'the' Real Exchange Rate (RER)

There are two main ways of measuring changes in a country's competitiveness: the first is by comparing changes in some domestic price index with changes in the prices of its major trading partners, after using market exchange rates to express domestic and foreign prices in terms of some common currency. The second is to compare changes in the prices of the traded goods – imports and exports – produced by the home country with changes in the prices of the non-traded goods that it produces.

The RER is conventionally defined as the price of traded goods relative to the price of non-traded goods (that is, the second concept), but is conventionally measured as the ratio of the average price level of foreign trading partners to the domestic price level, with all prices converted to a common currency using market exchange rates (that is, the first concept).[16] This conventional measure is easier to calculate than the average price of traded to non-traded goods, because somewhat arbitrary judgements are needed in practical attempts to classify particular goods as being tradable or non-tradable.

Provided that foreign taxes and trade barriers and the relative prices in foreign countries of traded and non-traded goods do not change – or at least that any changes in these variables in one foreign trading partner are roughly offset by opposite changes in others – this conventional index of the RER is an index of the border prices of traded goods relative to the average domestic prices of both traded and non-traded goods. The two RER concepts are therefore likely to be highly correlated, and this is borne out by studies that have calculated both.[17]

Just as a 'nominal depreciation', or 'devaluation', means a fall in the value of the domestic currency relative to foreign currencies, so a 'real depreciation' means a fall in the price of domestic goods relative to foreign goods; or, using the second of the above RER concepts, a fall in the prices of non-traded goods relative to traded goods. These definitions are adopted here because their use is so widespread; unfortunately this convention has the disadvantage that a real depreciation means an increase in the RER. An analogous source of possible confusion arises because the nominal exchange rate is conventionally defined as the price of foreign currency in terms of domestic currency. A nominal depreciation or devaluation therefore means an increase in the nominal exchange rate.

RER Overvaluation

'RER overvaluation' is more often used than defined. The definition used here is that the RER is overvalued if the correction of market failures would cause it to depreciate. Although it is often claimed that the RER must be overvalued if it has appreciated by a substantial amount over the preceding few years, this claim need not be true because RER appreciation is sometimes a symbol of success. This can happen because ongoing productivity growth will raise non-traded prices rise relative to traded prices if, in accordance with the Balassa–Samuelson hypothesis, the opportunities for productivity growth in non-traded sectors are more limited than those in the sectors producing traded goods.[18]

In some instances, however, RER appreciation can be a symptom of overvaluation and impending problems. The two most important causes of this phenomenon are mistakes in banking policy and mistakes in monetary policy. Government guarantees of banks combined with inadequate checks on excessive risk taking by banks can generate a spending boom based on excessively risky investments.[19] A by-product of such a boom is the appreciation of the RER. The monetary policy mistake which has been made most often by developing countries has been to peg the exchange rate while expanding domestic credit at a faster rate than that consistent with a fixed exchange rate. The motive for such an expansion of domestic credit is often to finance a budget deficit; the result is an appreciation of the RER, as the prices of non-traded goods and factors rise relative to the pegged prices of traded goods. A similar situation can also arise if the authorities try to stabilise the nominal exchange rate in order to slow down an ongoing inflation.

The 'Need for Real Depreciation' Argument for Retaining Capital Inflow Controls

Capital inflows caused by a fall in world interest rates, increased optimism about domestic prospects, or the liberalisation of capital controls cause the RER to appreciate. In this respect, their effects are similar to those of the so-called 'Dutch disease', in which the foreign exchange inflow from the development of North Sea oil contributed to a rise in the relative prices of non-traded goods in Holland, thus causing a recession in the traditional Dutch export industries.[20] Both capital inflows and oil discoveries increase the availability of foreign exchange thereby raising the demand for all goods; the supply of traded goods can be temporarily increased, to meet the higher demand, by borrowing from abroad and running a current account deficit, but the supply of non-traded goods can only be increased by increasing their relative prices. Restoration of equilibrium between the supply and demand for non-traded goods requires an appreciation of the RER: the prices of non-traded (or 'home') goods must appreciate relative to the prices of traded (or 'foreign') goods. When this happens, exports contract both because of the original increase in domestic demand and because resources are drawn into the non-traded goods industries by the rise in the domestic prices of such goods relative to those of traded goods.

There is no reason to believe that market forces would allocate too few resources to export industries, if trade were not restricted. Therefore, in the absence of trade barriers, the fact that capital inflows raise the prices of non-traded goods and contract exports would not provide a justification for trying to protect export industries, but would merely be a symptom of the beneficial effects of these events on economic development: the rise in the relative prices of non-traded goods would reflect a rise in real wages, driven by increased demand for labour.

However, in the presence of trade barriers, the export sector is inefficiently small and the sector producing import-competing goods is inefficiently large. Proponents of the 'need for real depreciation' argument for capital controls use this fact to argue that capital inflows should be restricted to avoid the additional contraction of the export-competing sector that would result from the appreciation of the RER which capital inflows would cause. This case is set out by Edwards (1984, p. 4 and 1987, pp. 27–8). Edwards argues that, on the one hand, when a liberalising economy opens its capital account there is likely to be a capital inflow and an appreciation of the RER while, on the other hand, a successful liberalisation programme requires a depreciation of the RER to assist the expansion of the export sector. His conclusion is that 'the capital and current accounts should *not* be opened at the same time. Moreover, in the transition period after trade has been liberalized, capital flows should be tightly controlled' (Edwards, 1987, p. 28). The very large real appreciations experienced by Korea in the late 1960s and by Chile, Argentina, and Uruguay in the late 1970s and early 1980s are often cited as examples of the need to restrict capital inflows to avoid real appreciation.

The 'need for real depreciation' case for restricting capital inflows during the process of trade liberalisation appears to have been made first by McKinnon (1973, p. 160) who stated that 'internal employment reallocation … may be upset by an unusually large inflow of foreign capital that inhibits the exchange rate from depreciating sufficiently'. McKinnon (1991, p. 116–17) argues not only that countries should restrict borrowing from abroad during trade liberalisation, but that aid from the World Bank and the IMF would harm the recipient country during a period of trade liberalisation, because it 'throws out the wrong long-run price signals in private markets' and would turn the RER against exporters and firms competing with imports, thus making it 'unduly hard for them to adjust to the removal of protection'.

It is argued here that there is in fact no presumption that trade liberalisation requires non-traded goods prices to fall relative to the average domestic prices of traded goods, and that the 'need for real depreciation' argument does not in fact provide a general presumption in favour of restricting capital inflows, even if tariff and non-tariff barriers have resulted in an inefficiently low level of trade. The flaw in the 'need for real depreciation' case for restricting capital inflows is that merely because one beneficial policy – namely, reducing tariffs – would cause the conventional proxy for the RER to rise, it does not follow that capital account liberalisation is harmful because it causes this index to fall. The implicit assumption that the conventional measure of the RER is a reliable indicator of welfare does not hold.

That the alleged need to restrict capital inflows is based on an inadequate analysis can be seen by focusing on imports rather than exports: by turning the RER against firms competing with imports, an inflow of capital would generally raise imports as well as reduce exports; since the assumed policy distortion is a tariff that makes imports too low, this is clearly a benefit of capital inflows and not one of their disadvantages.

Although there are really as many different 'RERs' as there are pairs of non-traded goods and traded goods, the use of a single measure of 'the' RER is generally a useful simplification. The exception to this generalisation occurs when the essence of the effect being analysed is a change in the relative prices of traded goods. In such cases – and the removal of import barriers is a prime example – it is important to distinguish between the 'import RER' and the 'export RER', defined, respectively, as the domestic prices of imports and exports, relative to the average price of non-traded goods. It is, therefore, misleading to claim that trade liberalisation requires a depreciation of 'the' RER. Relative to the prices of non-traded goods, the domestic prices of exports will indeed generally rise, but those of imports will generally fall. Trade liberalisation therefore causes the export RER to depreciate, but it causes the import RER to appreciate. The average domestic prices of all traded goods may either rise or fall relative to non-traded goods prices when trade barriers are lowered. Nothing of importance turns on which of these outcomes occurs.

Lal (1987, p. 291) argues that the real worry of opponents of capital account liberalisation is that it could lead to an 'overshooting' of capital inflows and the RER, that is, to initial changes in these variables that exceed their long-run changes, so that the eventual attainment of long-run equilibrium involves a period of capital outflows during which the RER depreciates. While conceding that such reversals are possible, Lal demolishes the argument that they constitute a ground for delaying capital account liberalisation by pointing out that such reversals may also occur when barriers to capital flows are removed even if all barriers to trade flows have already been removed. Therefore, if this argument for delaying capital account liberalisation is correct, 'it should apply to the liberalization of the capital account *at any time*, irrespective of whether or not trade liberalization has taken place.'[21]

Another frequently cited second-best argument for not liberalising the capital account when trade is restricted is based on the demonstration by Brecher and Díaz-Alejandro (1977) that under certain very special assumptions, an inflow of foreign capital must reduce the welfare of a small country. These assumptions are that there are just two factors, capital and labour; the country produces positive amounts of two commodities, whose world prices are given; imports are subject to a tariff; the import-competing sector is relatively capital-intensive and the return on capital received by foreign lenders and investors is equal to the domestic marginal value product of capital. The last of these assumptions implies that the domestic earnings of imported capital are not taxed; rather, imports of capital are implicitly assumed to be restricted by licensing, with licenses given away to foreign investors with no strings attached. If the domestic interest rate exceeds the world interest rate, foreign investors therefore receive more than the world interest rate.

The explanation of Brecher and Díaz-Alejandro's result is that their assumptions ensure that the indirect effects of liberalisation are harmful because it reduces trade, which is already inefficiently small, and that the direct benefits of (partial) liberalisation are zero. However, unless the capital account has already been liberalised to the point at which all remaining restrictions on capital mobility are trivial, in the sense that the domestic and world interest rates are equal, full liberalisation would produce the direct benefit for the home country of only having to pay the world interest rate for imported capital instead of the higher domestic interest rate that initially applies. The assumptions made by Brecher and Díaz-Alejandro implicitly prevent them analysing complete liberalisation, because if the domestic interest rate was initially above the world interest rate full capital account liberalisation in their model would cause the labour intensive industry to cease operating, thus violating an assumption that is crucial to their result that capital account liberalisation has no direct benefits. It follows that their result cannot be used to analyse full liberalisation of the capital account except in the trivial case in which capital controls have already been reduced to negligible importance.

It is not claimed here that it is impossible to construct theoretical cases in which capital account liberalisation exacerbates the inefficiencies due to trade barriers by enough to outweigh its direct benefits. It has merely been argued that, contrary to the arguments discussed, there is no presumption that it does this. The fact that it causes real appreciation does not even create the presumption that its indirect effects exacerbate the inefficiencies caused by trade restrictions, let alone that they do so by enough to outweigh the beneficial direct effects of removing capital controls.

4.5 'GOOD' AND 'BAD' CAPITAL INFLOWS?

Most controls and taxes on international capital movements discriminate among different types of capital flows. The view that countries should welcome FDI, but restrict portfolio investment and borrowing from foreign banks is very widely held. Even such an eminent proponent of free trade as Bhagwati (1998), who emphasises the qualitative differences between FDI and other forms of foreign investment that can arise when FDI is a vehicle for the international transmission of firm-specific technologies, supports restrictions on inflows of non-FDI capital.[22] In contrast, it was argued at the end of section 4.2 that such differences provide a case for taxing investments that embody firm-specific technologies more heavily than other forms of foreign investment.

A second rationalisation for favouring FDI is based on the view that it is less volatile than portfolio flows, bank loans or trade credits. Support for this view was provided by Frankel and Rose (1996) who found that countries with a relatively high ratio of FDI to foreign debt are significantly less likely to experience currency crises than countries with a relatively low ratio. A possible explanation for this finding is that the potential for rapid capital outflows to occur may sometimes be greater if liquid assets are held by non-residents than if they are held by residents. For example, a country that uses exchange controls can easily make it illegal for residents to transfer their bank deposits offshore, but could not pass a law to stop domestic residents repaying their short-term foreign loans without causing them to default on international obligations.

Claessens *et al.* (1995), however, found evidence that challenges the conventional view that FDI is more stable than other forms of capital flows. Using data for a sample of industrialised and developing countries, they found that information on the composition of capital inflows does not help in predicting the time series behaviour of net capital flows. They found no significant differences in the relative volatility of FDI, portfolio and other investment and contrary to popular belief, there was no statistically significant negative correlation between the volatility of net capital flows and the proportion of foreign direct investment in total foreign investment. The explanation suggested by Dooley (1996) is that precisely because wealth held in the form of factories is relatively hard to liquidate and move offshore, foreign direct investors have an incentive to hedge their exposure to fluctuations in the local economy by devices such as borrowing from local credit markets.

Even if a relatively high proportion of non-FDI flows in total inflows were generally associated with high volatility of total net inflows, there are several reasons for rejecting the conclusion that government policy should discriminate against portfolio and other investment and in favour of FDI. First, facilitating trade and direct investment requires providing a liberal regime for trade finance and bank loans and deposits. Thus, although leads and lags in trade payments provide a popular method of speculating against a pegged exchange rate, the role of short-term trade credits in financing international trade is sufficiently important that even control systems that restrict most forms of non-FDI capital flows usually provide exemptions for trade finance. For example, the controls operated by Malaysia since September 1998 do not apply to trade finance and Chile's VDR was not applied to suppliers' credits on imports nor to pre-shipment payments for exports. Second, access to offshore financial markets is one of the features that make a country an attractive destination for long-term capital flows. This was illustrated by the fact that the Bank of Korea liberalised foreign exchange transactions by foreign investors in 1998 in order to encourage FDI and portfolio investment. Another illustration of the same point is that in the aftermath of the 1997–98 debacle in Indonesia, it turned out that FDI firms owed $32 billion to offshore banks. This accounted for 48 per cent of Indonesia's total private non-bank external debts and 44 per cent of its total private sector external debts. It is most implausible to imagine that Indonesia could have insulated itself against the risk of sudden outflows by restricting private sector access to foreign bank credit without also reducing FDI.

In economies with managed exchange rates, the volatility of portfolio and other capital flows is greatly magnified by the almost universal central bank practice of tightening or easing monetary policy in an attempt to sterilise the effects of capital flows on the money supply.[23] For example, if the authorities attempt to sterilise the monetary effects of an initial capital inflow by contractionary monetary policy, the resulting interest rate rise will induce a further capital inflow. In developing countries, sterilisation by means of open market operations usually involves sales or purchases of short-term securities by the authorities; it therefore induces inflows or outflows of short-term portfolio capital.

In economies with flexible exchange rate regimes, it is particularly important to permit volatile movements in short-term capital because the central bank does not stand ready to meet day-to-day fluctuations in the supply and demand for foreign exchange by traders and long-term investors. These fluctuations must therefore be accommodated by private banks. If one separated out 'hot money flows', somehow defined, on the one hand, and all other international flows of 'goods and long-term investments' on the other, then under a pure flexible exchange rate system in which the monetary authorities never intervene in the exchange market, these two components would have to be equal and opposite because of the accounting identity that net sales of foreign exchange equal net purchases of foreign exchange. Restricting short-term capital flows so as to achieve some given reduction in their volatility would therefore increase the fluctuations in the spot exchange rate by the amount needed to achieve a matching reduction in the volatility of the trade flows and long-term capital flows that are financed by short-term capital flows.

4.6   OVERVIEW

First-best Arguments for Taxing Capital Inflows

If there are no market failures and if capital is in perfectly elastic supply to a small open economy at a given world interest rate, there is a strong case for not taxing the domestic earnings of foreign capital. This case is exactly the same as the traditional case for free trade in goods: taxing the earnings of foreign capital is inefficient because it results in domestic residents facing a price for capital that is higher than its opportunity cost to the home economy. The best way of raising tax revenue is by taxing the consumption of residents.

Sections 4.1 and 4.2 discussed three cases for taxing capital which result from departures from the assumption in the preceding paragraph that the home country faces a perfectly elastic supply of capital at the going world interest rate: first, the possibility of sovereign default makes the interest rates charged to domestic residents depend on the amount borrowed by the home country; second, non-resident investors sometimes have opportunities for earning monopoly profits in the home economy; and third, when foreign countries operate FTC systems, it may be possible to divert revenue from foreign treasuries to the domestic treasury without affecting the domestic interest rate, or the amount of capital inflow. These three cases provide 'first-best' justifications for taxing capital in the sense that they do not depend on the assumption that some other domestic policies have been badly set. Some second-best justifications for restricting capital inflows were considered in sections 4.3, 4.4 and 4.5; others are discussed in Chapter 6.

It was argued in section 4.1 that the sovereign risk argument for taxing capital inflow can only justify taxes that are lower than the taxes actually levied by most countries, other than tax havens. Harberger (1985) has shown that the appropriate tax rate implied by the sovereign risk case is approximately equal to the country risk premium. In normal times, the risk premia for developing countries are usually of the order of 1 percentage point per year: when the World Bank and the US Treasury can borrow in US dollars at 6 per cent per year, developing countries can 'normally' borrow in US dollars at about 7 per cent per year. Applying the Harberger approximation leads to an optimal tax on interest payments abroad of 1 percentage point per year. In the above example, the tax rate on interest payments abroad that is needed to raise the interest rate paid by borrowers from 6 per cent to 7 per cent per year is 16.7 per cent. By comparison, most developing countries charge much higher corporate taxes and the additional tax implicit in a 30 per cent unremunerated deposit requirement is 42.9 per cent.[24]

Obviously there is substantial variation in the risk premia among countries and over time. On some occasions, the annual risk premia for some countries have been much higher: perhaps 10 per cent or even more. But such high risk premia occur only during crises in which governments are anxious to encourage capital inflows, not to discourage them. The case for taxing inflows assumes that they always make default more probable; but in crises, any inflows that can be attracted make default less likely. The conclusion is that the case for the tax only exists when the rate implied by the Harberger approximation is relatively low.

A quite separate case for taxing the domestic earnings of foreign capital is provided by the fact that intellectual property rights, brand names and natural barriers to the transmission of firm-specific technologies give some foreign investors the opportunity to earn monopoly profits in the domestic economy. Some low rate of tax on the domestic earnings of these investors can be justified because it is a way of diverting some of their potential monopoly profits to the government of the home economy.

The third of the above arguments for taxing the domestic earnings of foreign capital is that when a small developing country imports capital from a country like the USA, which operates an FTC system, it might seem to have an opportunity to divert tax revenue from the US Treasury to its own treasury without affecting total tax payments by US investors, and therefore without discouraging US investment, simply by taxing the domestic earnings of foreign capital at a rate slightly below the rate of corporate tax in the USA. However, the case for such a tax is greatly weakened by two important complications.

First, the income from foreign subsidiaries of resident corporations is generally taxed when it is realised, rather than as it accrues. This provides a partial tax exemption for income earned abroad by subsidiaries. If income earned abroad is exempt from tax in the source country, the case for a tax in the capital-importing country disappears.

Second, although most capital-exporting countries operate FTC systems, most of them, with the exception of the USA, also provide some form of imputation system to alleviate the double taxation of dividends that occurs under the classical tax system still operated by the USA. Under an FTC system, foreign corporate taxes can be credited against domestic corporate taxes, but under an imputation system, the domestic corporate tax is only a withholding tax for most taxpayers. As a result of imputation, foreign tax credits are therefore wasted for a shareholder whose personal marginal tax rate exceeds the domestic corporate tax rate: each dollar of foreign corporate tax paid by its subsidiaries reduces the domestic corporate tax paid by the parent company by one dollar, but this reduces the income tax credits available to the shareholders by the same amount. The effect of imputation is therefore to convert what appear to be FTC and FTE systems into FTD systems. If capital is imported from countries that operate such systems, a country that is too small to influence the world interest rate harms itself by taxing the domestic earnings of foreign capital.

The combined effect of imputation and the taxation of foreign income on the basis of realisations is to convert the appearance of a free lunch by using domestic taxes to divert revenue from the treasuries of countries that operate FTC systems to the home treasury into a mirage.

The three 'first-best' factors discussed above might justify a corporate tax at, say, 20 per cent and a withholding tax on payments abroad at, say, 15 per cent, provided that foreign investors are allowed to use their imputation credits against their liabilities for withholding tax on dividends paid abroad. These rates are suggested only as very rough indications of suitable orders of magnitude. If they were adopted, net payments of withholding taxes would only be made on interest and royalty payments, and on dividends earned in 'tax-preferred' activities, such as those that receive investment grants or accelerated depreciation allowances.

With respect to the foreign income of domestic residents, countries have a selfish interest in operating an FTD system because from the purely selfish perspective of the home country, foreign taxes are as much a cost of operating abroad as foreign wages or any other part of operating costs. Since an FTD system can be achieved by combining imputation with an FTC system, a sensible overall system is to combine an imputation system with a low rate of corporate tax and a low rate of withholding tax on dividends, royalties and interest paid abroad.

Second-best Arguments for Restricting Capital Mobility

Section 4.3 dealt with the case for restricting capital outflows as a means for boosting seigniorage, that is, the revenue from printing money. If inflation is very rapid, and if budget deficits are financed by printing money or by extending central bank credit to the government, then the unilateral removal of outflow controls is not advisable because it raises the rate of a very inefficient tax, namely the inflation tax. This is very much a second-best rationalisation for temporarily retaining capital controls. It can also be used to rationalise all kinds of highly inefficient policies, not merely retaining capital controls: like the removal of capital controls, the removal of tariffs and export taxes would have adverse effects on inflation in the circumstances assumed. So would government spending on public goods. Since relying on rapid monetary growth to finance a large budget deficit is an extremely inefficient way of financing government spending, a government in the situation described above should speedily undertake a fiscal reform to eliminate the need for excessive seigniorage; once this has been done, the fiscal case for capital controls vanishes.

Section 4.4 deals with arguments for not removing inflow controls unless tariffs and export taxes have already been eliminated. It is certainly possible to construct models in which the indirect effects of capital account liberalisation are adverse and so large that they outweigh the beneficial direct effects.

Equally, however, the indirect effects may be beneficial. Section 4.4 argued that some commonly cited arguments which try to show that the indirect effects are normally harmful and large enough to offset the beneficial direct effects are invalid. In any case, the policy importance of second-best considerations is often quite small for two reasons. First, whereas the direct effects of capital account liberalisation are always beneficial, it is often hard to predict with confidence whether the indirect effects are harmful or beneficial. Second, opportunities to undertake particular reforms, or partial reforms, come and go as a result of political factors. If policy makers seize opportunities to liberalise whenever they arise, the overall effect of a sequence of reforms will be beneficial, even if there are occasional instances of movements in the wrong direction. Provided that each reform moves policy in the direction of removing all regulations and taxes that cannot be justified as part of globally optimal policies, any movements in the wrong direction must necessarily be temporary.

One popular argument for restricting capital inflows if trade is restricted is that they cause an appreciation of the RER which adversely affects exporting and import-competing industries. The first point to note is that capital inflows adversely affect exporting and import-competing industries even if trade is not restricted. However, they also normally benefit labour and factors that are specific to non-traded goods industries. If trade is restricted, moving resources out of export industries is inefficient, but moving them out of import-competing industries enhances efficiency. The existence of trade restrictions provides no presumption that shifting resources from traded to non-traded industries is inefficient.

Another frequently cited argument for restricting capital mobility is based on the claim that in the model of Brecher and Díaz-Alejandro (1977), an inflow of capital necessarily makes a country worse off if trade is restricted, if the import-competing sector is capital intensive and if licences to import capital are given away to foreign investors.[25] However, it was pointed out in section 4.4 that, even in this model, the complete removal of all capital controls would have a direct benefit to set against the indirect costs of liberalisation that are built into it, except in the trivial case in which capital controls have already been reduced to negligible importance. This benefit is that the total price paid to foreign investors for the use of their capital would be reduced from the domestic interest rate to the world interest rate.

The arguments for restricting capital flows until after the completion of trade liberalisation have acquired superficial plausibility because there are many examples of countries in which trade liberalisation has initially been followed by rapid capital inflows, that have subsequently turned abruptly to rapid outflows and then to exchange rate and financial collapse. These events probably have little do with the sequencing of current and capital liberalisation. Chile provides a classic example: the reforms of the late 1970s were followed by a currency crisis and financial collapse in 1982, despite the fact that the reforms had followed the conventional wisdom on sequencing: the liberalisation of the capital account was delayed until after the removal of most trade barriers.[26]

The most plausible explanation for the observed association of currency and financial crises with trade liberalisation programmes is that trade and financial liberalisation are often implemented together and financial liberalisation loosens the constraints that prevent banks and finance companies exploiting the opportunities for moral hazard provided by central bank safety nets for depositors. This is dealt with in Chapter 6.

Arguments for welcoming inflows of FDI, but discouraging inflows of portfolio capital, trade credits and bank loans and deposits at domestic banks were discussed in section 4.6, which referred to the empirical evidence that casts doubt on the claim that portfolio and other flows are more volatile than FDI. In any case, part of the observed volatility of portfolio capital is an endogenous response to attempts by central banks to sterilise capital flows by open market operations in short-term official securities. This strategy magnifies the volatility of capital flows, and if the authorities sterilise capital flows by buying and selling short-term securities, the induced volatility will be volatility of short-term portfolio flows.

Even if portfolio and other foreign investment flows were more volatile than net flows of FDI, this would not by itself justify different tax and regulatory treatment of different types of capital flows. Regulations cannot switch capital flows between alternative forms – for example, between bank loans and FDI – without inducing arrangements designed to hedge the altered risks. FDI projects are seldom financed entirely by foreign equity and may be financed largely by domestic or foreign bank loans. In addition, what is really a flow of debt or portfolio equity can, with some inconvenience, be relabelled as FDI. For example, China's restrictions on portfolio inflows have not stopped many domestic firms from setting up offshore subsidiaries in Hong Kong, in order to attract foreign capital by borrowing or by issuing equity and then making inward investments that can be officially described as FDI.

NOTES

1. Let the world interest rate, r^*, be a function of the amount of capital lent to the domestic economy, L, so that $r^* = r^*(L)$. Let ε be the elasticity of L with respect to r^* and let τ be the proportionate rate of tax on interest payments abroad, so that the domestic interest rate is $r^*[1 + \tau]$. At the optimum, $\tau = 1/\varepsilon$. Derivations of this formula can be found in Kemp (1964) and Jones (1967).
2. In the simplest version of the sovereign default case for restricting capital inflows, there is a single country-specific risk premium that is the same both for private and for publicly guaranteed domestic borrowers. This can be justified by assuming that non-residents who have lent to the private sector will be treated on the same terms as those who have lent to the public sector if the government imposes a moratorium on foreign debt service payments

which leads to a 'restructuring' – read 'reduction' – of contracted repayments. Evidence of the approximate realism of this assumption in the context of the Latin American debt crisis of the 1980s is provided by Folkerts-Landau (1985, pp. 326–7).

3. To confirm Harberger's result, assume that the schedule relating the contract interest rate, r_c, to the amount lent by foreigners, L, is linear with gradient γ: $r_c = r^* + \gamma L$, where r^* is the risk-free world interest rate and γ is some positive constant. In contrast to the true monopsony case, r^* is now assumed to be independent of L. The elasticity of the supply of loans with respect to the contract interest rate is $r_c/(\gamma L)$. Therefore, the optimal tax, expressed as a proportion of the contract interest rate, is $\gamma L/r_c$. The optimal tax per unit borrowed per period is therefore γL, which is also the per period country risk premium, $r_c - r^*$.

4. I am grateful to Ted Sieper for pointing out the need to take account of the effect on the observed risk premium of imposing the tax.

5. Applegate (1999) used data on bonds denominated in the same currencies (usually US dollars) to calculate the country-specific risk premia on annual interest rates for various developing countries relative to the rates paid by the World Bank before and after the onset of the Asian crisis. His graphs show that the premium for the Philippines rose from 1.2 per cent in February 1997 to 3.5 per cent in January 1998. Thailand's premium rose from an average of 0.8 per cent in the first half of 1997 to about 4 per cent in December 1997 and January 1998. Brazil's premium was usually between 2 per cent and 2.5 per cent in the second and third quarters of 1997 and then rose to between 3 per cent and 6.2 per cent in the last quarter. Argentina's premium briefly exceeded 9 per cent in early 1995, but was below 1 per cent during the first quarter of 1997. Indonesia's premium averaged slightly less than 1 per cent in the first half of 1997, but had risen to over 5 per cent by January 1998.

6. As noted in Chapter 3, Chile removed its VDR in 1998, and Korea accelerated the liberalisation of its restrictions on inflows in 1999.

7. I am grateful to Ted Sieper and Matt Benge for helpful comments on the issues relating to the taxation of foreign income. The analysis of this subsection is based on Benge (1999).

8. Suppose that the corporate income attributable to a representative resident shareholder is $100 before corporate tax and $80 after corporate tax at 20 per cent. If all the after-tax income is distributed, the shareholder receives a cheque for $80 and an imputation tax credit of $20. The shareholder's gross taxable income from the dividend is deemed to be $100, that is, the net dividend plus the imputation credit. An individual whose personal marginal tax rate is, say, 45 per cent would therefore have to pay an additional $25 in tax, and would have a disposable income of $55.

9. See Hartman (1985).

10. For a more complete treatment, see Bruce (1992). The basic point was made by Johnson (1970, pp. 44–5).

11. Base money is defined in section 2.2.

12. Fischer (1982) splits the present value of seigniorage revenue into a 'stock' component, which measures the cost to the government of buying back the outstanding stock of base money, and a 'flow' component, which measures the present value of all future money creation. To see that this approach gives the same answer as just using the nominal interest rate, note that if the stock of base money is initially R, if its real value is expected to grow steadily at rate g and if the rate of inflation is π, then the rate of growth of the nominal money supply is $\mu = \pi + g$. The real value of nominal additions to the money supply is μR. Since this real stream grows at rate g its present value is $\mu R/(r^* - g)$, where r^* is the real interest rate. This is Fischer's flow component. The total (stock plus flow) revenue from seigniorage is therefore $R(r^* - g + \mu)/(r^* - g) = iR/(r^* - g)$, where the nominal interest rate is $i = r^* + \pi = r^* + \mu - g$. Some authors (for example, McKinnon 1991, pp. 57–9) measure the revenue from seigniorage as the real value of nominal additions to base money. This ignores Fischer's stock component, but it is not a bad approximation to the correct formula in economies in which inflation makes the nominal rate much bigger than the real interest rate.

13. Cagan (1956).

14. Drazen (1989).

15. The notes to the table explain how seigniorage revenue was estimated; 'government current revenue' is defined as profits of state-owned enterprises plus on-budget revenue from fees and explicit taxes.
16. For example, Edwards (1989, pp. 7–8, 88) estimates the RER from the formula $\Sigma_i\, w_i\, [e_i.P_i^w]/[e_0 P_0^c]$, where e_i is the nominal exchange rate for trading partner i in units of its currency per dollar, e_0 is the home country's exchange rate in units of its currency per dollar; P_i^w is the wholesale price index for country i; P_0^c is the consumer price index for the home country and w_i is the share of country i in the trade of the home country.
17. Warr (1999a, 1999b).
18. Balassa (1964), Samuelson (1964).
19. This is analysed by McKinnon and Pill (1997).
20. See Corden and Neary (1982) and Corden (1984).
21. Lal (1987), p. 293.
22. The firm-specific features of some FDI and their role in the spread of technological innovations are emphasised by Hymer and Rowthorn (1970) and play a role in the product cycle theory of trade and investment of Vernon (1966). A survey of this approach is given by Bhagwati (1985).
23. Quantitative data on the extent of sterilisation are given in Chapter 7.
24. If there is a 30 per cent unremunerated deposit requirement, borrowers must pay interest on $100 in order to get the use of $70. This raises the effective interest rate by $100/70 = 1.429$. In Chile's case, the implicit tax rates on long-term borrowing were much lower, as explained in Chapter 3.
25. Recent examples of the use of Brecher and Díaz-Alejandro's analysis to support the case for capital controls include Reisen (1994, p. 117), Cooper (1998, p. 13) and Wilson (1999).
26. See Ffrench-Davis (1981), Edwards and Edwards (1991, pp. 111–12) and Velasco (1991, p. 123).

5. Speculative crises, default and contagion

In the aftermath of the speculative crises of the 1990s, the most popular arguments for capital controls have been based on the role of volatile capital flows in provoking crises. This chapter surveys the theoretical and empirical literature on speculative attacks on financial systems and exchange rates and examines why such attacks have generally led to much larger falls in real economic activity in developing than in industrialised countries.

5.1 DESTABILISING SPECULATION AND SPECULATIVE BUBBLES

Friedman (1953) set out the classic defence of speculation against those who regard it as harmful. He argued that those who correctly anticipate shortages, or gluts, can earn profits by buying when prices are below their future equilibrium levels or by selling when they are above them. Speculators with good information therefore earn profits and drive prices towards their equilibrium levels. Speculators with bad information do the opposite and are therefore destabilising; but, by buying high and selling low, they make losses. Market forces therefore sufficiently reward stabilising speculation and penalise destabilising speculation without any need for government intervention.

Friedman's claim that profitable speculation must be stabilising generated a search for counter examples which, more than 30 years later, showed that the claim is indeed too strong. Even when the invisible hand of self-interest guided by competition leads to efficiency, it need not always also lead to price stability. Hart and Kreps (1986) showed that speculation, which in their example involves purchase and storage of a commodity for subsequent resale, may in some circumstances increase price variability because, in situations in which future prices depend on uncertain future events, speculators buy when the probability of price appreciation is high and sell when this probability is low. This need not be equivalent to buying when prices are low and selling when they are high. Even in the Hart and Kreps counter example, speculation raises welfare: in the absence of market failures, the ability of speculators to store current output for future resale always raises efficiency, but larger price fluctuations may sometimes be more efficient than smaller ones.

Speculative episodes in which prices rise in booms and fall in slumps by amounts that are too large to attribute to new information about fundamentals are loosely referred to as 'bubbles'. The notorious stock market crashes of 1929 and 1987, in which prices fell abruptly by amounts which were very large relative to any new information about economic fundamentals, provide evidence in favour of the empirical importance of some version of the speculative bubble hypothesis with less than fully rational expectations. Shiller (1981) provided empirical evidence that stock market prices fluctuate by larger amounts, on average, than those that can be justified by subsequent fluctuations in dividends.[1]

Although Shiller's evidence suggests that market outcomes regularly differ in statistically significant ways from the predictions of models that assume fully rational behaviour, it does not follow that government intervention is desirable. If the government really has a comparative advantage over private speculators in information gathering, it could either publish its own forecasts or trade directly (and presumably profitably) in futures markets rather than try to stop private firms and individuals from engaging in speculation or arbitrage. The long history of government-organised commodity price stabilisation schemes which have lost money, despite being given subsidies and monopoly powers, suggests that any economies of scale in information gathering and processing are usually dwarfed by the incentives that lead to cost-padding in government agencies or to hidden subsidies for politically influential lobby groups.

5.2 CURRENCY CRISES WHEN THE COLLAPSE OF A FIXED EXCHANGE RATE SYSTEM IS INEVITABLE

Speculative attacks on fixed exchange rates in developing countries have often been preceded by sustained periods of growth of domestic credit at rates far in excess of the combined rate of growth of foreign prices and real GDP.[2] Krugman (1979) analysed such attacks in a model in which the government finances an ongoing budget deficit by adding to domestic credit and running down its foreign exchange reserves. In this model, the collapse of the fixed exchange rate system is inevitable because the monetary authorities must eventually run out of reserves.

The model is shown in Figure 5.1. The right panel shows the demand for base money, in real terms, as a function of the domestic interest rate. The world interest rate is r, and with the exchange rate fixed, at least temporarily, the domestic interest rate is also r. Point A in the right panel shows this initial position of temporary equilibrium. The demand for money is M_A.

The left panel in Figure 5.1 shows the movements over time in base money, official foreign exchange reserves and domestic credit. For the reasons set out in section 2.2, base money is equal to the sum of reserves and domestic credit. Suppose that at time 0, the authorities' foreign exchange reserves are just equal to M_A, but that the government finances an ongoing budget deficit by printing and issuing notes. With the demand for money unchanged, the private recipients

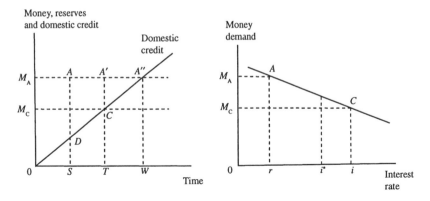

Figure 5.1   Inevitable and self-fulfilling currency crises

of these notes immediately convert them into foreign exchange so that the authorities are effectively financing the budget deficit by running down their foreign exchange reserves. Domestic credit initially grows over time at a rate equal to the budget deficit. At time S, domestic credit is equal to DS and reserves have shrunk from AS to AD. If the private sector was myopic, the government could continue to finance the unchanged deficit by running down reserves until time W, when reserves would be equal to zero.

If speculators are not myopic, what happens as reserves dwindle depends on what they expect the government to do when reserves run out. If they were confident that the government would then cut spending, or raise taxes, so as to balance the budget without resorting to money creation, even far-sighted speculators would not launch a speculative attack because there would be no reason for the demand for money to fall and the exchange rate to depreciate when reserves do finally run out. In Krugman's model, however, speculators anticipate that when the authorities run out of reserves, domestic credit will continue to grow steadily at the same rate as before: the budget deficit will be unchanged, but will thereafter be financed by printing money and allowing the exchange rate to depreciate. The switch from reserve depletion to inflationary finance as the mechanism for financing the budget deficit causes an increase in inflation and a fall in the demand for money. The rates of money creation and inflation needed to finance the given budget deficit are determined in the way analysed in Figure 4.1. With a budget deficit of D in Figure 4.1, the domestic nominal interest rate is i and the implied rate of inflation is $\pi = i - r$. At this higher interest rate, the right panel of Figure 5.1 shows that the demand for money would be only M_C.

If private money holdings remained unchanged until reserves run out at time *W*, the reduction in real money holdings at that time would be achieved by an abrupt depreciation of the domestic currency. Far-sighted individuals would be able to earn arbitrarily large profits by borrowing in domestic currency to finance holding foreign exchange at that time. Competition among far-sighted speculators would result in a speculative attack before time *W*. If many speculators have perfect foresight, they will compete away all the potential profits by launching a speculative attack at time *T*, when foreign currency reserves are equal to $A'C$, which is the amount by which the demand for money falls when the interest rate rises from *r* to *i*. At time *T*, the equilibrium in the right panel of Figure 5.1 will switch abruptly from point *A* to point *C*, where the new interest rate is compatible with the rate of inflation needed to finance the budget deficit, once reserves have run out. The fall in private money holdings, $M_A - M_C$, is equal to the foreign exchange bought from the authorities and used to finance private purchases of foreign bonds and securities.

The preceding analysis assumed that domestic credit is only changed by the gradual process of ongoing budget deficits. Flood and Marion (1998) show that the vulnerability of a fixed exchange rate system to speculative attack is increased if the monetary authorities are expected to expand domestic credit to sterilise a part of any reduction in the money supply due to a fall in foreign exchange reserves. Suppose that the authorities expand domestic credit by 50 cents for every dollar by which reserves fall. In the preceding example, instead of occurring when reserves have fallen to $A'C$, the speculative attack would occur at time *S* when they are twice this amount: speculators would finance the acquisition of $A'C$ of foreign currency assets using the $A'C$ of base money that they no longer wish to hold in this form and the remainder, $AD - A'C$, using the domestic credit advanced to them by the government in response to the fall in reserves of AD. In the extreme case in which the authorities are expected to try to expand domestic credit by one dollar for every dollar by which reserves fall, there is no initial level of reserves that is sufficient to prevent an immediate successful speculative attack.

It has been understood for a long time that the maintenance of a permanently fixed exchange rate system imposes a constraint on the permissible long-run rate of growth of domestic credit: it must not be expanded faster than the growth in demand for base money at the fixed exchange rate. The ultimate cause of the speculative attack in Krugman's model is that the authorities try to flout this constraint by using domestic credit expansion to finance a continuing budget deficit that is too large to be financed indefinitely in this way at a fixed exchange rate. The inevitable result is that foreign exchange reserves are depleted and the currency devalued.

By banning international capital movements, the authorities could delay the speculative attack, but could not prevent a devaluation from occurring: even if the current account were initially in surplus, the creation of domestic credit at a rate in excess of the growth in domestic demand for money at an unchanged exchange rate would eventually force the current account into deficit. Domestic prices would rise, and both residents and non-residents would switch their spending from domestic to foreign goods. Reserves would be gradually depleted, and the authorities would eventually be forced to devalue.[3] Even under the most severe capital controls, a modified speculative attack would occur. First, some capital flows would occur because of leads and lags in the payments for imports and exports: exporters would delay converting foreign currency into domestic currency and importers would buy the foreign currency needed to pay for imports at the earliest possible opportunity. Second, there would be increased importing and storing of the types of good for which shipping and storage costs are relatively low. Anticipating a devaluation, firms and households would have an incentive to convert their holdings of money and domestic currency-denominated assets into real assets. This would produce a spending boom which would add to the current account deficit and hasten the devaluation.

5.3   SELF-FULFILLING CURRENCY SPECULATION

Krugman's (1979) model is an example of a 'first-generation' speculative attack model. In these models, the breakdown of the fixed exchange rate system is inevitable because the authorities are attempting to pursue two policies which are not compatible in the long-run – the maintenance of a fixed exchange rate and the creation of domestic credit at a faster rate than that compatible with maintaining a fixed exchange rate. A second generation of models, beginning with Flood and Garber (1984) and Obstfeld (1986), sets out circumstances in which speculative attacks may be self-fulfilling, in the sense that multiple equilibria are possible, any one of which can be sustained indefinitely provided that everyone believes that it will be sustained.

By modifying the assumptions of the preceding section, it is possible to use Figure 5.1 to analyse a simple model of a self-fulfilling currency crisis. It is now assumed that the government has interest-bearing domestic currency-denominated debts and can finance its outlays either by income and sales taxes or by adding to domestic credit (thereby running down reserves, while the exchange rate remains fixed, or causing inflation, once reserves have run out). Suppose that if it can roll over its debts at an interest rate below i^*, which is shown in the right panel in Figure 5.1, the government would choose to balance the budget using income and sales taxes, and without adding to domestic credit. In this situation, reserves will remain constant if the demand for money remains constant. But now suppose also that if expectations of inflation cause the domestic interest rate to exceed $i*$, the levels of income and sales taxes needed to balance the budget, given the increased burden of outstanding government debt, would be so high that the government would prefer to print money and allow the exchange rate to float. Further, assume that following a successful speculative attack, the government would set monetary growth at the same rate as that assumed in the previous section, namely $(i - r)$.

Under the above assumptions, no speculative attack can succeed if domestic credit is less than CT and reserves are greater than $A'C$. But if reserves are initially positive, but less than $A'C$, and if domestic credit is less than $A''W$, but greater than CT, then two equilibria are possible. If each person expects the fixed exchange rate to be maintained, their expectations will be self-fulfilling. Because no inflation is expected, the interest rate is r and the demand for money is M_A; and because the interest rate is less than $i*$, the authorities do not expand domestic credit. Reserves can therefore remain unchanged. The equilibrium in the right panel will be at point A, and this equilibrium can be sustained indefinitely.

However, if each person expects the exchange rate to depreciate at $(i - r)$, these expectations will also be self-fulfilling because they will cause the authorities to begin to expand domestic credit at this rate. The interest rate will rise to i and the demand for money will fall to M_C. Even if the authorities sold off their remaining reserves at the old exchange rate, not all of this fall in desired money holdings could be accommodated by using money to buy reserves from the authorities at the old exchange rate since the fall in money demand is $A'C$, and since, by assumption, the pre-attack level of reserves is less than $A'C$. Part of the fall in real money holdings must therefore be met by a finite devaluation. Anticipating a finite devaluation, it would be in each individual's self-interest to use domestic currency holdings to buy foreign exchange from the authorities at the old exchange rate.

The possibility of self-fulfilling speculation in this model could be removed if the government denominated its debt in foreign currency rather than in domestic currency, and if it could credibly commit itself always to repay its debt in full. The reason is that a speculative attack would no longer affect the burden of the government's debts since this burden no longer depends on the domestic interest rate. The larger the penalties imposed by the international community for sovereign default, the more credible such commitments become. However, in the absence of a credible commitment never to default, a self-fulfilling speculative attack would again be possible. In the amended scenario, with the government's debt denominated in foreign currency, partial default would take the place of devaluation, and the penalties for default, such as loss of reputation and possible disruption to international trade and investment, would take the place of the costs of inflation. In this amended model, increased expectations of default might be self-fulfilling because, by raising the risk premium demanded by holders of government bonds, they would raise the cost to the government of not defaulting.

The model of potentially self-fulfilling expectations of partial default set out above is formally equivalent to the original model of potentially self-fulfilling expectations of devaluation. This is not surprising because devaluation is formally equivalent to a partial default on the authorities' commitment to maintain the real value of the currency.

There are many other possible ways in which multiple equilibria can arise.[4] For example, an expectation of devaluation may also be self-fulfilling if it results in money wages being set at higher levels than those that would be set if workers and employers were confident that the exchange rate would not be devalued. The reason is that if money wages have been set at relatively high levels, the authorities are under more pressure to reduce unemployment by devaluing than if wages had been set at lower levels. In this example, 'herding' behaviour is in the self-interest of employers and employees: a particular labour market contract should specify a high money wage if this is what other contracts specify, but not otherwise.

Multiple equilibria can also occur because speculation against a fixed exchange rate will be successful – and therefore profitable – if many speculators attack a currency at the same time, but unsuccessful – and therefore unprofitable – if only a few speculators join the attack. Herding behaviour is now in the self-interest of each speculator: each speculator gains from short-selling the domestic currency if others do the same, but not if they do not.

Although all the above examples involve speculation against a fixed exchange rate system, analogous problems can arise under a floating rate regime if speculators believe that speculation against the exchange rate or financial system may cause the authorities to abandon the monetary or inflation targets that are necessary for the stability of a floating rate regime. This is illustrated in section 8.5 which discusses the loss of credibility of Indonesia's monetary targets in 1997–98.

Some of the theoretical models in which multiple equilibria are possible make the equilibrium that actually occurs depend on some stochastic signal. The possibility of multiple equilibria now exists before the signal is observed, but the outcome is unique once the signal has been observed. If a currency's fundamentals are sufficiently weak that a speculative attack would succeed if the actions of speculators are coordinated, then a relatively small adverse event may trigger panic selling and large devaluations. For example, if speculators can at best observe only an imperfect estimate of the true fundamentals, then it may sometimes pay them to disregard the information about fundamentals that they themselves have received and instead copy what others are doing.[5]

Such models of imperfect information help to explain 'financial contagion'; that is, the possibility that a speculative attack on one currency, or bank, may trigger attacks on other currencies, or banks, in apparently similar circumstances.

In financial crises, as in flu epidemics, the existence of contagion does not imply that 'fundamentals' are irrelevant: countries and banks with strong fundamentals may resist, or avoid, speculative attacks, just as many individuals manage to resist contagious diseases for various reasons, such as having been vaccinated, having high natural immunity or avoiding contact with carriers. The importance of fundamentals is illustrated in the amended version of the model of Figure 5.1 used in this section: no speculative attack can succeed if official foreign exchange reserves are kept above $A'C$ and if domestic credit is kept below CT. Only if domestic credit is expanded until reserves fall into the 'danger zone' below $A'C$ can a self-fulfilling speculative attack be successful.

5.4   BANKING PANICS AND DEFAULT

Banking Panics

Banking panics are a classic example of the self-fulfilling speculation that can occur when multiple equilibria exist. Many of their features are captured in the well-known model of Diamond and Dybvig (1983). Like the currency crisis models in which speculation is self-fulfilling, it is a multiple equilibrium model. In the 'good' equilibrium, banks provide liquidity services by allowing risk-sharing among a group of depositors who are unsure whether they will be able to leave their deposits untouched for long enough to finance long-term investments or whether they may need to make early withdrawals. In the 'bad' equilibrium, depositors who do not really need early withdrawals nevertheless panic and demand them because, if enough others also panic, a bank whose assets are illiquid will be forced into bankruptcy even though it would be solvent in the absence of a panic. Despite being very stylised, the model illustrates how bank runs can occur, how they can result in a real loss of output, and why depositors may benefit from the ability of banks to suspend the convertibility of deposits in a crisis.

Diamond and Dybvig propose a tax-financed compulsory deposit insurance scheme which would prevent bank runs and unnecessary early withdrawals. It is therefore often claimed that their model provides a rationale for compulsory government deposit insurance. However, this claim is misleading for two reasons. First, their assumptions implicitly rule out the important possibility that a bank run may be an efficient response to a bank being insolvent, rather than merely illiquid. Second, the cause of unnecessary panics in their model is the assumption that demand deposits involve 'sequential service contracts': banks must service each withdrawal demand in turn, without taking account of the total volume of early withdrawals being demanded. If the total is large relative to the bank's resources, sequential service will result in those at the front of the queue for early withdrawals being repaid in full, while those at the back get nothing. Expectations of panic are self-fulfilling because the bank will fail if enough depositors panic. Therefore, if others are panicking, it is in the interest of each depositor to demand an early withdrawal regardless of their true liquidity needs.

However, what is crucial to the success of Diamond and Dybvig's proposed deposit insurance scheme is not the government's ability to levy taxes, but an assumed informational advantage which allows it to levy the appropriately calculated tax on those making early withdrawals before these individuals can consume the amounts withdrawn, and before any productive investments have been interrupted unnecessarily. Without this information, the ability to levy taxes would not be sufficient to achieve full efficiency, and with it a private bank could arrange an optimal contract without the need to levy taxes: rather than offering sequential service contracts, the bank would offer conditional contracts in which the interest rates paid to those making early and late withdrawals would depend on the volume of early withdrawals. The rates would be the same as those provided, net of tax, to those making early and late withdrawals under Diamond and Dybvig's proposed arrangements. Those making late withdrawals would always be assured of receiving a higher return than those making early withdrawals and would therefore never have an incentive to demand early withdrawals unless they genuinely needed them.

The Real Costs of Default

If borrowers and lenders were risk-neutral and if default was merely the result of borrowers being occasionally presented with the opportunity to avoid repaying debts while also avoiding any penalty for non-repayment, then an increase in the probability of default would merely be accompanied by an equal increase in 'contract' interest rates, that is, the interest rates written into the contracts that specify how much the borrower is legally supposed to repay. Just as the effects of inflation for both borrowers and lenders can be neutralised by an increase in the nominal interest rate, leaving the expected real interest rate faced by both borrowers and lenders unchanged, so – if default involved transfers, but not waste – the effects of default on both borrowers and lenders could be neutralised by an increase in the contract interest rate, leaving the expected net-of-default interest rate unchanged.

A slightly more realistic model of default than the one just presented would involve debtors being occasionally presented with the opportunity to incur costs of, say, 80 cents in order to avoid repaying each dollar of contracted debts. As long as the proportion of costs to avoidance is less than one, debtors have an incentive to default whenever they get the opportunity to do so. The real costs associated with bankruptcy and default can thus provide a partial explanation for the large declines in real output that are often associated with financial crises. However, in the absence of bargaining costs, even the presence of default costs would not prevent debtors and creditors adjusting the amounts of contracted repayments to neutralise the effects of default risk. For example, in a situation in which the debtor has the opportunity to incur costs of 80 cents to avoid repaying each dollar of debt, the creditor could offer to accept 40 cents per dollar of originally contracted debt and to forgive the remaining 60 per cent. This would make both debtor and creditor better off by 40 cents per dollar of originally contracted debt than they would be if the debtor defaulted and incurred the costs of doing so. Therefore, in the absence of bargaining costs, even the presence of default costs would merely convert opportunities for default into opportunities to demand partial debt forgiveness without any wasting of resources. If the possibility of partial debt forgiveness is anticipated by both borrowers and lenders at the time that contracts are written, it can be incorporated into the contract interest rate thereby again neutralising the effects of default on borrowing and lending decisions as in the previous paragraph.

By combining default costs with bargaining costs and the collective action problems associated with bargaining among a large group of creditors, it is possible to rationalise the occurrence of costly defaults rather than mere partial debt forgiveness.[6] In most cases, the legal costs of bankruptcy proceedings are only a small part of the full costs of default. If a bankrupt firm has been managed by its owners, and if the creditors succeed in acquiring the assets, the firm-specific skills of the original owners will be wasted and the assets may have to be disposed of at fire-sale prices. Alternatively, even if the original owners and managers of an insolvent firm are able to prevent a court-ordered transfer of their assets to creditors, they are unlikely to be able to obtain new working capital. The result in such cases is that corporations can be left in a state of limbo in which their productive assets can neither be seized by creditors nor efficiently utilised by the original owners.

In some developing countries, formal bankruptcy procedures are almost completely moribund. In these countries, creditors try to protect themselves against possible default by insisting on very high levels of collateral as security for loans. Provided that the value of the collateral always exceeds the outstanding debts, this kind of system functions adequately even though it makes borrowing more expensive than it would be if the legal system gave better protection to creditors. The occasional bankruptcies of small firms result in the seizure of their assets by banks owned by the politically and economically powerful conglomerates to which they are likely to be indebted.

Relatively primitive credit systems in which bankruptcy laws do not operate and creditors are protected only by their ability to foreclose on well-secured loans can break down completely in a major economic downturn that reduces the value of collateral to less than the value of the loans that it was supposed to secure. Because these problems became particularly acute in the Asian crisis countries, the IMF programmes for Indonesia, Korea and Thailand provided for new, or radically amended, bankruptcy laws. Indonesia's recovery was delayed by the reluctance of its new commercial court to enforce the amended bankruptcy law against debtors.[7] Malaysia benefited from the fact that its bankruptcy system, which had been copied from British law in 1965, was more effective than those of Indonesia, Korea and Thailand.

Indonesia had the least effective bankruptcy system of all the Asian crisis countries: only a few hundred bankruptcy cases were filed in the entire period between 1905 and 1998.[8] It also had the highest proportion of insolvent corporations: by mid-1998 almost half of all Indonesian corporations were insolvent.[9] In September 1998, a new commercial court began to administer the newly amended bankruptcy law. At the same time, the government also implemented the 'Jakarta Initiative', a mediation framework, designed by the IMF and the World Bank, within which debtors and creditors could negotiate out-of-court bargaining over the terms of debt standstills or partial debt forgiveness. As of June 1999, 234 firms with combined debts of about 20 per cent of total Indonesian corporate debt were enrolled in the Jakarta Initiative and temporary or final agreements had been reached in 22 cases covering about 3 per cent of total corporate debt.[10] The slow rate of progress reflects the fact that, even under the amended bankruptcy law, many debtors continue to regard debt repayment as voluntary.

If bankruptcy laws are ineffective, financial crises can severely disrupt property rights and cause potentially valuable assets to be underutilised. The greater effectiveness of bankruptcy systems in industrialised than in developing countries is probably the main reason why financial crises have involved much larger falls in real income in the latter countries than in the former. The greater efficacy of bankruptcy procedures in Malaysia than in Indonesia, Korea and Thailand helps explain why Malaysia was less severely affected by the Asian crisis than the other three countries. The extreme inadequacy of Indonesia's bankruptcy procedures helps explain why it was more severely affected by the crisis than any other country.

One of the factors that contributed to the self-fulfilling nature of the speculation against the Asian financial systems is that a depreciation of the RER can cause the collapse of financing arrangements in an economy in which bankruptcy laws are ineffective and many foreign currency-denominated debts are secured against domestic assets. A sufficiently large and abrupt fall in the dollar value of these assets removes the incentives for debtors to repay. If the fire-sale value of collateral is less than the amount of the loan it was intended to secure and if the debtor has many creditors, there is no easy way of restructuring debts to keep assets productively employed. Until bad debts have been cleared, new loans will not be forthcoming and without sufficient working capital enterprises are forced to operate below full capacity. Banks are unwilling to offer large debt write-downs to any one firm, for fear of provoking demands for similar write-downs from their other debtors, while debtors are unwilling to accept anything less than large write-downs of debt if bankruptcy laws do not function. To try to raise liquidity, firms have an incentive to sell off stock, movable items of capital and even real estate, thus further depressing the RER.

Refusal to repay debts can also be contagious because of effects related to reputation and credit ratings: before the recent Asian crisis, one of the reasons why large firms chose to repay debts to foreigners, even when they were located in countries with ineffective bankruptcy procedures, was their desire to preserve their international credit ratings. However, once the credit ratings of all firms in the countries affected by the Asian crisis had been severely downgraded, and once very few foreign banks were willing to extend new loans to any firm in the affected countries, this motive became much less powerful. Similar effects operated through reputation for firms too small to have formal credit ratings: reputation became much less valuable when almost all domestic and foreign banks stopped extending any new loans.

In addition to increasing the incentives for others to default, each individual default also reduces the ability of creditors, suppliers and employees of the defaulting debtor to meet their own commitments. As a result, if bankruptcy procedures do not transfer assets from defaulting debtors to their creditors, a few individual defaults can develop into chains of bad debts that may cause the collapse of most of the financial system.

The chains of bad debts produced by financial crises help explain both herding behaviour and contagion. Because a formerly solvent firm can become insolvent if its debtors do not repay on time, if its creditors call in their loans or if its customers reduce their purchases, it is rational for every firm to respond to an observed increase in the economy-wide rate of defaults by cutting back on purchases, reducing lending, delaying debt repayment and hoarding money. The fact that such economy-wide attempts to increase liquidity will be self-defeating in aggregate only adds to the urgency of each individual firm's attempts to increase its liquidity at the first sign of a financial crisis before the others have had time to do so.

The failure of bankruptcy procedures to transfer ownership of assets from technically insolvent enterprises to their creditors has led to problems in the Asian crisis countries, and particularly in Indonesia, that have much in common with those experienced by Eastern Europe and the former Soviet Union during their transitions from central planning to capitalism: in both cases, large and potentially valuable enterprises failed to operate at full capacity because of a breakdown in property rights. In the transition from communism to market-based economic systems, property rights broke down because governments no longer possessed the coercive powers that had been necessary to enforce the old communist state order systems and because privatisation and the creation of market-based tax systems took time.[11]

The waste that results from financial crises is not confined to instances of actual default. The functioning of even relatively simple economies involves firms and households coordinating their plans by means of networks of unwritten understandings and mutually consistent expectations. When these networks are broken they are hard to mend and the resulting disruption can involve a large fall in real income. Part of the declines in real output in the countries of Eastern Europe and the former Soviet Union during their transitions from communism to capitalism can plausibly be attributed to the fact that these networks of informal understandings and expectations are essential to the working of a capitalist economy and take a long time to develop; part of the large declines in real output in countries suffering from financial crises can be attributed to the fact that these crises severely damage these informal networks.

5.5   EMPIRICAL EVIDENCE ON BANKING AND BALANCE OF PAYMENTS CRISES

Eichengreen *et al.* (1995) analyse the empirical aspects of currency crises using quarterly data for 20 OECD countries in the period 1959–93. They measure 'exchange market pressure' as a weighted average of three variables: the depreciation of the nominal exchange rate, the reduction in foreign exchange reserves and the rise in nominal interest rates. All changes are measured relative to Germany, which is therefore completely immune to speculative pressure, so defined. For each country, they construct a 'crisis variable', which is equal to one, indicating the occurrence of a 'crisis', if their speculative pressure variable is more than two standard deviations above its mean, and is otherwise equal to zero. Even if the central bank succeeds in avoiding a devaluation, a crisis can occur, according to this definition, if reserves are run down sufficiently rapidly or if interest rates are raised sufficiently.

Eichengreen *et al.* (1995) found that trade deficits, reserve losses, expansionary monetary policy and relatively high unemployment are leading indicators of devaluations and that the reverse of these phenomena are leading indicators of revaluations. The probability of the occurrence of crises is increased by domestic credit expansion; this is often undertaken in response to rising unemployment and leads to inflation and reserve losses. They found that capital outflows typically occur shortly before a crisis and that severe monetary tightening sometimes enables governments to resist a speculative attack; milder monetary tightening does not usually prevent a devaluation but does help to prevent a major crisis, while intervention to sterilise a balance of payments deficit typically results in a major currency crisis.

The common patterns observed by Eichengreen *et al.* (1995) in currency crises in OECD countries are consistent with the predictions of both the first and second-generation speculative attack models. Work by Moreno (1995) and Frankel and Rose (1996) shows that some of these patterns also occur in developing countries. Moreno (1995) found that currency crises in the countries of the Asia-Pacific region are usually associated with rapid growth of domestic credit and large budget deficits. Frankel and Rose (1996) studied over 100 developing countries in the period 1971–92 and also found that rapid growth of domestic credit tends to be associated with a 'currency crash', defined as an annual depreciation in the dollar value of the domestic currency of at least 25 per cent in total, and at least 10 per cent more than in the previous year. They found that currency crashes are also associated with slow output growth, RER appreciation, low reserves, high foreign interest rates and a low ratio of foreign direct investment to total external debt. They found no evidence that budget or current account deficits raise the probability of a currency crash, after controlling for these effects.

Kaminsky and Reinhart (1999) distinguish between financial crises and balance of payments crises. Their data set covers 20 countries in the period 1970–95 and also includes developing as well as industrialised countries. They classify an event as a banking crisis if the authorities intervene in the financial system to provide large subsidies to important financial institutions, or to take over such institutions, or to force them to close or to merge with other institutions; their definition of balance of payments crises is similar to that of Eichengreen *et al.* (1995).[12] According to these definitions, there were 25 banking crises and 71 balance of payments crises in the 20 countries in the period studied.

Kaminsky and Reinhart (1999) found that a much higher proportion of the financial systems in the 20 countries they studied had been liberalised in the period 1980–95 than in the period 1970–80. They also provide strong evidence that deregulated financial systems are more liable to financial collapse than heavily regulated ones. These two facts explain why the proportion of the countries in their study that experienced banking crises more than quadrupled from 1.5 per cent per year in the period 1970–79 to 6.9 per cent per year in the period 1980–95.

They found that the probability of a balance of payments crisis is higher in the 12 to 18 months following a banking crisis than at other times. However, they found no indication that the occurrence of a balance of payments crisis increases the probability of a banking crisis in the subsequent 12 to 18 months. In fact, after controlling for financial liberalisation, they found that the prior occurrence of a balance of payments crisis appears to make the occurrence of a banking crisis slightly less likely, but the estimated effect was not statistically significant. The proportion of countries experiencing balance of payments crises rose only from 12.5 in the period 1970–79 to 14.4 per cent per year in the period 1980–95.

Kaminsky and Reinhart (1999) also estimated the average time paths of macroeconomic variables in the 18 months before and after crises. In their data set, as in that of Eichengreen *et al.* (1995), balance of payments crises are usually preceded by a large loss of reserves. Reserves usually rise immediately after a devaluation. The RER, as measured by the ratio of foreign to domestic consumer prices in a common currency, typically follows a 'sawtooth' pattern in which domestic goods gradually lose competitiveness between devaluations, and then regain it very abruptly as a result of the large devaluations which usually define when the crisis is deemed to have occurred. The excess of domestic currency interest rates over interest rates on dollar-denominated assets also generally rises sharply in the months just before and after a crisis, and then declines. Declining output growth, accelerating monetary growth and deteriorating terms of trade were also found to be leading indicators of crises.

Kaminsky *et al.* (1998) studied the predictive properties of various potential leading indicators of currency crises suggested by earlier empirical studies. For each indicator, they defined a threshold which when crossed corresponded to an alarm that a crisis was liable to occur within the next 24 months. Setting a threshold that is seldom crossed reduces the number of false alarms, but raises the probability of failing to warn of real crises. Setting a threshold that is often crossed reverses the probabilities of these two types of potential error. Country-specific thresholds for each indicator were chosen so as to minimise its noise-to-signal ratio, defined as the ratio of false alarms to correct warnings. The appreciation of the RER relative to its trend was the indicator with the lowest noise-to-signal ratio. It gave a false alarm on 5 per cent of the occasions when no crisis occurred, but correctly predicted 25 per cent of the crises that did occur. Whereas the unconditional probability of a crisis was 28 per cent, the conditional probability when this alarm rang was 67 per cent. The next four most useful indicators were the prior occurrence of a banking crisis, the growth rate of exports, the growth rate of stock market prices in dollars and the growth rate of the ratio of broad money (M2) to international reserves. The RER and the occurrence of a banking crisis were also the two indicators with the longest average lead times, which were 17 and 19 months, respectively.

Sachs *et al.* (1996b) studied the speculative pressures associated with the 'tequila crisis' of 1994–95, which most strongly affected Mexico, but also had significant repercussions on Argentina, Brazil, Venezuela and the Philippines. They construct a crisis index similar to that of Eichengreen *et al.* (1995) and use it to measure differences in the intensity with which this crisis affected 20 developing countries. They also look for explanations of the severity of these effects using indicators of the 'fundamental' strengths and weaknesses of these economies. Their crisis index is a weighted average of the nominal devaluation of each currency against the dollar over this period, and the percentage reduction over the period in foreign exchange reserves. They found that the three variables which did best in explaining why countries experienced crises, as measured by this index, were: first, the extent to which countries had experienced a boom over the period 1990–94 in bank lending to the private sector; second, the vulnerability of their foreign exchange reserve position, as measured by the ratio of the broad money supply to reserves; and third – for countries with low foreign exchange reserves according to this criterion, but only for such countries – their loss in competitiveness between 1986–89 and 1990–94, as measured by the increase in their domestic consumer prices relative to a weighted average of the corresponding increase in consumer prices in the USA, Japan and the EU, measured in a common currency. Of these three effects, only the interaction between low reserves and loss of competitiveness was statistically significant at the 5 per cent level; however, the lending boom variable only just failed to be significant at this level. After controlling for these three effects, Sachs *et al.* (1996b) did not find statistically significant effects either for capital inflows or for current account deficits.

Berg and Patillo (1998) studied the ability of three models that had been specified and estimated before the Asian crisis to predict the events of 1997. The three models were Sachs *et al.* (1996b), Frankel and Rose (1996) and Kaminsky *et al.* (1998), which had appeared as a working paper in July 1997. Berg and Patillo conclude that the forecasts of the first two models for the period after that for which they had been estimated were 'no better than guesswork'. In contrast, the third of these models produced 'alarm signals' – defined as an estimate that the probability of a crisis in the following 24 months was more than 25 per cent – that were statistically significant predictors of subsequent crises, even though they explained only 28 per cent of the variation in actual crisis rankings. The unconditional probability of a crisis in 1997 in the countries studied by Berg and Patillo was only 27 per cent, but the conditional probability of a crisis, given that the model of Kaminsky *et al.* (1998) had sounded an alarm, was 37 per cent.

Contagion

The probability that the speculative attacks on most East and South East Asian countries in 1997 were independent events that just happened to occur within a few months of each other is so low that the hypothesis that it was a coincidence can be dismissed in favour of the hypothesis that contagion was involved. In Indonesia, the stock market continued to rise and the rupiah continued to trade at the strong side of Bank Indonesia's intervention band right up until shortly after the Thai authorities abandoned their defence of the baht. Subsequent events showed that the fundamentals of Indonesia's financial system were weak, but it is very implausible to suggest that speculators would have suddenly guessed, or discovered, that this was the case if Thailand's financial and exchange rate systems had not succumbed to speculative attacks.

Calvo and Reinhart (1996) assemble more systematic evidence of contagion in the form of the striking correlations across Latin American countries for several variables that can be thought of as proxies for investor confidence. These countries' risk premia, as measured by yields on Brady bonds, were highly correlated at the time of the Mexican crisis in late 1994 and early 1995; so, too, were their stock market indices, converted to dollars. Calvo and Reinhart also found that, even after controlling for world interest rates, capital inflows to the larger Latin American countries in the period 1979–93 played a statistically significant role in explaining the inflows to the smaller ones, but inflows to the smaller countries were not significant determinants of inflows to the large countries.

A study by Eichengreen *et al.* (1996) used the quarterly data from their 1995 study to provide quantitative estimates of the importance of contagion in causing currency crises. They found that, after controlling for the influence of a wide range of contemporaneous and lagged macroeconomic variables, the probability of a crisis in any given country in any given quarter is increased by about 8 percentage points if at least one other country in their group experiences a crisis in that quarter. These findings were not sensitive to minor changes in the definitions of 'crisis' or 'speculative pressure', and there is evidence of contagion both in the period 1959–78, before the formation of the European Monetary System, and in the period 1979–95, after its formation.

Eichengreen *et al.* (1996) recognise that the appearance of contagion in their data might have arisen because they defined 'crises' with reference to events in a 'base' country – Germany: a strengthening of the mark relative to all other currencies would cause the appearance of 'speculative pressure' on all other currencies, and if these pressures were sufficiently large, they could cause the impression of contagion. Evidence that the appearance of contagion in their data is not entirely due to this explanation is provided by the fact that the goodness of fit of the equation that they use to predict crises in any given country is improved by weighting the crisis variables for other countries by their trade links with the given country. They conclude that currency crises are transmitted, at least in part, via bilateral trade ties. For example, if a crisis in some given country reduces its import demand, and results in a devaluation of its currency, there will be increased incentives for the countries which export to it to devalue so as to counteract the fall in their exports that would otherwise occur as a result of both price and income effects.

Eichengreen *et al.* (1996) also test whether crises in a given country are more likely to be precipitated by crises in countries which have similar macroeconomic characteristics than by crises in dissimilar countries. When trade links were also allowed for, this channel for the transmission of crises appeared not to be significant in their data set. However, in the 1997 Asian crisis, there are not strong trade links between the affected countries. Goldstein (1998, pp. 17–22) suggests that before the collapse of the baht, international investors and regulators had ignored available warning signals and had been misled by published statistics, which overestimated official reserves and underestimated short-term debts. The collapse of the baht acted as a 'wake-up call' to investors, who then short-sold the currencies and securities of countries that had financial characteristics in common with Thailand. To test this hypothesis, Goldstein and Hawkins (1998) assembled data on a number of possible indicators of vulnerability, such as credit growth, the ratios of short-term external debt to foreign exchange reserves and to GDP and the ratio of broad money to reserves. They show that the variables that suggested that Thailand was especially vulnerable to a crisis were also those that roughly predict the intensity with which the other countries were affected by the Asian crisis.

5.6   OVERVIEW

Numerous models have been developed that can account for many of the features of currency crises. Models of bank runs have many similarities with models of exchange rate crises because the failure of a commercial bank to repay its depositors in full is analogous to the devaluation of a supposedly fixed exchange rate by a central bank.

In the theoretical literature, there is a clear distinction between 'first-generation' models of currency crises, in which the breakdown of a supposedly fixed exchange rate system is inevitable, because the government is following a strategy that cannot be sustained for ever, such as financing expenditure by running down foreign currency reserves, and 'second-generation' models, in which the exchange rate system could be maintained indefinitely, but can nevertheless break down if enough speculators expect it to do so and if the government responds to speculative pressure by a policy shift that validates the speculators' beliefs. In practice, the distinction between the two types is blurred because a situation that is invulnerable under one set of beliefs may be liable to collapse under another. Both first and second-generation models can be illustrated by the simple geometric analysis of Figure 5.1. An unsatisfactory feature of the models of currency crises is that their properties depend crucially on arbitrary assumptions about how speculators expect the authorities to react in a crisis and on each person's beliefs about the expectations of everyone else.

Empirical studies of currency crises have confirmed the importance of some of the variables that indicate vulnerability in the theoretical models. For instance, rapid expansion of domestic credit increases the probability of crises and so does a high ratio of the broad money supply to foreign exchange reserves. Liberalised financial systems are more vulnerable to crises than repressed ones, as are countries whose RERs have appreciated by large amounts. There is empirical confirmation of the importance of contagion in the sense that the existence of a crisis, or crises, in other countries increases the likelihood of any given country experiencing a crisis.

Despite the finding of significant associations between the occurrence of crises and the indicators of vulnerability listed above, empirical studies are a very long way from being able to predict crises at all accurately. The tests by Berg and Patillo (1998) of the success in predicting the crises of 1997 of three models that had been estimated before 1997 showed that only one of these models, Kaminsky *et al.* (1998), did better than pure guesswork. Although the conditional probability of a crisis when this model sounded an alarm was significantly higher than the unconditional probability of a crisis, 63 per cent of its alarms were false alarms and it nevertheless failed to give warnings of 75 per cent of the crises that actually occurred.[13] Further evidence of the difficulty of predicting currency crises is the magnitude of the profits and losses made during them: if they were perfectly predictable, all investors would earn a normal rate of return on their portfolios, regardless of their currency composition.

Some of the policy implications of currency crisis models are clear: if a government wishes to keep the exchange rate fixed, it should avoid large-scale sterilisation of the monetary effects of balance of payments deficits and it certainly must not finance budget deficits by adding to domestic credit at a rate in excess of the growth in demand for base money at the fixed rate. To reduce the probability of self-fulfilling speculative attacks, governments also need to make their policy commitments credible by choosing policy rules that are likely to be compatible with their own long-run self-interest and by designing institutions that will ensure that these rules are followed even when there might otherwise be transitory benefits from breaking them. However, it may pay to introduce escape clauses that allow the strategy followed by the government in normal circumstances to be abandoned in extreme circumstances. Escape clauses raise the probability of a speculative attack if the circumstances that trigger them become more likely, but minimising the probability of speculative crises is not the sole object of policy. The choice of specific rules and the design of institutions for reducing the risk of currency crises are dealt with in Chapters 7 and 8. Chapter 6 deals with designing policies to reduce the frequency and severity of financial sector crises.

NOTES

1. Shiller (1989, Chapter 4) surveys the debate generated by his 1981 paper.
2. The empirical evidence is surveyed in section 5.5.
3. A formal analysis of the effects of using capital controls to defend a (temporarily) fixed exchange rate in the face of excessive growth of domestic credit is given by Wyplosz (1986).
4. Obstfeld (1996) surveys the ways in which the possibility of self-fulfilling speculative attacks can arise.
5. See, for example, Banerjee (1992).
6. McKibbin (1998, 1999) shows that many of the features of the 1997–98 Asian crisis, including in particular the real and nominal depreciation of the Asian currencies, can be accounted for by postulating an increase in default risk in the affected countries on the assumption that default costs use up all the potential benefits to defaulters of avoiding debt repayment.
7. The January 2000 Letter of Intent from the Indonesian government to the IMF implied that this reluctance was the result of 'governance problems' within the judiciary and went on to propose measures to combat corruption in the judiciary.
8. For more details on the inadequacy of bankruptcy law in Indonesia see Lindsey (1998).
9. Kawai (1999, p. 9).
10. Kawai (1999, pp. 8–9).
11. Fane and Nash (1998) argue that Georgia's economic collapse and descent into hyperinflation in the period 1991–94 was due to the breakdown of property rights that occurred when the old communist state order system collapsed before the implementation of privatisation or the creation of a functioning tax system.
12. Kaminsky and Reinhart (1999) classify an event as a balance of payments crisis if the index of exchange market pressure rises by more than three standard deviations above the mean.
13. Berg and Patillo (1998, Table 2, p. 114).

6. Banks, moral hazard and prudential regulations

This chapter deals with the excessive risk-taking that is induced by bail-outs of insolvent or illiquid firms. The major recipients of bail-outs financed by taxpayers are the depositors at banks and other financial institutions. In addition, particularly in developing countries, insolvent commercial and industrial firms may receive what amount to bail-outs financed by their creditors (who are often banks) because ineffective bankruptcy procedures prevent creditors taking over the assets of defaulting debtors.

6.1 BANK SAFETY NETS AND MORAL HAZARD

Most governments provide two 'safety nets' for depositors at financial institutions. The first is to guarantee, implicitly or explicitly, that depositors will be bailed out in the event of bank failure. The guarantee may take the form of compulsory deposit insurance. In countries without explicit deposit insurance, governments often deny that they will bail out depositors at banks that fail, but nevertheless almost always provide deposit guarantees and bail-outs at times of financial crises in the hope of restoring confidence. The second safety net is the creation of a central bank whose functions include acting as the 'lender of last resort'; that is, lending to banks and other financial institutions during a financial panic, if it believes that they are merely illiquid rather than insolvent.

Taking the assets and liabilities of the banks and finance companies as given – as they are in an immediate short-run crisis situation when a bank run has developed – the provision of safety nets clearly reduces the incentives for depositors to withdraw their deposits and increases the probability that banks will be able to survive. However, it is not clear whether the provision of safety nets reduces or increases the frequency and severity of financial crises in the long run once account is taken of the fact that safety nets encourage banks to take risks that they would otherwise avoid. This happens because shareholders in banks that lend at high interest rates to risky projects benefit if a good outcome occurs, but share losses with taxpayers if a bad outcome occurs. Safety nets give banks an incentive to lend to less creditworthy borrowers than they otherwise would, to diversify their loan portfolios less than they otherwise would and to gamble on exchange rate movements, rather than to hedge their foreign currency assets and liabilities. Banks also have an incentive to exploit the differentials between the relatively low interest rates on liquid short-term claims and the higher rates on illiquid long-term claims, by using deposits that can be withdrawn on demand to finance illiquid and long-term loans, in the hope that short-term liquid borrowings can be rolled over.

Safety nets also give banks an incentive to operate with high ratios of debt, in the form of deposits, relative to equity. Banks and other financial institutions take considerable advantage of these incentives: the equity to assets ratios of US banks were 30 per cent to 35 per cent on average in the late nineteenth century, 20 per cent in 1910 (shortly before the creation of the Federal Reserve System) and 13 per cent in 1930 (shortly before the introduction of compulsory deposit insurance).[1] At the end of 1990, insured savings and loan institutions (S&Ls) in the USA had liabilities other than equity that exceeded their equity by a factor of 33; this factor was 14 for commercial banks and 11 for domestic finance companies. For non-financial sector firms it was only 0.8.[2] The proportion of short-term debt to total debt is also usually much higher for banks than for industrial and manufacturing firms. The potential benefit to a bank from being highly leveraged is that equity is generally a more costly source of finance than insured deposits because equity investors cannot expect the bail-outs on which depositors can count in the event of bank failure.[3]

The paradox that the provision of safety nets may exacerbate financial risks reflects the fact that they are a form of insurance and insurance generates 'moral hazard' and 'adverse selection'. Moral hazard is the increase in the probability of an accident ('hazard') that occurs because people and firms ('moral agents') who have taken out insurance have less incentives to take precautions than those who are uninsured. Just as smoothing out a speed hump may increase road accidents, so reducing the costs to depositors of bank failure may make banks riskier, not safer. Adverse selection is the bias, encountered by insurance companies, which arises because individual purchasers of insurance usually have more accurate information than the insurer on the probability that they will suffer the event against which they are insuring. At a given premium, insurance is more valuable to bad risks than good ones.

Insurance can create outright fraud, as well as moral hazard: the more difficult it is for regulators to monitor the risks taken by banks, the greater are the incentives for business groups to set up their own banks in order to channel guaranteed (and therefore low interest) deposits to firms in the same group at interest rates that do not reflect the risks being taken.

Moral hazard problems are not limited to banks and other finance companies. Because limited liability is a form of insurance that ensures that shareholders do not bear the full brunt of all losses incurred by the corporations they own, these corporations have incentives to engage in excessive gambles. The important difference between the moral hazard problems associated with banks and other corporations is that the private firms and individuals that lend to limited liability corporations have incentives to monitor them, and use loan covenants to restrict the extent to which they can gamble, whereas government safety nets largely transfer these incentives and responsibilities from depositors to regulators. Many of the proposals for improving the efficiency of deposit insurance schemes seek to make regulatory sanctions and safeguards resemble those used by the private creditors and guarantors of risky corporations as closely as possible.

6.2   RATIONALISATIONS FOR GOVERNMENT REGULATION OF FINANCIAL INSTITUTIONS

Bagehot's Supposed Rationalisation for Last Resort Lending

The most celebrated proposal for last resort lending is that of Bagehot (1873): 'in a panic the holders of the ultimate Bank reserve (whether one bank or many) should lend to all that bring good securities quickly, freely, and readily. By that policy they allay a panic, by every other they intensify it'.[4] By a 'good security', Bagehot meant one that 'in ordinary times is reckoned a good security' because it is commonly pledged and easily convertible in such times.[5] Because the market values of loans are very hard to measure, regulators and central bankers focus mainly on their book values, as written down by accounting conventions on when to classify loans as 'doubtful', or 'bad'. When a bank is in severe financial difficulties, its own best estimate of the true value of its loans is likely to be far less than the book value revealed to regulators. There is therefore a great danger that last resort loans will be given to banks which are not just illiquid, but also insolvent. Bagehot's qualification that last resort loans should be made only against 'good securities' was his way of trying to ensure that they would go only to those banks that are merely illiquid. Banks that could not offer good securities would be left to fail under his proposal. He also recommended that last resort loans should be made at a very high rate of interest in order to discourage applications by institutions that could survive without them. The conventional modern justification for setting high interest rates is to reduce moral hazard.

Bagehot is regularly interpreted as advocating that last resort lending should be the responsibility of the central bank and much of Bagehot (1873), including the above quotation, creates this impression. However, this quotation leaves open the question 'whether one bank or many' should hold the banking reserve and he describes the fact that the Bank of England kept almost the entire banking reserve as an anomaly, but one that is 'so fixed in our system that we cannot change it if we would' (*ibid.*, p. 159). In Bagehot (1866), he argued that a system in which one bank holds the entire banking reserve 'is not a natural, an expedient, or an universal system, or one that we should prescribe where a country has its banking system to choose, and is not controlled by an imperious history'.[6] In other words, if its choice has not already been made, a country should *not* create a central bank to act as lender of last resort!

The final nail in the coffin of attempts to use Bagehot to justify central bank last resort lending is that there is little reason to believe that past history is as imperious as he asserted: commercial banks would probably quickly start holding their own liquid reserves in substantial quantities if central banks stopped providing emergency loans and regular discount facilities at interest rates that do not reflect their true cost. This is illustrated by recent events in Hong Kong, which are described in more detail in section 8.3. In October 1997, without announcing a radical change in the way it planned to conduct monetary policy, the Hong Kong Monetary Authority (HKMA) nevertheless abruptly reduced the access of commercial banks to its discount facilities. The banks responded by increasing their deposits at the HKMA by a factor of more than seven in just three months.

Collective Action Rationalisations for Last Resort Lending

Some modern defenders of last resort lending, such as Sachs (1995), rationalise it as a way of overcoming the collective action problems, discussed in Chapter 5, that can result in individual depositors and potential lenders deciding not to roll over their deposits, or extend new loans, to a solvent but illiquid bank simply because each knows that the bank will fail if most other depositors and potential lenders act in the same way. If the central bank can really distinguish insolvent from illiquid banks, it can lend to the latter without incurring losses because it is large enough to arbitrage this potential market failure, which may be too big to be arbitraged by any individual firm or household.

The test of whether this rationalisation of last resort lending holds in practice is whether the central bank's last resort loans are profitable. In fact, even a central bank as sophisticated as the US Federal Reserve has a poor track record in distinguishing between illiquid and insolvent banks. Benston and Kaufman (1997, pp. 148–9) cite a US House of Representatives study which found that in the S&L crisis of the late 1980s, 90 per cent of the banks that received extended credit from the Federal Reserve System subsequently failed. Providing last resort loans to a bank that would otherwise be insolvent, or almost insolvent, is especially dangerous because such banks have little or nothing to lose, and everything to gain, from massive gambles, which would save them if successful and would merely impose still larger losses on the government if unsuccessful. Benston and Kaufman (1997, pp. 140–2) show that the largest losses during the S&L crisis arose because bankrupt, or nearly bankrupt, institutions got more extended opportunities to gamble with other people's money than they did in the days before deposit insurance when bank runs would have quickly closed them down. The discussion in section 8.5 of the resolution of the 1997–99 Indonesian banking crisis shows that the misuse of last resort loans by banks can be very much more costly, relative to GDP, in developing countries.

Safety Nets, Financial Stability and the Payments System as a Public Good

If they actually helped to reduce the severity and frequency of financial crises, safety nets could be rationalised on the ground that financial stability and the functioning of the payments system have some of the attributes of a public good, since widespread confidence in the smooth functioning of the financial system is necessary for conducting almost all commercial transactions. However, the public good argument for government intervention in the financial system must take account of the fact that deposit insurance and last resort lending have adverse long-term effects on financial stability that should be set against their beneficial short-term effects. Whether government intervention in the financial system strengthens or weakens it must be decided empirically and the answer need not be the same at all times, or in all countries.

US historical experience provides no support for the view that having a lender of last resort reduces the probability of bank failures: in the period 1875–1913, when there was no central bank, the proportion of commercial banks which failed each year averaged 0.9 per cent; in the period 1914–33, after the creation of the Federal Reserve System but before the introduction of compulsory deposit insurance, the average rate of bank failures was more than four times higher at 3.8 per cent per year even though the average rate of general business failures fell very slightly between these two periods. Even in the period 1914–28, which is chosen to exclude the bank failures of the Depression years, the rate of bank failures was half as high again, at 1.35 per cent per year, as in the period 1875–1913. In contrast, the average rate of general business failures fell between these two periods from 1 per cent per year to 0.9 per cent per year.[7]

The introduction of deposit insurance in the USA did largely eliminate bank runs, but – depending on the precise periods chosen for comparison – did not much alter the direct cost of bank failures to depositors and taxpayers taken together. As noted in section 6.1, banks were much more highly capitalised in the period before the introduction of compulsory deposit insurance and the creation of the Federal Deposit Insurance Corporation (FDIC) in 1934 than they are now. As a result, losses to depositors at all US commercial banks in the period 1865–1933 – which includes the bank failures of the Great Depression – averaged a trivial 0.21 per cent per year.[8] Since the introduction of deposit insurance, the direct costs of bank failures have been met by insurance premia and by taxpayers. The premia charged have varied very sharply over time.[9] Shaffer (1997) argues that the long-run break-even level of the premium is between 0.09 per cent and 0.15 per cent per year. In addition to the costs of deposit insurance borne by bank depositors, US taxpayers had to spend $200 billion on bailing out the S&Ls. This is about 5.9 per cent of the average level of the liquid liabilities of the consolidated financial system (M3) in the late 1980s; dividing this cumulative cost evenly over the period 1983–89 gives an average annual cost to taxpayers which was equivalent to 0.8 per cent of M3.[10] This is roughly equal to the average annual cost of bank losses to depositors, as a percentage of bank deposits, in the worst four years of the Great Depression.[11] These estimates suggest that the direct costs of bank failures in the USA since 1933 have been similar to, or perhaps slightly less than, those in the period before the introduction of compulsory deposit insurance. The results depend on exactly which periods are chosen for comparison.

It seems likely – although it would be hard to prove – that by spreading the cost of bank failures and largely eliminating bank runs, deposit insurance has contributed to macroeconomic stability. If, as a result, there have been fewer and less severe recessions than there would otherwise have been, these economy-wide gains would dwarf the small effects of insurance on the direct costs of bank failures.

In developing countries, whose regulatory and legal systems are much less sophisticated than those of the USA, the provision of deposit guarantees has been enormously costly to taxpayers: since 1982 there have been more than 20 cases in which these costs have exceeded 10 per cent of annual GDP and about 10 in which the costs have been of the order of a quarter of annual GDP.[12] The cost to the Indonesian government of making good the guarantee given to depositors in 1998 is officially estimated to exceed 50 per cent of annual GDP.[13] In addition, banking crises in developing countries have been associated with very large falls in GDP. The most plausible explanation for the spate of financial crises in developing countries is the moral hazard created by the combination of government guarantees to depositors, weak systems of prudential control and ineffective bankruptcy procedures.

The Inevitability of Depositor Bail-outs

The benefit of last resort loans, deposit insurance or deposit guarantees is that they help to avert bank runs, or at least to limit their severity. In a crisis situation these benefits are immediate. The main social cost of providing bail-outs is excessive risk-taking by banks, generated by moral hazard. This cost is spread out over long periods. The reason that it is very hard for governments to resist the political pressures to provide bail-outs for depositors in failed financial institutions is that the political process makes governments focus excessively on the short-term benefits, and to neglect the long-term costs, which may well be incurred by their successors in office. This is an example of a phenomenon highlighted by Kydland and Prescott (1977): in the absence of penalties for breaking promises, governments (like firms and individuals) may have incentives not to keep to commitments that would be beneficial if they could be made binding.

Calvo *et al.* (1993, p. 144) note that: 'As recent experience in the United States and Latin America shows, it may not be possible to state credibly that bank deposits are not fully guaranteed by the government if banks run into financial difficulties. As a result, banks may end up receiving free deposit insurance'. There have been numerous examples of countries which proclaimed that depositors would not be bailed out, but which provided bail-outs as soon as major crises occurred. Despite having announced that the government would not bail out private creditors, the Chilean government felt obliged to take responsibility for the foreign debts of failed Chilean banks in 1983–84 when foreign banks threatened to disrupt trade credits to Chile and argued that the failure of Chilean banks demonstrated dereliction of its supervisory duties by the central bank.

Although some form of bail-out of depositors appears to be almost inevitable, it is not inevitable that it must include last resort lending, as well as deposit insurance, or deposit guarantees. Section 8.5 uses Indonesia's experience in 1998 to argue that the massive costs to taxpayers of bailing out banks in developing countries in the aftermath of financial crises confirms that central banks are quite unable in practice to distinguish between insolvent banks and illiquid, but potentially solvent ones. Last resort loans therefore generate an acute adverse selection problem for central banks: the banks that are willing to pay the central bank's penalty rate on last resort loans are those judged to be especially bad risks by other participants in the money market. By lending to weak banks, the central bank not only loses its own funds, but also helps the weak banks to gamble away depositors' funds.

The seeming inevitability of bail-outs, even when governments have previously denied that they would be provided, was demonstrated once again in the Asian crisis in which government treatment of depositors and other creditors in troubled banks became increasingly more generous and comprehensive as the crisis progressed.[14] The IMF programmes in Thailand, Korea and Indonesia called for the eventual replacement of the blanket guarantees issued during the crisis by compulsory, but limited, deposit insurance. However, the aim of limiting deposit guarantees is unlikely to be achieved since the same forces that led governments to replace informal guarantees by extensive formal ones when crises occurred can also be expected to induce them to replace limited deposit insurance by more extensive bail-outs in similar circumstances in the future. Probably the only way in which most governments could credibly remove the perception that depositors will always be bailed out in a crisis would be by introducing constitutional amendments. Even they might be ineffective. In the absence of such constitutional restraints, the *de facto* existence of government provided safety nets creates a very strong case both for some kind of prudential regulation and also for charging banks for the deposit insurance that they receive.

6.3   FINANCIAL LIBERALISATION AND FINANCIAL CRISES

A crude form of protection against the vulnerability of financial sectors to panics and speculative attacks was provided by the policies of financial repression that were widespread in developing countries until the 1980s. The increasing frequency of financial crises is partly due to the very widespread adoption of financial liberalisation without the implementation of prudential controls powerful enough to limit the moral hazard created by financial safety nets.[15]

The very widespread adoption of financial liberalisation is demonstrated by a survey of 9 industrialised and 25 developing countries in the period 1973–96 by Williamson and Mahar (1998). Their results show that 31 of the 34 countries studied relaxed credit controls, 31 relaxed interest rate controls, 31 relaxed barriers to entry into the financial sector, 26 relaxed controls on international capital flows and 16 privatised some financial institutions.[16] Government regulation of the internal operation of financial institutions was reduced in 9 of the 24 countries for which data on this control are presented. In none of the 34 countries was the extent of regulation increased for any of these six criteria. For all criteria except privatisation, the proportion of developing countries that liberalised was higher than the proportion of industrialised countries that did so. The main reason for this was simply that more industrialised countries were already fully liberalised at the beginning of the period. Williamson and Mahar deliberately selected countries that had engaged in some financial liberalisation in the period studied; however, since they excluded China and the countries in Eastern Europe and the former Soviet Union, which have also undertaken quite extensive, if only partial, financial liberalisation, and since all the largest developing countries other than China were included, their results must be fairly representative of what has occurred in the developing world as a whole.

The 1997–98 Asian crisis fits the pattern, noted in section 5.5, that the liberalisation of financial sectors is often followed by a financial crisis.[17] Indonesia, Malaysia, Thailand, Korea and the Philippines all liberalised their financial systems by removing or relaxing controls on interest rate ceilings, reserve ratios and forced lending to 'priority' sectors. Restrictions on the entry of new banks and the setting up of new bank branches were also relaxed.

Cole (1995) notes the growth of a consensus among economists that prudential regulations should be strengthened before controls over the financial sector are relaxed.[18] This recommendation was not followed in Indonesia where the financial sector was deregulated in the 1980s, and prudential controls were not tightened until the 1990s. In contrast, as pointed out by Cole (1995), the sequencing adopted by Thailand followed conventional wisdom. The sequencing of reforms in Malaysia after 1983 was similar to that in Thailand except that Malaysia retained more financial controls. In the end, the different approaches to sequencing made no difference: all these countries had implemented elaborate systems of prudential controls well before the onset of the crisis of 1997–98 and their prudential controls all turned out to have been inadequate.

Moral hazard is an important part of the explanation for the frequency of financial crises following the removal of financial repression because many of the regulations which are relaxed when financial sectors are liberalised are also crude ways of restricting the scope for aggressive banks to exploit government safety nets for depositors. Quantitative limits on bank lending and on the establishment of branch networks restrict attempts by banks to expand their scale in order to take advantage of the subsidies to risk-taking that safety nets offer. Interest rate ceilings can have similar effects. If all lending rates are at a controlled ceiling, banks will prefer safe loans to risky ones; but if lending rates are not controlled and risks are partly borne by the government, competition will force banks to charge risk premia that reflect only the part of the total risk that is borne by the bank. As a result, excessively risky investments will be undertaken and will be financed by government guaranteed deposits. Similarly, if all banks must offer the same deposit rate, depositors with less than complete confidence in implicit government guarantees will avoid supplying funds to more risky banks; but if deposit rates are not controlled, and if depositors have high (but not total) confidence in government guarantees, then small increases in interest rates will enable risk-taking banks to attract more deposits and expand their loan portfolios. Finally, regulatory barriers to entry provide existing banks with valuable monopoly rights that they will be reluctant to jeopardise by excessive risk-taking; in effect the 'franchise value' of scarce banking licences will make true capital higher than the book value of capital.

The reduction, or abolition, of the minimum reserve ratio (RR) – that is, the ratio of a commercial bank's reserves of cash and deposits at the central bank to its own deposit liabilities – usually forms part of financial liberalisation. Indeed the use of minimum RRs is often classified as a form of financial repression because it imposes a tax on holding bank deposits.[19] This criticism is justified if deposit guarantees are fully financed by explicit deposit insurance premia. But in most developing countries this is not the case, and non-interest-bearing required reserves can then reduce the subsidy to banking which safety nets otherwise provide. Required reserves at the central bank constitute suitable collateral for last resort loans and minimum RRs also help to counter the incentive for banks with access to government-subsidised safety nets to hold less than the socially optimal ratio of liquid reserves to total assets. The trend among developing countries to reduce or remove RRs, without introducing explicit self-funding insurance schemes, and while continuing to provide banks with last resort loans and *de facto* deposit guarantees, is therefore a subsidy to risk-taking rather than the replacement of wasteful regulations by efficient market forces.

A proposal with strong similarities both to setting minimum RRs against deposits and to the Chilean VDR discussed in section 3.4 is that banks should be required to place a zero interest deposit at the central bank in proportion to their borrowings from non-residents.[20] In contrast to a standard VDR, non-bank domestic borrowers from non-residents would not be required to place deposits because their loans would not be guaranteed. Like the Chilean VDR, this proposal would be unlikely to make a large contribution to preventing crises. Thailand, for example, was not saved from the 1997 crisis even though, from June 1996 onwards, Thai banks had been required to place deposits at the Bank of Thailand equal to 7 per cent of their foreign liabilities, in either domestic or foreign currencies, with a maturity of less than one year.[21] The case for such deposits is rather that they would at least make banks and the non-residents that lend to them pay for the implicit government guarantees that they usually receive. As in Chile after the 1982 crisis, foreign creditors of domestic banks in the Asian crisis countries were bailed out along with domestic depositors. If the proposed requirement is viewed as a charge for implicit guarantees, a bank with a low capital adequacy ratio (CAR), as defined in section 6.4, should be required to make proportionately larger non-interest-bearing deposits than one with a higher CAR. The main objection to this proposal is that by charging for implicit guarantees of foreign loans to domestic banks it would further expand the scope of government guarantees over the financial sector. Like arguments against compulsory deposit insurance, this objection would have more force if it were not for the fact that such guarantees are almost invariably provided in any case.

6.4 PRUDENTIAL SUPERVISION AND REGULATION OF THE FINANCIAL SYSTEM

Kane (1995) notes that by insuring a bank's deposits, the government acts as a guarantor of its ability to meet demands for withdrawals. Just as it is efficient for a private guarantor to protect itself by surveying and regulating the risks taken by a firm that it has guaranteed, so it is efficient for the government to survey and regulate the risks taken by banks whose deposits it has insured. This section surveys the two main ways of trying to limit the risks induced by government deposit guarantees: the 'Basle' approach, based on setting minimum CARs backed up by supplementary prudential regulations, and the 'Chicago Plan', which proposed the setting of 100 per cent RRs on demand deposits.

A third approach would be to allow banks to contract out of the government's deposit insurance scheme by buying deposit insurance from an approved private guarantor. The responsibility of the government regulators would then be confined to insuring deposits at banks that did not opt for private insurance and to deciding which private guarantors to approve – major international banks and insurance companies would be the obvious candidates. The government might also choose to act as the guarantor of last resort for the private guarantors. This proposal is unlikely to be practicable in most developing countries because foreign guarantors would probably be at a comparative disadvantage in trying to monitor local banks, or to collect bad debts from local firms through the bankruptcy courts; as a result, the fees they would charge for guarantees would probably be prohibitive.

The Chicago Banking Plan

An extreme version of the proposal that banks should have to hold high cash reserves is the plan proposed by a group of Chicago economists as a solution to the bank failures in the USA in the period 1930–33. These economists accepted the desirability, or inevitability, of government protection of the payments system, but hoped to avoid other government interventions in the financial system. They proposed that 'narrow' banks – defined as those that accept demand deposits – should have to hold 100 per cent reserves against deposits, while all other financial institutions should be unregulated except that they could not provide cheque facilities since this would be an exclusive privilege of narrow banks. To make demand deposits absolutely safe, they would have priority over time deposits and all other claims in the event of bankruptcy.

An antecedent of the Chicago Plan was the proposal for banking reform in 1824 by David Ricardo, which was implemented in Britain by Sir Robert Peel's Bank Charter Act of 1844. This Act separated the Bank of England into a lending department and a note issue department, and required the latter to hold gold reserves equal to 100 per cent of the notes that it issued. Phillips (1995) suggests that Peel's Act and the Chicago Plan share a common defect: 'Peel's Act only applied to bank notes and demand deposits were a substitute, whereas the Chicago Plan only applied to demand deposits when time deposits were a close substitute'.[22] Some advocates of the Chicago Plan argue that the substitutability between demand deposits and time deposits is too low to be important.[23] Even if this was once true, it is unlikely still to be the case, given the ingenuity with which innovative financial entrepreneurs have found ways to provide the essential services of demand deposits, without actually coming within the legal definition of demand deposits.[24] To allow demand deposits at narrow banks to compete with unregulated substitutes, it would therefore be necessary to pay interest on commercial bank deposits at the central bank at a rate sufficient to allow narrow banks to leave the charges and interest rates on demand deposits roughly unchanged, despite the imposition of the 100 per cent required RRs. Proposals of this type have been made by Friedman (1960), Pierce (1991), Merton and Bodie (1993) and Miller (1995).

To guarantee the efficient working of the payments system, Merton and Bodie recommend that government insurance of demand deposits continue to be compulsory, but that banks accepting demand deposits should have to provide the insurance agency with collateral in the form of Treasury bills equal to 100 per cent of the deposits insured. The effect of this proposal would be very similar to a requirement that commercial banks must hold 100 per cent reserves against demand deposits, and that they should receive interest on these reserves at the rate paid on Treasury bills.

Under this proposal, banks with insured demand deposits would be allowed to accept uninsured time and savings deposits. Merton and Bodie also recommend that uninsured money market mutual funds should be allowed to offer cheque-writing privileges, as long as they value their assets at their market prices and do not create the illusion of offering perfectly risk-free deposits.[25] One problem with this concession is that it would mean that the payments system would not be fully guaranteed; another is that it is not clear how regulators would prevent uninsured institutions creating the illusion that they offered risk-free demand deposits.

Since 100 per cent RRs on demand deposits are intended to be a substitute for high minimum CARs, their effectiveness should be judged on the assumption that financial institutions are highly leveraged. In this case, it would be the holders of non-guaranteed deposits who would bear the brunt of any bank losses. Under the Merton and Bodie proposal there would be nothing to prevent a run on savings deposits and promissory notes, nor to prevent holders of maturing time deposits from deciding not to roll them over. If there were a run on non-guaranteed deposits the government would be subjected to the kinds of pressures that have led to the issuing of blanket guarantees during financial crises, even in countries whose governments had denied that they would ever provide bail-outs. It is therefore unlikely that a government that adopted the Merton and Bodie proposal would be able to make a credible commitment not to bail out holders of uninsured time deposits, savings deposits and promissory notes. Even if such a commitment could be made, the proposal would not solve the problem that widespread failures of private banks could occur and would lead to the payments system having to be operated, at least temporarily, by the government.

Minimum Capital Adequacy Ratios

The most direct way for a guarantor, whether public or private, to protect itself against non-performance by a firm that it has guaranteed, is to insist that the firm keep a high ratio of capital to other liabilities: like the deductible amount in a contract insuring assets against possible loss, capital in a guaranteed firm is both a buffer between these losses and the contingent liability of the guarantor, and also a check on moral hazard, because small losses are borne entirely by shareholders in the guaranteed firm.[26] If banks are subject to high capital adequacy requirements, the problems facing bank regulators are reduced to ensuring that the requirements are met and that the risk of banks incurring losses greater than their required capital is very small. The effectiveness of setting high minimum CARs is demonstrated by the fact that the banks with the highest capital ratios have generally been the ones best able to withstand crises.[27]

The 1988 Basle Capital Accord, which was drawn up by representatives of the central banks and bank supervisory authorities of Luxembourg, Switzerland and the G–10 countries, provides a framework which was fully adopted by these countries and has also been followed more or less closely by most others.[28] A survey of 140 countries in 1996 found that 92 per cent of them set capital requirements for banks that are defined as a percentage of risk weighted assets.[29] The Accord proposed that banks should be required to have 'core capital' equal to at least 4 per cent, and 'total capital' equal to at least 8 per cent of their 'risk weighted assets'. Core capital, or tier 1 capital, comprises the issued value of common stock plus accumulated profit reserves and some types of preferred stock. It excludes the value of bank licences and other forms of goodwill, and loan-loss reserves against identified bad or doubtful loans. Supplementary capital, or tier 2 capital, comprises preferred stock not included in tier 1 capital, loan-loss reserves up to 1.25 per cent of risk-adjusted assets and subordinated debt, which is defined as debts that rank behind all other claims except equity in the event of bankruptcy. Total capital is the sum of core and supplementary capital.

A bank's total risk weighted assets are calculated by placing each asset in one of four categories. The first category has a zero risk weight and includes cash and central government securities; the second category has a risk weight of 20 per cent, and includes inter-bank deposits, fully backed local government bonds and the securities of government agencies; the third category has a weight of 50 per cent and includes other local government bonds and first home mortgages; the fourth category has a weight of 100 per cent and covers everything else. Thus, a bank which held just cash and central government securities would have risk weighted assets of zero, while a bank which held only loans to corporations would have risk weighted assets equal to its total assets. The face values of off-balance sheet items are converted to balance sheet equivalents using rules of thumb: for example, stand-by letters of credit are counted in full, but only half of the unused portion of lines of credit are counted. The rationale for this is that the bank is fully liable for letters of credit, but may be able to cancel a line of credit, and faces no credit risk until the credit is drawn down.

Supplementary prudential regulations (that is, those other than the CAR) are like the covenants imposed by private guarantors: their purpose is to reinforce capital adequacy requirements by surveillance and direct controls on easily measurable variables. Almost all countries set limits on banks' net foreign currency exposure, on their loans to related firms and on large loans to individual borrowers. In each case, the ceilings are usually set as a proportion of capital. The justification for restrictions on bank lending to related firms is that it restricts the opportunities for fraudulent transfers of insured deposits from banks to other firms in the same group. Apart from this potential for fraud, such lending would be no more risky than bank lending to any other single large borrower. Because shell companies can be placed between banks and ultimate borrowers, and because the authority and practical ability of bank regulators to conduct audits and inspections usually does not extend beyond the banks themselves, it is hard to enforce effective restrictions on large individual loans, or on lending to related firms.

In addition to setting prudential ratios between various balance sheet items, supervisors normally require the reporting by financial institutions of detailed accounts, including information on all large individual loans. This information provides the basis for moral suasion backed up by the supervisor's discretionary powers, which may include the power to dictate the terms and availability of last resort loans, and the ability to close down institutions that are judged to be unsound.

Does Setting High Minimum Capital Adequacy Ratios Cause Waste?

The advantage of setting a high minimum CAR is that it would reduce the moral hazard created by safety nets for depositors. The main disadvantages that have been suggested are a possible increase in agency costs for bank shareholders and a possible loss of economies of scope between the making of bank loans and the accepting of deposits. It is argued below that these factors are unlikely to be important, at least in developing countries and over a wide range of possible increases in the minimum CAR.

Merton and Bodie (1993, pp. 13–14) argue that one of the costs of equity, relative to debt, is the agency cost to shareholders of monitoring managers. However, there are two reasons for doubting that a requirement that forced banks to replace some deposits by equity would induce excessive expenditure on monitoring. First, since monitoring is like a public good, whose benefits can be shared by all shareholders, raising the equity share in total assets makes it possible for shareholders to have both more total monitoring and lower expenditure on monitoring per dollar of capital invested. Second, efficiency requires managers to be monitored; since deposit insurance removes the incentives for depositors to engage in monitoring, it must be done either by regulators, or by equity investors, or by holders of subordinated debt. If raising the equity share in total assets leads to increased monitoring of managers by shareholders, it will have the beneficial side-effect of reducing the need for monitoring of managers by regulators. Admittedly, the objectives of owners and regulators are not always identical: small losses are of no concern to regulators, and the magnitude of losses is of no concern to owners if it exceeds the value of initial capital. However, since actions that raise the probability of small losses will often add to the probability of large losses, and vice versa, the objectives of owners and regulators will often be quite similar.

One way in which setting too high a minimum CAR might induce waste would be if the regulation destroyed possible economies of scope, due to synergies between the lending and deposit taking activities traditionally undertaken by banks. This is unlikely to be the source of significant inefficiencies because CARs could be raised without altering the total volume of bank loans and deposits (except in ways that are intrinsically desirable because they result from the diminution of moral hazard): provided that they were not prevented from doing so by regulations, banks could issue new equity to non-bank institutional investors, such as pension funds, insurance companies and mutual funds, and use the proceeds to buy some of the industrial and commercial shares originally held by the institutional investors. To induce the institutional investors to take up the bank equity, its price would have to fall, and to induce them to sell their holdings of industrial and commercial shares the prices of these shares would have to rise. To reflect the increased cost of finance, banks would presumably raise all lending rates, and the institutional investors would seek to reduce the risks taken by banks by requiring them to raise interest rates on the most risky loans relative to the general level of lending rates. The institutional investors would presumably wish to institute increased monitoring of bank managers. These are all desirable ways of reducing moral hazard. Since the volume of deposits need not change, and since the change in total loans would reflect merely the reduction that would occur because of reduced moral hazard, there would be no interference with any synergies that may exist between making loans and taking deposits.

A possible economy of scope between deposits and loans is suggested by Flannery (1994) who argues that even in the absence of government intervention it would be efficient for banks to finance a relatively high proportion of illiquid assets with short-term liabilities. He assumes that creditors can roughly observe the risks taken by a bank, but argues that trying to restrict these risks by writing covenants would be very costly. 'This makes short-term debt an unusually valuable contracting device for banking firms: changes in bank risk will be promptly reflected in banking costs, leaving banks free to acquire any investment that seems profitable' (p. 321). To the extent that it is quantitatively important, Flannery's argument implies that one of the potential costs of any deposit insurance scheme is that it prevents the efficient operation of the signalling device that he describes. However, the argument does not imply that setting high CARs is an inefficient way of limiting the moral hazard created by deposit insurance because when deposits are insured the potentially useful signalling role of short-term debt that he describes would barely operate: risk-taking by a bank would have only very muted effects on the interest rate paid on deposits insured by a government agency. When deposits are insured, the signalling role described by Flannery is played by the interest rate on subordinated debt, which is a component of regulatory capital.

Even if setting excessively high CARs was very wasteful, there would be a strong case for large increases in the current minimum CARs in developing countries. Banks with CARs near the 8 per cent minimum have abnormally low ratios of equity to debt relative to other businesses and the obvious explanation for this pattern of financing is that government guarantees make bank deposits a heavily subsidised source of finance. Raising minimum CARs would move bank financing towards, not away from, the patterns that would be observed if deposits were insured in competitive private markets. Even if minimum CARs were doubled, from 8 per cent to 16 per cent, they would be below the average levels observed in developing countries with strong banking systems and similar to the levels observed in the USA before the creation of safety nets for depositors.[30]

Problems with Enforcing Minimum CARs

The main problems in relying on high minimum CARs to limit moral hazard are that both bank capital and the riskiness of assets are hard to measure. At present, regulators rely on accounting measures of capital, as recorded on banks' balance sheets. The stock market value of bank equity may differ from the book value of shareholders' equity for several reasons. Strong banks are reluctant to revalue their assets because doing so increases their liability for corporate tax. The book value of shareholders' equity also excludes 'goodwill' and the scarcity value of the bank's licence. For strong banks, with regulatory capital well in excess of the minimum required, measured capital therefore usually understates true capital, and often by large amounts.[31] However, the opposite is likely to be true for weak banks: this is because a bank that is in danger of being suspended by its regulators can artificially exaggerate its true capital by rolling over bad loans so as to avoid making accurate provisions for probable losses.[32] In the case of banks which are so weak that they are almost insolvent, or would actually be insolvent in the absence of government safety nets, the value of expected government bail-outs may give their shares some positive market value.

A crude, but useful, way of dealing with the problem of measuring capital for regulatory purposes would be to redefine it as the lower of the book and market values of the bank's equity and subordinated debt. To make this proposal viable, banks would have to be listed on stock exchanges. Admittedly, the market value of an insured bank exceeds the concept of capital that is appropriate for regulatory purposes because it includes the value of the put option which is implicit in the shareholders' ability to transfer all their assets and liabilities to the government at a zero price. But this objection is not fatal, because book values are also far from ideal. Market values can be measured without lags and it would be much harder for managers to conceal a serious problem of non-performing loans from the share market than to delay its effects on the book value of equity. To the extent that more prompt observation of capital led to more prompt government intervention in a troubled bank, the value of the put option described above would be reduced, and so therefore would the conceptual error involved in using market values to measure capital for regulatory purposes.

It is also hard for regulators to measure the riskiness of assets. The Basle convention contains obvious biases, such as treating all government securities as having zero risk even though some developing country government bonds are given junk bond status by financial markets. Even if these easily corrected biases were removed by using credit ratings in assigning risk weights, it would still be hard to overcome the problem that since the institutions actually making loans, or entering into derivatives contracts, necessarily have an informational advantage over the supervisors looking over their shoulders, they can partially disguise the real risks that they are taking.

One suggested way of measuring risk is to require banks to make their own assessments of the risks they face, and then impose penalties on those whose assets fluctuate in value by more than could be expected, given their own assessments. One problem with this proposal is that banks may be able to disguise losses for long periods by rolling them over. A second problem is that it would not allow regulators to detect the existence of extremely small probabilities of very large losses. Suppose that in addition to the 'normal' risks that it faces, a bank also faces a one in a thousand chance of losing everything. It would have no incentive to declare the exceptional risk to regulators: if the disaster does not happen, regulators have no way of knowing of its existence, if it does happen, all is lost anyway. If the occurrence of the disaster could be used as evidence that managers knew the risks the bank faced, they could be prosecuted. Often however it would be hard or impossible to prove that the probability of the disaster was known to managers in advance. Despite these reasons for believing that self-assessment of risk is liable to result in the camouflaging of small losses and the underestimation of the risks of major disasters, it is likely to be a considerable improvement on the crude risk weighting system that is currently used.

The EU and the Basle Committee have proposed that banks should be able to choose whether to meet traditional CARs or to hold capital equal to three times their own assessments of their 'value at risk', defined as the biggest loss which the bank could incur in the next 10 days with 1 per cent probability.[33] This proposal would reduce the cost of capital requirements for the safest banks, but would do nothing to overcome the more serious problem of reducing the risks taken by the most risky banks, which could stick with the traditional 8 per cent CAR requirement.

A second way of trying to assess the risk faced by banks would be to use the interest rates paid on subordinated debts. Again, this measure would probably be an improvement on current procedures, but would be highly imperfect: if subordinated debt is to be an effective buffer against bank runs, it must be impossible for its holders to withdraw their loans at short notice; but the fixed contract interest rates on long-term debts cannot provide an accurate guide to short-term fluctuations in risk.

Regulators face increasingly difficult choices as a troubled bank's capital adequacy approaches the specified minimum level. On the one hand, if a bank with very low, or negative, capital is allowed to continue to operate, its owners and managers have an incentive to 'bet the bank on a gamble on resurrection'. On the other hand, closing down a bank whose CAR falls below the legislated minimum is likely to reduce general confidence in the whole financial system. Kane (1995) argues that regulators have an incentive to allow managers of troubled banks to gamble on resurrection: a bank failure is a stigma on the careers of the regulators and politicians that allowed it to fail, and even the postponement of such a failure may allow them to shift some of the blame to their successors.

The best solution to these problems is called 'prompt corrective action'. It was partially implemented in the USA in the 1991 FDIC Improvement Act, although this Act has been criticised for not imposing sufficiently large differentials in insurance premia between weak and strong banks and for allowing regulators too much discretion.[34] Ideally, legislation would set a range of CARs and a corresponding range of regulatory actions: above the 'minimum satisfactory CAR', that is, the highest CAR in the range, banks would be classified as 'sound'. Such banks would be subject to minimal supervision and reporting requirements, would be charged low insurance premia and would be given wide discretion over the risks that they can take, although limits would still be set on loans to related firms and to individual large borrowers. Banks with lower CARs would have to pay progressively higher insurance premia and would be subjected to additional prudential controls, which could include frequent reporting, compulsory auditing, supervision of new loan approvals and restrictions on derivative trading and foreign exchange exposure. They would have to draw up and implement satisfactory plans for raising new capital.

To minimise the risk of regulators trying to cover up the weaknesses of the banks for which they are responsible, it is desirable to restrict their discretion and oblige them to take specified measures as soon as banks fall into the CAR range in which such measures are supposed to be applied. Well before capital falls close to zero, it is important that the regulators take over the operation of an insured bank to prevent the owners staking the insured deposits on very risky investments.

To reduce the risk of regulatory intervention causing panics, and to increase the probability that regulators have time to intervene well before a bank's capital falls to zero, it is important to set the minimum satisfactory CAR at a high level. Benston and Kaufman (1997) suggest that the appropriate ratio is the ratio observed for financial institutions whose liabilities are not insured, such as insurance companies. A good case can, in fact, be made that banks should be required to have even higher CARs than those of non-insured financial institutions. First, they need to operate more cautiously than other financial institutions because their deposit liabilities are more liquid than the liabilities of most other financial institutions. Second, the importance of the payments system to the rest of the economy implies that banks should be made even safer than they would choose to be under the influence of market forces alone. Third, the opportunities for banks to abuse government deposit insurance schemes by exaggerating their reported capital and understating their measured risk justify requiring banks to have higher CARs than those chosen by institutions whose liabilities are not insured by the state.

6.5   REGULATION AND SUBSIDISATION OF THE FINANCIAL SECTOR

While government intervention in the financial system is conventionally rational-ised by the need to reduce risk-taking, its ultimate effect, at least in developing countries, is to increase risk-taking. This section lists three types of government intervention that lead to this result and shows that each is related to the desire of governments to protect politically influential domestic groups.

First, it is very common for governments of developing countries to force banks to deviate from normal commercial principles to lend at relatively low interest rates to borrowers whom the government wishes to help. Compulsory long-term lending to priority sectors, such as agriculture, industry or low-income housing has accentuated the mismatch between short-term deposits, and long-term and illiquid assets.[35] Second, the governments of most developing countries have protected their banking sectors by restricting entry by foreign banks, or by restricting branching by those foreign banks that were admitted. This makes the domestic banking sector much more vulnerable to a crisis than would otherwise be the case. If banks are globally diversified, a downturn in one economy or region does not have such adverse effects on the quality of their loan portfolios as it does in a closed system, in which all banks are lending only to domestic firms, which are all exposed to the same economy-specific risks. This effect partly explains why the economic crisis of 1997–98 resulted in the collapse of some financial systems, but not others: in Singapore and Hong Kong the shares of foreign banks in the total assets of all banks were 80 per cent and 78 per cent, respectively; in Indonesia, Korea and Thailand these shares were 4 per cent, 5 per cent and 7 per cent, respectively.[36]

The third form of risk-augmenting protection is the setting of CARs that are far too low given that deposits are explicitly or implicitly guaranteed. Just as the rules of the World Trade Organization (WTO) limit the extent to which governments can subsidise their agricultural and industrial sectors, so the Basle Capital Accord limits the extent to which the major industrial countries can subsidise their banks by allowing them to finance loans with government guaranteed deposits. The extent of financial failures in the last 20 years in the USA, Japan and Scandinavia suggests that this ceiling on protection by subsidisation of risk is much too low even in industrial countries.

6.6 OVERVIEW

The financial crises in Asia in 1997–98 reinforce the earlier Latin American evidence that the systems of prudential regulation that were introduced when financial repression was eased have often been ineffective. Since severe financial repression, including capital and exchange controls, is prohibitively inefficient, the main options for trying to reduce the huge cost of banking crises in developing countries are:

1. to abolish safety nets for depositors altogether and stop trying to regulate the financial sector;
2. to replace the current approach to regulation, based on CARs, surveillance and other subsidiary controls, by setting 100 per cent RRs on demand deposits, as proposed by the Chicago Plan;
3. to tighten the subsidiary controls – such as surveillance of banks, limits on large individual loans and on loans to related borrowers and limits on foreign exchange exposure – that are currently used to supplement the existing international standard of an 8 per cent minimum CAR;
4. to increase minimum CARs very substantially;
5. to use a Chilean-style VDR to limit inflows of short-term and portfolio capital.

Option (1) has certain attractions: even in the USA, financial safety nets have a poor track record and in developing countries the risks they induce are the main source of financial crises. However, the pressures on a government to guarantee bank deposits during a financial crisis appear to be almost irresistible. Perhaps reformers should push for the introduction of constitutional amendments to prohibit bail-outs. However, the case for such amendments is not clear-cut: the skill with which supreme courts find ways around constitutional provisions, when it is politically expedient to do so, might make them ineffective and the economy-wide benefits of a sound financial system do provide a potential case for safety nets, if adequate prudential controls for dealing with moral hazard can be devised. Whatever the merits of constitutional amendments to restrict bail-outs, there is no prospect of their speedy introduction; as long as government promises not to provide bail-outs continue to lack credibility, there is an overwhelming case for prudential controls to limit the moral hazard created by the safety nets.

The disadvantage of option (2), the Chicago Plan, is that implementing it would induce innovations that would reduce the role of demand deposits at regulated banks, and expand that of non-guaranteed time deposits, savings deposits and promissory notes. In a crisis, governments would still face heavy pressures to bail out all depositors.

Option (3), to strengthen surveillance and other existing prudential controls, without greatly increasing the minimum CAR, seems to be the preferred option of the multilateral agencies and major governments. In the wake of the Asian crisis, there have been numerous criticisms of the existing prudential controls in developing countries and calls for tighter controls to be implemented in the future. The case against option (3) is that it has failed so often in the past. The need for strict prudential regulation of banks was part of the conventional wisdom long before the Asian crises of 1997–98, and, as noted earlier, elaborate prudential controls had already been set up in Malaysia, Korea, Indonesia and Thailand well before 1997. Commentators such as Cole (1995, p. 251), Browne (1997, pp. 349–52), Djiwandono (1997, pp. 342–5) and Montgomery (1997, p. 4) expressed at least guarded praise for the new controls, subject to reservations about the effectiveness of their implementation. It turned out however that there had indeed been a chasm between the controls that existed on paper and those that the regulators had been able to implement. Bank Indonesia was apparently aware of the problem because it has now published time series data, which go back to before the start of the crisis, on the number of banks violating the main prudential controls.[37]

The official proposals for strengthening financial sectors also include recommendations for improved bankruptcy procedures and for the opening of financial sectors in developing countries to competition from international banks. If the courts prove willing and able to enforce the new, or amended, bankruptcy laws in Indonesia, Thailand and Korea, they will make a major contribution to reducing the risks of financial collapse. The WTO's General Agreement on Trade in Services (GATS) requires a gradual opening of closed banking sectors to foreign competition, and the IMF agreements with Indonesia, Thailand and Korea provide for accelerated financial opening in these countries. Free entry by international banks will strengthen domestic banking systems by helping to diversify their asset holdings. The Basle Committee on Banking Supervision (1999) published a consultative paper on possible revisions to the Capital Accord which recommended an increase in the risk weights assigned to relatively risky assets and the setting of risk weights of more than one for the most risky categories.[38] This is another highly desirable reform.

Increased risk weights in CAR formulas, improved bankruptcy procedures and opening of financial sectors to international competition are all measures that deserve support. But they are unlikely to be sufficient while CARs remain at 8 per cent. Even with improved bankruptcy procedures and internationally diversified financial sectors, there is no reason to expect that the probability of an 8 per cent fall in the value of bank assets will ever become negligible, no matter how closely supervisors attempt to monitor and control risk taking. Yet, even if all assets were given a risk weight of unity, such a relatively small fall in asset values would cause the failure of a bank with a CAR of 8 per cent.

The reform that would do most to reduce the excessive fragility of financial sectors in developing countries is option 4. The existing 8 per cent CAR has proved inadequate in industrialised countries and banks in developing countries need higher CARs than those in industrialised countries. In developing countries, bank supervision is less sophisticated than in the industrialised countries and banking sector regulations are harder to enforce because many banks are owned either by governments or by politically well-connected businessmen. The terms of trade of developing countries are more volatile than those of industrialised countries and the risks faced by financial institutions are further increased by the opportunities that ineffective bankruptcy procedures offer to recalcitrant debtors. Real exchange rate fluctuations are also relatively large in developing countries and any large relative price movements make banking dangerous: those that lose from the price change may be unable to repay their contracted debts, while those that gain merely continue to repay what had been contracted. Very abrupt real exchange rate depreciation contributed to an explosion of non-performing loans in the Asian crisis countries in 1998. This was also a cause of non-performing loans in the Chilean exchange and financial crisis of 1982–83, in the Argentine financial crisis of 1980, and in other Latin American cases, including Uruguay and Colombia in the early 1980s.[39] Developing countries are also particularly vulnerable to contagion effects in which bank failures – often associated with speculation against the exchange rate – in one economy reduce confidence in the banking systems and currencies of the economies which trade with it, or have similar characteristics. Such effects were powerfully illustrated both by the Asian currency crisis of 1997–98 and by the spill over effects of the Mexican crisis of 1994–95.

In addition to very substantial increases in minimum 'satisfactory' CARs, there is also a need for rules that oblige regulators to take 'prompt corrective action' whenever CARs fall below these satisfactory levels. Banks with more than the minimum satisfactory CAR would be exempt from all other controls, except limits on loans to related firms and individual large borrowers, but those with less than the satisfactory minimum would be subject to increasingly onerous prudential controls of the types listed in section 6.4 and proposed by Benston and Kaufman (1993, 1997). If they achieved nothing else, the threat of these onerous prudential controls would give banks a strong incentive to keep their CARs above the minimum satisfactory level. Regulators should be forced to take over weak banks well before their capital falls close to zero. Implicit guarantees should be replaced by compulsory deposit insurance with the premia set to make the schemes self-funding. Banks with more than the minimum CAR should be rewarded by having relatively low insurance premia. As argued in section 6.4, capital should be defined for regulatory purposes as subordinated debt plus whichever is the lower of the book and market values of equity.

International comparisons provide at least some indication of the appropriate level for the minimum CAR. The actual risk-based capital ratios of the banking sectors of Singapore, Hong Kong and Argentina in 1995 were 18.7 per cent, 17.5 per cent and 18.5 per cent, respectively, whereas in Indonesia, Korea and Thailand the reported values of these ratios were 11.9 per cent, 9.3 per cent and 9.3 per cent, respectively.[40] Ineffective rules on making provisions for bad and doubtful loans in Indonesia, Korea and Thailand meant that the true CARs in these countries were much lower than the reported ones, especially for the weakest banks.

Folkerts-Landau (1996, p. 104) suggests that in developing countries the minimum required CAR should 'probably be close to double' that required in industrialised countries. In contrast, Musch (1997, p. 138) argues that imposing a higher CAR in developing countries than in industrial countries would place banks in developing countries at a competitive disadvantage. For the time being, concern for regulatory neutrality is somewhat academic, since domestic banks in most developing countries are often protected from competition from international banks by regulatory barriers to entry and branching.

All banking systems could be made much safer, while preserving regulatory neutrality, if the Basle Capital Accord were amended to increase CARs for banks in all countries and to increase the risk weights on loans to borrowers resident in developing countries, unless the borrowers had good credit ratings from international ratings agencies. If this were done, and if developing countries fully opened their financial sectors to international competition, the present need for higher CARs in developing than in industrialised countries could be greatly reduced. If the Basle Accord is not reformed in this way, individual developing countries should raise their own CARs unilaterally. Although it is politically difficult for an individual country to do this, it is not impossible: Argentina has set a minimum CAR of 11.5 per cent.[41]

An appropriate initial target might be to raise the risk weights on assets in developing countries by between 50 per cent and 100 per cent, and to impose a phased increase in minimum CARs in all countries to, say, 16 per cent over five years. These reforms, combined with complete opening of financial sectors, would probably reduce the spate of financial crises of the last two decades to acceptable levels. However, even with CARs of 16 per cent, banks and finance companies would remain very highly geared relative to almost all non-financial institutions and further increases in minimum CARs might be required. Many international banks already have CARs of 16 per cent or more; many others would probably be able to reach this level merely by revaluing their assets to reflect their true market values. However, many developing country banks would have to reduce their holdings of assets with high risk weights and acquire less risky ones. Banks would have to raise the interest rates charged to risky projects and to reduce the interest rates on loans to less risky ones, thus reflecting the desired object of the policy: to switch investment from risky projects to less risky ones.

The potential for last resort lending to allow failing banks to gamble away government resources was noted in section 6.2. This point, and the appropriate monetary strategy to adopt during a financial crisis, are discussed in more detail in section 8.5, which uses Indonesia's experience in the financial crisis of 1998 to highlight the seemingly impossible problems that central banks confront in trying to make such loans without incurring large losses. Because it is almost impossible in practice for central banks to distinguish between insolvent banks and solvent but illiquid banks, and because adverse selection makes last resort loans much more attractive to banks that are likely to fail than to those that are likely to repay, most last resort loans go to institutions that subsequently fail. This has occurred not only in developing countries, such as Indonesia in 1998, but also (as noted in section 6.2) in the USA in the S&L debacle.

Providing last resort loans to banks that are probably insolvent defeats the whole purpose of prompt corrective action: regulators should be trying to close down institutions that are likely to absorb the funds of the deposit insurance agency, but providing them with last resort loans allows them to continue using deposits (and the last resort loans themselves) to gamble on resurrection. In the absence of deposit insurance it would be impossible for governments to resist the pressures to provide last resort loans, but if deposits are insured or guaranteed this need not be the case. This provides a powerful, if cynical, justification for deposit insurance: even in economies in which it cannot be justified as a way of reducing the probability and magnitude of recessions, it is much the lesser of two evils, at least one of which seems to be almost inevitable.

Even those economists who favour the eventual removal of capital controls usually recommend that restrictions on inflows – option 5 – should not be relaxed until 'adequate' prudential regulations are in place to ensure the strength of the financial sector. However, it was argued in Chapter 3 that Chile's inflow controls probably had little effect on its avoidance of currency and financial crises in the 1990s, and the evidence from multi-country econometric studies on the effectiveness of inflow controls as safety devices is inconclusive: Rossi (1999) finds that they have a perverse, but statistically insignificant effect on the probability of banking crises, but are significantly associated with a reduced probability of currency crises.[42] He also finds that they are significantly associated with relatively slow GDP growth.

Since even the countries with the strongest traditions of prudential regulation can experience financial and currency crises, delaying the removal of inflow controls until prudential regulations are 'adequate' is liable to be a recipe for never removing them. The position taken here is that if a country experiencing rapid inflows has not set a high minimum CAR, then it should do so. During a period of rapid inflows the political constraints on raising the minimum CAR are weaker than usual and raising it would not only slow inflows in general, but – in contrast to an across-the-board VDR – would particularly discourage inflows that finance risky investments that are viable only because potential losses would be cushioned by government bail-outs. If a minimum CAR of 16 per cent, or more, is already in place, the risk of a financial crisis is probably small even if inflows are very rapid. In either case, imposing a general tax on inflows appears likely to do some harm and little good.

NOTES

1. See Benston *et al.* (1986, especially pp. 63–4), and Kaufman (1994).
2. Estimates derived from Flannery (1994, p. 321).
3. Rojas-Suárez and Weisbrod (1996a, p. 71).
4. See p. 164 in the 1920 edition.
5. See p. 189 in the 1920 edition.
6. Cited by Fischer (1999).
7. The estimates in this paragraph of average bank and business failure rates are unweighted averages of the data on annual failure rates in Benston *et al.* (1986, pp. 54–7).
8. See Benston *et al.* (1986, p. 64).
9. For many years, the annual insurance premium set by the FDIC was only 0.08 per cent of insured deposits. By 1994, however, the insurance premia charged by FDIC ranged from 0.23 per cent per year, at the strongest banks, to 0.31 per cent per year at the most risky (Berger *et al.*, 1995, p. 405). Since 1996, the premia have ranged from nothing, for the strongest banks, to 0.27 per cent per year at the most risky; since 98 per cent of deposits in 1998 were at banks that paid no premium, the average was only 0.001 per cent (FDIC, 1999).
10. The $200 billion estimate is taken from Ryan (1996, p. 245). The period to which the losses should be attributed is arbitrary: Ryan states that the budgetary payments by taxpayers were spread over three years; presumably, the losses were incurred by banks over a much longer period.
11. Benston *et al.* (1986, p. 64).
12. See the studies referred to by Calomiris (1998).
13. See section 8.5.
14. Fane and McLeod (1999).
15. McKinnon (1973, 1991), Diáz-Alejandro (1985), Kaminsky and Reinhart (1999).
16. All the findings summarised in this paragraph are obtained by comparing the classifications in Table 1 of Williamson and Mahar (1998), of the restrictiveness of controls in 1973 and 1996.
17. McKinnon and Pill (1997) provide a simple model of this process.
18. See McKinnon (1991, Chapter 1) and Edwards (1998, p. 12).
19. Rojas-Suárez and Weisbrod (1996a, p. 65) criticise reserve requirements as an inefficient tax on banking.

20. This proposal has been made by Greenspan (1998).
21. Bank of Thailand (1996), pp. 114–15.
22. Phillips (1995, pp. 90, 165) attributes this criticism to Allais and cites a 1934 letter from Henry Simons to Irving Fisher, which shows that Simons was aware of the problem: 'Little would be gained by putting demand deposit banking on a 100% basis, if that change were accompanied by [an] increasing disposition to hold, and increasing facilities for holding, liquid "cash" reserves in the form of time deposits'.
23. This was Irving Fisher's position. See Phillips (1995, p. 92).
24. Mishkin (1992, pp. 307–11) lists examples of financial innovations developed by US banks to exploit loopholes in regulations that attempted to impose minimum RRs and ceilings on interest rates on cheque accounts.
25. Merton and Bodie (1993, p. 19).
26. The CARs of banking groups must be measured on a consolidated basis if deposit insurance is to be equivalent to insurance of assets with a deductible equal to capital. Otherwise, cross-holdings of shares, which are counted as part of the deductible of the bank that issued them, are also part of the insured assets of the bank that holds them.
27. de Krivoy (1996, p. 179).
28. The history of the Basle Capital Accord is summarised by Padoa-Schioppa (1997).
29. Musch (1997, p. 137).
30. Only after the creation of the Federal Reserve System in 1914 did the average ratio of equity to assets for US commercial banks fall below 16 per cent. See Berger *et al.* (1995, p. 402).
31. In June 1998, *Euromoney* published data on the 50 largest banks in the world as measured by market capitalisation and on the 50 largest as measured by book value of equity. The total market capitalisation of the 37 banks that were in both these groups was 2.7 times the book value of their equity.
32. Rojas-Suárez and Weisbrod (1996b, pp. 12–13) show that concealment of non-performing loans from bank supervisors is a more serious problem in Argentina, Chile, Venezuela, and Mexico than in industrial countries: the official estimate of the ratio of non-performing loans to total bank loans in Chile just before the onset of its 1982 financial crisis was lower than the corresponding ratio in the USA in 1989. The other three Latin American countries had ratios of non-performing loans to total loans, just before the onset of each of their financial crises in the 1980s and 1990s, which were similar to that observed in Finland at the end of 1992, although the Finnish crisis was proportionately much less expensive to resolve than the Latin American ones.
33. International Monetary Fund (1996, pp. 136–7).
34. Those making such criticisms include Miller (1995) and Benston and Kaufman (1997, pp. 149–50).
35. de Krivoy (1996).
36. Goldstein and Turner (1996, Table 6, p. 35).
37. Bank Indonesia (1999a, pp. 92–3).
38. Basle Committee on Banking Supervision (1999, paragraph 23).
39. Gavin and Hausmann (1996, p. 43).
40. Goldstein and Turner (1996, Table 4, p. 26).
41. Caprio *et al.* (1996).
42. Rossi (1999) finds that outflow controls are associated with increased probabilities of both currency and banking crises, but that only the former effect is statistically significant. He also finds that outflow controls are significantly associated with relatively rapid GDP growth.

7. Monetary and exchange rate policies

This chapter deals with the implications of capital mobility for macroeconomic policy. Section 7.1 describes how capital flows affect aggregate demand under fixed and flexible exchange rates and how capital mobility alters both the effectiveness of monetary and fiscal policies and the ability of automatic stabilisers to moderate the effects on aggregate demand of monetary and expenditure shocks. Section 7.2 argues that attempts to 'sterilise' capital flows under a fixed exchange rate system – that is, to vary domestic credit in order to offset part, or all, of the effects of capital flows on the money supply – are likely to be both inefficient and destabilising. Section 7.3 produces evidence of the very great extent to which developing countries have sterilised the monetary effects of balance of payments flows. This is particularly notable in developing countries with conventional central banks. Even some countries with currency boards have engaged in very considerable amounts of sterilisation, though to a lesser extent, on average, than those with conventional central banks. Section 7.4 provides an overview.

7.1   CAPITAL FLOWS, STABILISATION POLICY AND THE EXCHANGE RATE SYSTEM

Capital Flows and Aggregate Demand Under Alternative Exchange Rate Regimes

The monetary policies adopted by the authorities when the exchange rate is fixed can be thought of as being on a spectrum, which shows how they adjust NDC in response to changes in official foreign exchange reserves. It follows from the simplified balance sheets set out in section 2.2 that the change in the supply of base money (M0) is equal to the sum of changes in NDC and net foreign assets (NFA):

$$M0 = NDC + NFA,$$
$$\Delta M0 = \Delta NDC + \Delta NFA,$$

where $\Delta M0$, ΔNDC and ΔNFA indicate the changes in M0, NDC and NFA. The increase in official foreign exchange reserves is the dominant element in ΔNFA.[1] Since the balance of payments surplus in any period is equal to the change in official foreign exchange reserves, it follows that how the central bank adjusts domestic credit in response to a change in official foreign exchange reserves determines the overall effect on the money supply of balance of payments surpluses or deficits under a fixed exchange rate system.

At one end of the spectrum is full sterilisation of the monetary effects of balance of payments flows: the authorities try to hold base money constant by expanding domestic credit if the balance of payments is in deficit, and by contracting domestic credit if it is in surplus. At the other end of the visible spectrum is a textbook currency board system under which the board leaves domestic credit unchanged, so that a balance of payments deficit causes the monetary base to fall dollar-for-dollar with official foreign exchange reserves. In the invisible spectrum, beyond even currency board purity, is the textbook 'rule' of the gold standard which, though seldom followed even in the pre-World War I gold standard period, required a central bank to contract domestic credit if the balance of payments was in deficit and to expand domestic credit if the balance of payments was in surplus. If followed, this rule would lead to even smaller fluctuations in foreign exchange reserves than the currency board rule of holding domestic credit constant. Attempts by the monetary authorities to sterilise the effects of capital flows on the money supply are analysed in the next section. This section analyses the properties of a fixed exchange rate system when the central bank follows a currency board policy of holding domestic credit constant.

In the absence of sterilisation, capital inflows used to finance purchases of either domestic securities or non-traded goods unambiguously expand aggregate demand under a fixed exchange rate regime. A capital inflow that is used entirely to finance spending on traded goods would have no effects on employment, the exchange rate, the money supply or foreign exchange reserves under either a fixed or a flexible exchange rate regime. Inflows of capital that finance the purchase of domestic securities raise the prices and therefore lower the yields of these securities; this reduction in domestic interest rates stimulates investment spending, reduces savings at any given level of income and allows the demand for money to rise to match the increased supply produced by the capital inflow. The same qualitative effects on spending occur directly if capital inflows are used to finance the purchase of non-traded goods.

The effects on aggregate demand of capital inflows that result from a fall in world interest rates, or an increase in the expected profitability of domestic investment, are quite different under fixed and flexible exchange rate regimes. The reason is that the effects of capital flows on the money supply are quite different in the two cases. Consider the fixed exchange rate case first. To keep the exchange rate fixed, when there is a capital inflow, the monetary authorities must buy the incoming foreign exchange and thereby add to the supply of base money in circulation. Inflows therefore directly add to the supply of base money and outflows directly reduce it. In contrast, under a flexible exchange rate system, the central bank does not allow capital inflows to raise the money supply; since it does not intervene in the foreign exchange market, each dollar of capital inflow used to finance increased spending on non-traded goods must lead to an appreciation of the exchange rate that is sufficient to contract net exports (that is, exports minus imports) by a dollar.

In both the flexible exchange rate case and the fixed exchange rate case, a capital inflow that is caused by a fall in world interest rates or an increase in the expected profitability of domestic investment leads to an appreciation of the real exchange rate. However, because of the different responses of the money supply in the two cases, the effects on aggregate demand, employment and the average price level are quite different. Whereas, in the fixed rate case – as explained above – the real appreciation is achieved by a rise in the price of non-traded goods, with the price of traded goods held constant, the real appreciation in the flexible rate case is achieved by an appreciation of the nominal exchange rate (which reduces the domestic currency prices of traded goods), combined with a rise in the price of non-traded goods. In the flexible exchange rate case, the expansionary effects of a capital inflow on the sectors producing non-traded goods are therefore approximately neutralised by the contractionary effects of the induced exchange rate appreciation on the sectors producing traded goods.[2] Nominal GDP and the average domestic price level therefore rise by less in the flexible exchange rate case than in the fixed exchange rate case, and if nominal wages and non-traded prices are not perfectly flexible, a flexible exchange rate system has the substantial advantage, relative to a fixed exchange rate system, of reducing the fluctuations in aggregate employment and output arising from any given fluctuations in net capital flows.

Capital Flows and Stabilisation Policy[3]

In a flexible exchange rate system, capital mobility helps to insulate an economy against fluctuations in consumption and investment demand for non-traded goods: higher demand for these goods raises the domestic interest rate and attracts an inflow of foreign capital. The resulting appreciation of the exchange rate has a stabilising effect on aggregate demand and employment because it reduces the demand for tradable goods. This stabiliser does not operate under a fixed exchange rate, because the monetary authorities respond to the capital inflow by raising the money supply and holding the exchange rate fixed. Therefore, in a fixed exchange rate system, the more open is the capital account, the weaker is the automatic stabilisation of shocks to the demand for goods.

Next, consider how capital mobility affects the fluctuations in aggregate demand that result from monetary shocks under alternative exchange rate systems. The results are the opposite to those just derived for shocks to spending on non-traded goods: capital mobility helps to insulate the economy against monetary shocks under a fixed exchange rate, but magnifies their effects on aggregate demand under a flexible exchange rate system. The reason for this difference is that whereas interest rates rise in response to a macroeconomic stimulus, such as fiscal expansion, which operates through the goods market, they fall in response to a stimulus that operates through the money market, such as an increase in the supply of money.

The fact that in an economy with a fixed exchange rate capital mobility reduces the effects of monetary shocks, but magnifies those of fluctuations in the demand for goods, means that when the exchange rate is fixed capital mobility weakens monetary policy and strengthens fiscal policy. In the case of a small country with a fixed exchange rate and perfect capital mobility, an open market purchase of securities by the central bank has no effect on the money supply, nor on aggregate demand. It is entirely offset, without any change in prices or interest rates, by a capital outflow financed by using the money injected by the open market operation to buy foreign exchange from the central bank.

Conversely, the fact that in an economy with a flexible exchange rate capital mobility dampens the effects of shocks to the goods market, but magnifies those of monetary shocks, means that when the exchange rate is flexible, capital mobility strengthens monetary policy and weakens fiscal policy.

7.2 STERILISATION OF CAPITAL FLOWS UNDER A FIXED EXCHANGE RATE SYSTEM

The discussion in section 7.1 of the effects of capital inflows on aggregate demand under a fixed exchange rate assumed that the monetary authorities hold domestic credit constant. In practice, most central banks try to 'sterilise' the monetary effects of capital flows by varying domestic credit. The directly expansionary effects of capital inflows on the money supply under a fixed exchange rate system occur because capital inflows increase official foreign exchange reserves. To sterilise these direct effects, the central bank may contract domestic credit by selling securities denominated in domestic currency. Similarly, outflows can be sterilised by open market purchases of such securities. In addition to open market sales of securities, sterilisation can also be achieved by changing the ratios of reserves to deposits that banks are required to hold, or by shifting public sector deposits between the commercial banks and the central bank. These regulatory methods of sterilising balance of payments flows are analysed in the final subsection below. Until then, it is assumed that sterilisation is done by open market operations in domestic currency-denominated securities.

Sterilisation by Open Market Operations in Government Securities

The model of section 2.2 shows that the effects on official foreign exchange reserves of changes in world interest rates are magnified if the authorities sterilise the monetary effects of these shocks rather than keeping domestic credit constant. To see why, first note that even when domestic credit is held constant, a rise in the world interest rate leads to a fall in official foreign exchange reserves because, as explained in section 2.2, with domestic credit unchanged, it raises the domestic interest rate and lowers the domestic share price. Therefore the LM schedule in Figure 2.2 must shift to the left. This means that the supply of base money must fall. With domestic credit held constant by assumption, the fall in base money must be achieved by an equal fall in official reserves. If the monetary authorities sterilise the contraction of the money supply by expanding domestic credit (that is, by buying domestic currency-denominated securities), the LM schedule is returned to its original position, and the BB schedule in Figure 2.2 must shift back towards the origin. The new equilibrium will therefore be at a lower domestic interest rate and higher domestic share price than if domestic credit had been held constant. At the new world interest rate, both these effects of domestic credit expansion produce additional capital outflow: they reduce non-residents' demand for both domestic shares and domestic currency-denominated securities and they increase the private sector's demand for foreign currency securities. The overall capital outflow is therefore larger if the authorities sterilise its monetary effects than if they hold domestic credit constant. This is also true if the capital outflow is produced by a fall in the expected profitability of domestic investments.

Although effects that operate through the current account cannot be analysed using the model of section 2.2, it is clear that sterilising the monetary effects of current account imbalances also magnifies their effects on reserves. A fall in world prices relative to domestic prices, or an exogenous switch in demand from domestic to foreign goods, would generate a current account deficit and falling official foreign exchange reserves, at least in the short run. If domestic credit is held constant, the money supply will fall, thereby reducing the prices of domestic non-traded goods and switching domestic production towards tradables, while domestic consumption is switched towards non-tradables. Both these switches will help restore current account balance. But if domestic credit is expanded to prevent the money supply falling, these self-correcting mechanisms will also be prevented from operating.

Sterilisation of the monetary effects of balance of payments imbalances therefore raises the probability that the authorities will run out of foreign exchange reserves as a result of random shocks in the demand for base money. In addition, by revealing that they are unwilling to follow the traditional rules for ensuring their ability to defend a fixed exchange rate, monetary authorities who engage in sterilisation also signal their lack of commitment to the policy of defending the supposedly fixed rate.

Since capital flows are more interest-elastic in the long run than the short run, reserves which are initially large enough to permit the sterilisation of a rise in world interest rates may turn out to be too small to allow this policy to be maintained indefinitely. If investors come to believe that the central bank's long-run policy contains an inconsistency of this type, there will be a speculative attack on the currency.

The Dangers and Inefficiencies of Sterilisation

The analysis of capital inflows in section 7.1 showed that inflows that result from a fall in the world interest rate, or a rise in the expected profitability of the domestic economy, lead to real appreciation under either a floating exchange rate system or a fixed rate system in which domestic credit is held constant. In contrast, under a fixed exchange rate system in which domestic credit is varied to sterilise the monetary effects of capital inflows, the private sector can be completely insulated from all changes due to a capital inflow that takes the form of purchases of domestic currency-denominated securities by non-residents: the monetary authorities issue the domestic currency-denominated securities that non-residents want to buy, and they hold the foreign exchange that non-residents use to buy them. Prices and interest rates remain unchanged and the private sector is completely insulated from any of the potential effects of the inflow.

If the inflow takes the form of investment in shares or non-traded fixed assets, complete insulation would only be possible if the authorities reduce their holdings of shares (if they have any), or their purchases of non-traded goods, so as to accommodate the increased demand by non-residents. However, if non-traded fixed assets and shares are close substitutes in portfolios for domestic currency-denominated securities, sterilisation of capital flows by open market operations in such securities will largely insulate the private sector from the potential effects on prices and interest rates of all kinds of capital flows.

Because sterilisation can insulate the private sector from the effects of capital inflows, Kenen (1993, p. 245) and Reisen (1994, p. 220) argue that it is a first-best response to a capital inflow that is not accompanied by an increase in the demand for domestic money. Reisen explains this argument as follows:

> capital inflows cause the domestic currency to appreciate in real terms, unless there is sterilized intervention on the foreign exchange market. The nominal exchange rate appreciates when it is flexible; the domestic price level rises when the nominal rate is pegged. With either fully flexible or pegged exchange rates, the real appreciation of the exchange rate resides in the failure of the monetary authorities to supply the mix of assets which domestic and foreign investors are now demanding. The authorities do nothing in the floating rate case, they issue money in exchange for assets in the fixed rate case. They should issue bonds instead, by engaging in sterilized intervention (*ibid.*, p. 217).

There are two objections to this recommendation that the authorities should try to sterilise the monetary effects of capital flows. First, by focusing on stabilisation

policy – implicitly understood as trying to minimise the effects on the private
sector of whatever has caused the inflow or outflow of capital – it neglects the
fact that it is far from optimal to minimise the private sector's adjustment to the
opportunities which give rise to capital flows. Rather, in the absence of market
imperfections, it is optimal to allow the private sector to adjust fully to any
change in the external environment; and a blanket attempt to sterilise market
forces is not the best way to handle imperfections if they exist. For example, a
fall in world real interest rates means that foreign capital has become cheaper,
and the optimal response to such a fall is to import more foreign capital. To
absorb the additional capital, imports must rise relative to exports and the sectors producing traded goods must therefore contract relative to those producing
non-traded goods. To provide incentives for factors to move from traded to
non-traded goods sectors and to encourage firms and households to switch demand towards foreign goods, the real exchange rate must appreciate. In the
absence of sterilisation, capital inflows resulting from a fall in world interest
rates do indeed cause an appreciation of the real exchange rate under either a
floating or a fixed exchange rate regime. This real appreciation is the short-run
manifestation of the optimal long-run response to the opportunities provided
by lower real world interest rates and it is therefore a *disadvantage* of sterilisation that it inhibits this efficient adjustment. The same criticism can be made of
capital controls, which even more directly inhibit efficient adjustment to changes
in world interest rates.[4]

Second, by shielding the private sector from the need, or opportunity, to
adjust, the monetary authorities expose themselves to increased risk because
sterilisation involves them in breaking the rules that are needed to maintain the
stability and credibility of a fixed exchange rate system. If the ultimate outcome
of sterilisation is a speculative attack on the currency which the authorities are
unable to resist, the private sector eventually suffers shocks which are much
more destabilising than those that result from either of the policies analysed
in section 7.1.

Sterilisation of inflows also has the potential to undermine the credibility of
the authorities' commitment to maintain a fixed exchange rate system: by raising
the proportion of public debt that is denominated in the domestic currency, it
allows the authorities to reduce domestic taxation (or increase spending) if they
do subsequently devalue, and, since it raises both the amount of public debt
denominated in domestic currency and the premium of the nominal interest rate
on this debt over the world interest rate, it obliges them to raise domestic taxation
(or cut spending) if they do not subsequently devalue.[5]

In developing countries, uncertainties about future inflation make long-term
bonds very risky and therefore cause the markets in long-term government
securities to be thin, or non-existent. In these circumstances, sterilisation by
open market operations involves the selling (or buying) by the authorities either

of Treasury bills, or of certificates of deposit, including those issued by the central bank itself. If the securities used by the authorities for sterilising capital flows are short-term ones, then the magnified and induced capital flows will also be flows of short-term securities. Sterilisation therefore raises the volatility of short-term portfolio capital flows.

Why Sterilisation is not a Good Way to Reduce Inflation under a Fixed Exchange Rate

Under a fixed exchange rate, capital inflows directly add to the monetary base and are therefore sometimes described as 'inflationary'. This is part of the reason why the monetary authorities usually try to sterilise them. It is argued in this subsection that describing capital flows in this way is totally misleading if they occur in response to an increase in the domestic demand for money, and substantially misleading even if they occur for reasons which are exogenous to the domestic economy, such as a fall in world interest rates or a decision by foreign portfolio managers to raise the share of the assets of developing countries in their portfolios.

Consider first the case in which the capital inflow occurs in response to an increase in the domestic demand for money. Obviously, this would not be inflationary: no prices need change, since the increase in the money supply is matched by the increase in demand which generated it. Such an endogenous increase in the money supply in response to an exogenous increase in demand is clearly quite different to an exogenous increase in the money supply in a closed economy (or in an open economy with a flexible exchange rate): this latter case is inflationary precisely because, in the absence of an exogenous increase in money demand, induced price increases are needed to raise the demand for money to match the increased supply.

Next, consider the case in which a capital inflow to an economy with a fixed exchange rate occurs for reasons that are exogenous to the domestic economy and in which the domestic demand for money is initially unchanged. Regardless of whether the inflow finances purchases by foreigners of goods or bonds, the resulting stimulus to aggregate demand would raise the prices of domestic physical and financial assets, and thereby stimulate domestic investment and raise the prices of non-traded goods and factors. With the prices of traded goods determined by world prices and the fixed exchange rate, the average domestic price level would indeed increase, but this rise in average prices would be a once-over effect: the relative prices of non-traded goods and factors would rise only by enough to remove the original excess demand. This once-over increase in the average price level is not 'inflation' in the generally accepted sense of the term, since it can only occur if relative prices change, and since it is not part of a process that can continue indefinitely.

Capital inflows can accurately be described as inflationary if they result from a secular increase in the rate of inflation in the country to whose exchange rate the domestic currency is pegged. However, if this inflation is judged to be too rapid, the appropriate policy response is to float the exchange rate, or shift the peg to a more stable currency. If instead the authorities try to hold down domestic inflation by sterilising the resulting capital inflows, they create a conflict between long-run policy objectives that cannot be sustained indefinitely. Either the domestic rate of inflation must rise, or the supposedly fixed exchange rate must be abandoned.

Since the 1970s, most developing countries with fixed exchange rates have pegged their currencies to the dollar, or to baskets of currencies in which the main weights are assigned to the dollar, the yen and the mark. During this period, very few developing countries have managed to avoid devaluing relative to these three currencies by large amounts. Complaints about importing inflation by pegging to these currencies can therefore more accurately be described as complaints about the large short-run fluctuations in aggregate demand that result from the volatility of capital flows under a fixed exchange rate system. Again, the appropriate policy response is to float the exchange rate, not to sterilise.

Sterilisation by Monetary Regulation

The cost of sterilising capital inflows by open market operations is borne by the central bank and the government in the form of higher interest rates on public debt. In developing countries, sterilisation of inflows by open market operations often involves selling short-term central bank bills. In such countries, the policy directly eats into central bank profitability. Rather than bear the costs themselves, the authorities usually try to shift them onto the commercial banks by raising the required ratios of bank reserves to deposits. As a result, the large reductions in required RRs that had accompanied the processes of financial deregulation in Indonesia, Thailand and Malaysia were partially reversed in the mid-1990s in order to reduce the costs to central banks of sterilising capital inflows. Although the attraction of this option to governments and central banks is obvious, this form of monetary contraction is subject not only to the same objections as those already raised against sterilisation of capital flows by open market operations, but also to the objection that it increases the implicit tax on banking to which required reserve ratios are equivalent.[6]

Yet another way in which the monetary authorities can shift the cost of sterilising capital inflows onto others is to require public sector enterprises to switch their deposits from commercial banks to the central bank. This policy has the potential to cause a severe monetary contraction because liquidity is drained from the commercial banks, which must raise interest rates to attract new deposits, or else reduce lending.

7.3 THE EXTENT OF STERILISATION UNDER CURRENCY BOARDS AND CENTRAL BANKS

Table 7.1 documents the great extent to which countries have sterilised the monetary effects of balance of payments flows. The reported sterilisation coefficients are defined as the amount by which the authorities contract NDC within the current quarter in response to each unit increase in NFA. Denote this amount by φ. Since the supply of base money is equal to NDC plus NFA, a unit increase in NFA will be associated with an increase of $(1 - \varphi)$ in base money, provided that the authorities do not change base money for other reasons. A sterilisation coefficient of unity indicates complete sterilisation in the sense that any change in the monetary base due to a change in the domestic demand for money, or to a capital inflow induced by a fall in world interest rates, is fully sterilised by an equal and opposite change in NDC. At the other end of the spectrum, a sterilisation coefficient of zero will be observed if the monetary authorities act like a textbook currency board and never vary domestic credit.[7]

To estimate the reported sterilisation coefficients, quarterly changes in the domestic currency values of NDC and NFA were adjusted by subtracting an estimate of the appreciation of NFA due to exchange rate changes from the actual change in NFA and adding it to the actual change in NDC. The adjusted changes in both variables were then expressed as ratios of the value of the monetary base at the start of the quarter. Let the resulting adjusted variables be denoted $\Delta NDC^*/M_{-1}$ and $\Delta NFA^*/M_{-1}$. The former variable was regressed on a constant and the latter variable, and the reported sterilisation coefficients were obtained as minus the coefficient on the latter variable.

The reported coefficients obtained in this way probably exaggerate the true extent of sterilisation. This is because if capital mobility is very high and if the authorities sometimes contract or expand NDC for reasons other than to sterilise balance of payments flows, the reported sterilisation coefficients would be close to unity, although the true causality in this case would run from changes in NDC to changes in NFA, rather than from NFA to NDC.[8] Since there is no reason to expect this bias to be greater for systems operated by central banks than for those operated by currency boards, the reported coefficients can be used to show, at least qualitatively, differences in the extent to which conventional central banks and currency boards engage in sterilisation. In most cases, the upward bias is probably not very serious, since the results are dominated by observations when there were large capital flows associated with economic booms or speculative crises, such as the 'tequila crisis'; in these cases, causality clearly ran from capital flows to changes in domestic credit, not the other way round.

Table 7.1   *Extent of sterilisation in selected countries, 1990–99*

Country/period	Sterilisation coefficient[a]	Country/period	Sterilisation coefficient[a]
Argentina, 1991(2)–95(1)	0.73*	Latvia, 1993(4)–97(2)	0.56*
Argentina, 1995(2)–98(4)	0.20	Malaysia, 1990(1)–97(2)	0.96*
Brazil, 1994(3)–97(2)	0.67*	Mexico, 1990(1)–97(2)	1.00*
Chile, 1990(1)–97(2)	0.27	Mexico, 1990(1)–94(3)	0.76*
Colombia, 1990(1)–97(2)	0.77*	Pakistan, 1990(1)–97(2)	0.90*
Estonia, 1993(1)–98(4)	0.09	Papua N.G., 1990(1)–97(2)	0.71*
Hong Kong,[b] 1994(2)–99(1)	0.93*	Philippines, 1990(1)–97(2)	1.09*
Hong Kong,[c] 1994(2)–99(1)	0.74*	Russia, 1995(3)–1997(2)	0.61*
India, 1990(1)–97(2)	0.68*	Singapore, 1990(1)–97(2)	0.94*
Indonesia, 1990(1)–97(2)	0.83*	Sri Lanka, 1990(1)–97(2)	0.63*
Korea, 1990(1)–97(2)	0.82*	Thailand, 1990(1)–97(2)	1.12*

Notes:
a.   Sterilisation coefficients are defined in the main text. A coefficient of unity implies complete sterilisation of the monetary effects of foreign exchange flows; a coefficient of zero implies no sterilisation. The data for Hong Kong were supplied by the HKMA. All other data were obtained from IMF, *International Financial Statistics* CD-ROM.
     In most cases the first observation is for changes during the first quarter of 1990 – denoted 1990(1) – and the last observation is for changes during 1997(2). However, missing data necessitated using later starting dates for Estonia, Latvia and Russia. Periods of very rapid exchange rate change make the measurement of the revaluation of foreign assets and liabilities unreliable and were therefore excluded. For this reason, the first observation used for Brazil is for the third quarter of September 1994, and the last observations used for all the non-currency board countries is for the second quarter of 1997, just before the large devaluations that occurred during the emerging markets crisis. For Argentina, the first observation used is for the second quarter of 1991, immediately following the introduction of the currency board, and for each of the three currency board countries included in Table 7.1, the last observation used was the last observation available.
b.   Hong Kong included Exchange Fund Bills (EFBs) in base money from September 1998, but excluded them from base money up to and including August 1998. See section 8.3 for a discussion of EFBs and the definition of base money in Hong Kong. The series used in calculating this regression excluded EFBs throughout. NFA is defined as the foreign currency assets of the Exchange Fund, converted to HK$ at HK$7.80 = US$1. In October 1998, US$19.3 billion was transferred from the Land Fund to the Exchange Fund. In deriving the NFA series used here, this amount was deducted from the Exchange Fund's foreign assets in October 1998 and all subsequent months.
c.   The series used in calculating this regression included EFBs in M0 throughout. In other respects, the comments in note b apply here too.
*   Coefficients that are significantly different from zero at the 5 per cent significance level are indicated with asterisks.

Table 7.1 shows that Estonia is the only country among those studied to have largely avoided sterilising balance of payments flows. On average, the Bank of Chile has only sterilised just over one quarter of the monetary effects of balance of payments surpluses. Except for Chile, the countries with traditional central banks – namely all those in Table 7.1, except Argentina, Hong Kong and Estonia – have engaged in sterilisation to a very large extent.

Since introducing its currency board in 1991, Argentina has usually avoided large-scale sterilisation of balance of payments surpluses; however, there have been two major exceptions to this generalisation. The first occurred in the third quarter of 1992 when an increase in NFA equal to 67 per cent of base money was almost totally sterilised by a 65 per cent contraction in NDC. The second occurred during the speculative attack that followed the Mexican crisis when a reduction in NFA in the first quarter of 1995, equal to 38 per cent of the monetary base at the start of the quarter, was sterilised by an expansion of domestic credit equal to 19 per cent of the monetary base, so that the decline in base money was limited to 19 per cent. Since these two observations greatly affect the results for Argentina, Table 7.1 reports separate estimates for the period ending with changes during the first quarter of 1995 and for the period beginning with changes during the second quarter of 1995. In the first period, Argentina engaged in sterilisation to the same extent as several countries with traditional banking arrangements, but since the second quarter of 1995, it has operated much more like a textbook currency board.

Estimates for two different periods are also reported for Mexico. The first is for the full period; the second is for the period ending with changes during the third quarter of 1994, and therefore excluding the massive sterilisation of outflows in late 1994 and early 1995. In the period before the start of the 'tequila crisis', Mexico's policy involved much less sterilisation than that of most of the other countries with conventional central banks.

The table implies that there has been a very high degree of sterilisation in Hong Kong, but this effect is probably spurious. There are two reasons why the upward bias in all the estimated sterilisation coefficients is likely to be larger for Hong Kong than for most other countries. First, the HKMA holds large foreign currency deposits on behalf of the government; if the government finances an outlay in HK dollars by running down its deposits at the HKMA, and if the HKMA merely transfers the government's deposit to that of the banks at which the cheques written by the government are deposited, without altering its holdings of foreign exchange, there has been an increase in base money, matched by an increase in NDC rather than NFA. If the government kept its own offshore foreign currency deposits and if it financed its onshore expenditure by running them down and converting the foreign exchange to HK dollars at the HKMA, the effects on the domestic private sector would be the same as in the previous case, but the rise in base money would now be matched by a rise in measured NFA rather than in measured NDC. Second, the HKMA has been trying to deepen the market in HK dollar-denominated securities by issuing its own bills; to prevent this contraction of domestic credit causing a credit squeeze, it used the proceeds to buy foreign exchange.

7.4   OVERVIEW

If the authorities decide to abolish capital controls, there is a strong case for adopting a flexible exchange rate to reduce the effects on aggregate demand of volatile capital flows. And if capital mobility is high and the exchange rate is flexible, the appropriate tool for stabilisation policy is monetary policy, rather than fiscal policy.

Most developing countries have ignored this conventional advice. First, except in the aftermath of exchange rate crises, most have adopted fixed, or 'managed', exchange rate regimes. Second, even in economies with fixed exchange rates and fairly open capital accounts, stabilisation policy has regularly involved the use of monetary contraction to prevent 'overheating' – meaning a situation in which aggregate demand exceeds the economy's productive capacity.

In the instances in the 1990s when the authorities were concerned with 'overheating' in the rapidly growing Asian economies, booming consumption and investment were accompanied by large capital inflows. Both the spending booms and the capital inflows were due partly to optimistic expectations about future growth, and partly to falling world interest rates in the early 1990s. In these circumstances, the widespread use of contractionary monetary policies in fixed exchange rate systems was totally inappropriate for two reasons: first, given high capital mobility and fixed exchange rates, monetary policy has little effect on aggregate demand. Second, section 7.2 showed that sterilisation magnifies the capital flows which would otherwise occur in response to given underlying changes in world interest rates and domestic investment opportunities, and therefore magnifies the fluctuations in the authorities' holdings of foreign exchange reserves that such underlying changes produce.

Table 7.1 shows that sterilisation has been pervasive in countries with conventional central banks and even Argentina, and perhaps Hong Kong, have deviated a great deal from the no-sterilisation rule of a textbook currency board on some occasions.

Sterilisation of capital outflows was an important contributing factor in the Mexican crisis of 1994–95 and in the crises in Thailand and Korea in 1997.[9] In each case, the monetary authorities tried to sterilise capital outflows by expanding domestic credit in the hope of holding down domestic interest rates and protecting weak financial institutions. In each case, these actions magnified the outflows that would otherwise have occurred and the authorities ran out of foreign exchange reserves and were forced to devalue. Between end-June 1996 and end-June 1997, the reported on-balance sheet NFA of the Bank of Thailand (BOT) fell by an amount equal to 44 per cent of the initial level of the money base (M0). However, the BOT pursued such a vigorous sterilisation policy that the increase over this period in NDC (as measured by reported on-balance sheet items) was 74 per cent of the initial level of M0.[10] The monetary base therefore rose by 30 per cent (74 per cent – 44 per cent). The true fall in NFA and the true rise in NDC were far larger than the ones reported, because the BOT's balance sheet did not show the foreign exchange liabilities and baht assets created by its foreign exchange swap transactions. These transactions arose because the BOT accommodated speculation by buying baht in the spot market and then swapping baht for dollars, while contracting to repurchase baht later at a specified exchange rate.[11] This device allowed the BOT to conceal the true extent to which it had used up its foreign exchange reserves by expanding domestic credit. Unfortunately, it also resulted in the BOT building up future foreign exchange liabilities for itself and allowing speculators to take positions against the baht without diminishing their baht liquidity.

NOTES

1. The main difference between official foreign exchange reserves and NFA is that the central bank's foreign currency liabilities must be subtracted from the former to arrive at the latter.
2. To the extent that sectors producing non-traded goods are generally more labour-intensive than those that produce traded goods, the net effect of the capital inflow and induced exchange rate appreciation is to expand aggregate employment, or raise real wages, or both.
3. This section follows Mundell (1968, Chapter 18), which is the classic reference on the effects of monetary and fiscal policy under fixed and flexible exchange rates when capital is highly mobile.
4. Sieper and Fane (1982, pp. 255–6).
5. Calvo (1991) sets out a model of an economy in which the demand for money increases because of the implementation of a monetary stabilisation programme. If domestic credit is left unchanged, the increased demand for money is met by a capital inflow. But if this capital inflow is sterilised by sales of domestic currency-denominated debt by the monetary authorities, the government has an incentive to inflate and devalue in the future. Because investors anticipate this, the nominal interest rate rises and the demand for money therefore rises by less than in the no-sterilisation case.
6. It was noted in Chapter 6 that in the absence of formal deposit insurance, the setting of a minimum RR can be rationalised as a crude approximation to the insurance premia which banks should be charged for deposit guarantees. However, if the RR is set at the appropriate level to impose this charge, it cannot simultaneously be varied to shift the costs of sterilisation from the central bank to the commercial banks.
7. See the discussion of currency boards in section 8.1.
8. Many studies, of which Kouri and Porter (1974) is a well-known example, attribute the finding of a strong inverse correlation between changes in NDC and NFA to high capital mobility.
9. For a discussion of Mexico's sterilisation of capital outflows in 1994, see Sachs *et al.* (1996a). Korea's sterilisation of capital outflows in 1997 is discussed in section 3.3.

10. The increase in on-balance sheet net domestic credit of Bht. 294 billion can be roughly accounted for by the BOT's lending to the finance companies: its claims on non-bank financial institutions, net of their deposits at the BOT, rose by Bht. 302 billion in this period, while the other elements of on-balance sheet net domestic credit fell by only Bht. 8 billion.

11. If the BOT's swap transactions are brought onto its balance sheet, the fall in NFA in the 12 months to end-June 1997 becomes Bht. 759 billion and the rise in NDC becomes Bht. 877 billion. As percentages of initial base money, the revised estimate of the growth in NDC in the 12 months to the end of June 1997 is 222 per cent and the fall in NFA is 192 per cent. These estimates are derived by adjusting the changes reported by the BOT (see Fane and McLeod, 1999, Table 1) to allow for the BOT's estimated swap contracts at mid-1997 of about $23 billion (*Wall Street Journal*, 22 August 1997) or Bht. 583 billion at the end of June 1997 exchange rate. The level of swaps at mid-1996 is assumed to be negligible.

8. The credibility of monetary and exchange rate policies

This chapter surveys the ways in which monetary and exchange rate policies can be made credible. It begins with a discussion of currency boards, because they are the institution with the best record for keeping fixed exchange rates fixed. Currency boards are sometimes criticised on the ground that they cannot provide safety nets for commercial banks. This issue is set out in section 8.2 and the successes and difficulties of Hong Kong's currency board system in dealing with the speculation arising from the Asian financial crisis is analysed in section 8.3. Section 8.4 deals with the credibility of commitments to keep to targets for monetary growth, or inflation, under flexible exchange rate regimes. The first part of section 8.5 uses Indonesia's experience in 1997–98 to illustrate what can happen in a flexible exchange rate system when credible monetary targets are not followed. The second part of section 8.5 discusses the proposal, made in February 1998, to try to restore monetary policy credibility in Indonesia by setting up a currency board. The final section provides an overview.

8.1 CURRENCY BOARDS

The institutional arrangement for operating a fixed exchange rate system which has the best track record for resisting speculative attacks is the currency board. Under a 'textbook' currency board system, the board is established by legislation that gives it only one responsibility: to buy or sell whatever amounts of the domestic base money may be offered or demanded at some specified rate against some chosen foreign currency.[1] This means that a textbook currency board cannot operate an independent monetary policy by expanding or contracting domestic credit. Provided that the board is set up with foreign currency reserves in excess of the supply of domestic base money, that its running costs are small, that it earns some interest on its foreign currency reserves, that it does not pay interest on its domestic currency liabilities and that it is not responsible for bailing out failed banks, the board will always have enough reserves to be able to buy back whatever domestic currency is presented to it. Therefore, if a currency board nevertheless devalued, it would be because it (or the government) had chosen to devalue, not because it had literally been forced to do so. Real-world currency boards deviate from the textbook model in varying degrees. Schuler's survey of currency board history provides only one instance of a currency board that devalued: the East Caribbean Currency Authority devalued by about 30 per cent in 1976 when it switched from sterling to the US dollar as its reserve asset.[2]

The purpose of a currency board is to allow a country that would not otherwise have a strong reputation for monetary stability, 'the home country', to tie its currency to one of the world's strongest currencies, for example, the US dollar, and at the same time make sure that the home government collects most of the seigniorage revenue from the issuing of the base money used in the home country.[3] If the home country simply used a foreign currency – as in Panama, where US dollar notes and balboa coins are legal tender and there are no separate Panamanian bank notes – most of the seigniorage from issuing the base money used by its residents would accrue to the foreign government, unless an arrangement could be reached by which the foreign government agreed to transfer this revenue back to the home country. As a result of the rapid recent growth of interest in complete 'dollarisation' in several countries, most notably Argentina and Ecuador, a bill to formalise the arrangements under which the USA would transfer most of the seigniorage revenue to a country that adopted the dollar as its sole legal tender was introduced into the US Senate in 1999.

In the nineteenth and early twentieth centuries, currency boards were widely used by Britain to provide its colonies with a source of revenue and to overcome the problems created by the occasional failures of private note-issuing banks.[4] On achieving political independence, the new nations severed their monetary links to their former rulers. This was done partly because currency boards subordinate the national currency to a foreign one, whereas independent governments want the prestige of having a central bank and a fully independent currency and monetary policy. In addition, most newly independent countries have had ambitious development plans and limited tax raising capacities. The abolition of currency boards allowed them to collect the additional revenue from seigniorage that can be obtained by setting inflation at rates well above those of the world's major currencies. Except in the very smallest countries, the seigniorage revenue that can be had from moderate inflation far exceeds the fixed costs of setting up a central bank.

Despite their partial eclipse in the period after World War II, the very successful record of currency boards in the few very small countries that retained them has led several developing countries and countries making the transition from communism to market economies to introduce currency boards as a way of restoring the credibility of promises to halt rapid inflation. The most important examples of countries that have either adopted currency boards, or similar arrangements under other names, are Argentina, Bulgaria, Hong Kong, Estonia and Lithuania.[5] Currency boards have been seriously considered by Russia, Brazil and Indonesia.

The two most important examples of currency boards are Argentina and Hong Kong. The Hong Kong system is analysed in detail in section 8.3 below. Argentina's adoption of currency board rules for its central bank is notable for the subsequent improvement in its inflation record. In the six years after the currency board system was introduced in 1991, annual inflation averaged only 7 per cent, and in the period 1994–97 it averaged only 1 per cent. In stark contrast, Argentina's inflation record had previously been among the worst in the world: in the period 1970–91 annual consumer price inflation averaged 240 per cent and the consumer price index increased by a factor of 140 billion.[6]

In the wake of the Mexican peso crisis, Argentina successfully resisted a very large speculative attack on its currency and banks. Argentine banks lost their access to international financial markets and their deposits fell by almost one fifth between the beginning of the crisis and the end of March 1995.[7] Argentina's success in avoiding a devaluation and major financial collapse was due partly to the strong reputation of its currency board system. This limited speculation and made it easier for the government to organise a $2 billion loan from domestic and foreign private lenders. However, not all of this success can be claimed as proof of the benefits of currency boards: the government was helped by a $5 billion loan package provided by the IMF, the World Bank and the Inter-American Development Bank, and the central bank broke the textbook rules for currency board operations both by reducing the required reserve ratios of the commercial banks and by expanding net domestic credit by 19 per cent of base money, so that the actual fall in base money in the first quarter of 1995 was 'only' 19 per cent, whereas, as noted in section 7.3, the fall in NFA was equal to 38 per cent of the initial level of base money.

Although Argentina's fixed exchange rate system withstood the speculative pressures of 1995, its real GDP contracted by 2.8 per cent between 1994 and 1995 and the unemployment rate rose to 16 per cent. GDP growth did recover in 1996 and 1997, but the growth between 1997 and 1998 was only 3.9 per cent and unemployment remained high. Similarly, although Hong Kong's linked exchange rate system survived the speculative pressures of 1997–98, its real GDP fell between these two years by 5.2 per cent and the unemployment rate, which had been only 2.1 per cent in June 1997, rose steadily to reach 6.4 per cent by August 1999.

8.2 FINANCIAL FRAGILITY UNDER CURRENCY BOARDS AND CENTRAL BANKS

Although there is no limit to the extent to which speculators may short-sell a currency by borrowing in it to finance the acquisition of foreign currency-denominated assets, such speculation does not directly involve the currency board, since it is essentially a bet about the future value of the exchange rate which is made between the speculators and the banks or other traders who lend to them in domestic currency-denominated assets. However, it does have adverse consequences for the financial system and for the conduct of the government's economic policy: if speculators expect the 'fixed' exchange rate to be abandoned, there is no ceiling on the level to which domestic currency interest rates might rise, and this might result in the government deciding to devalue rather than endure the consequences of very high interest rates for employment and the financial system.

A currency board that only issues base money in exchange for foreign exchange cannot act as a lender of last resort, and one that has reserves that only just exceed the supply of base money cannot bail out depositors in failed banks. One possibility would be to have a currency board and dispense with safety nets for commercial banks. This option would be less politically unpalatable than it may initially appear, if, as is often the case in countries with currency boards, many of the local banks are branches of international banks whose head offices can obtain last resort loans in their home countries. A second possibility would be for the currency board to have reserves in excess of base money, or to borrow abroad, to finance bail-outs for depositors in failed banks; if it broke the 'no sterilisation' rule, it could also engage in some last resort lending. This is approximately the option that Argentina and Hong Kong have chosen. A third possibility would be for the government to make the currency board responsible only for the convertibility of the currency, and to set up an adequately endowed 'bank supervisory board', which would be responsible for last resort lending and bailing out failed banks.

In practice, despite (or because of) the limitations on the ability of currency boards to act as lenders of last resort to domestic banks, banks in currency board systems actually have a much better record of surviving speculative crises than those in systems operated by central banks. Schuler (1992, Chapter 9) states that:

> Bank failures in currency board systems were rare. British imperial banks dominated in most currency board systems, and no imperial bank failed after the Oriental Bank Corporation in 1884. The imperial banks' size, easy access to the London money market, and international scope made them very strong. Because most had branches in more than one colony, they were able to spread risks effectively.

Schuler reports only two twentieth century instances of failures of non-local banks in currency board systems; the most important of these was the 1991 failure of the Bank of Credit and Commerce International, which had branches in many countries. Schuler notes that, in comparison to international banks, 'local banks in currency board systems have been far more prone to failure and to runs'. Nevertheless, the record even of local banks is far better in currency board systems than in central bank systems. Schuler notes that some local banks failed in Palestine in 1940 and in Nigeria in the 1950s. Several local banks were taken over by the Exchange Fund of Hong Kong during the banking panic of 1983–86 and most of the domestically incorporated banks in both Djibouti and Brunei failed during the 1980s; a large private bank failed in Estonia in 1992 and over half of the private banks failed to survive the banking crisis in Lithuania at the end of 1995.[8] In the Argentine financial crisis of 1995, only one small bank failed; however, the central bank provided $2 billion of last resort loans to weak banks, of which at least $300 million is unlikely to be recovered, and taxpayers face an additional bill of about $3 billion to finance bank restructuring.[9] These amounts are small in comparison to the costs to taxpayers of financial collapse in systems managed by central banks.

Part of the explanation for the greater fragility of financial institutions in countries with central banks relative to those with currency boards, as Hanke *et al.* (1993) note, is that the financial systems in the former countries have been relatively much less open to international competition than those in the latter. Opening a financial system to entry by international banks allows it to reduce its exposure to the economy-specific risks which can lead to the collapse of closed financial systems. In addition, as Hanke *et al.* (1993) also point out, the relatively good performance of commercial banks in currency board systems is consistent with the view that last resort lending – which is much less prevalent under currency boards than under central banks – often does more to weaken financial systems in the long run than to strengthen them. Section 8.5 uses the 1998 economic debacle in Indonesia to illustrate the dangers and difficulties of last resort lending.

8.3 HONG KONG'S LINKED EXCHANGE RATE SYSTEM[10]

The Hong Kong dollar has been pegged at HK$7.80 per US dollar since 1983. The basic legal framework under which Hong Kong's 'linked exchange rate system' operates is Ordinance 12 of 1995 (originally 54 of 1935). This ordinance does not mention a currency board and is sufficiently vague to be compatible with the floating exchange rate system which operated between 1974 and 1983 and with the currency board systems which pegged Hong Kong's currency first to the pound sterling until 1971, and then to the US dollar between 1971 and 1973, and again after 1983. The system is now managed by the HKMA, which was formed in 1993 by the merger of the Exchange Fund, which had managed the currency from 1935 onwards, with the Office of the Commissioner of Banking.[11]

The exchange rate is not fixed by legislation and the credibility of the HKMA's commitment to the fixed rate comes partly from its large foreign exchange reserves, partly from the fact that the fixed rate has been maintained for so long, and partly from the fact that, according to opinion polls, the general public strongly supports the system. If the peg were abandoned, it would badly damage the reputations of those responsible.

One difference between Hong Kong's monetary arrangements and those of a textbook currency board is that the HKMA does not undertake to convert notes presented to it by the public. This difference is very minor: it really involves no more than the contracting out by the HKMA to three commercial banks (the 'issue banks') of the inconvenience of dealing with the general public's supply and demand for foreign currency at the retail level. Three designated commercial banks are entitled to issue HK dollar notes up to the amount of their 'Certificates of Indebtedness' (CIs), which are HK dollar-denominated non-interest-bearing liabilities of the Exchange Fund (EF). The issue banks can acquire CIs from the EF, or redeem them, at a rate set by the government. It is this official exchange rate for CIs that has remained fixed at exactly HK$7.80 per dollar since 1983. Nominally, HK dollar notes are the liabilities of the private issue banks, whereas CIs are the liabilities of the HKMA; but given the one-to-one correspondence between the two, HK dollar notes are, in effect, HKMA notes 'printed with advertisements for the three note issuers' (Schuler, 1999). These advertising rights are the issue banks' quid pro quo for having to deal with the general public.

The major difference between Hong Kong's linked exchange rate system and a textbook currency board is that the HKMA has used monetary policy to accommodate most demands by commercial banks to settle day-to-day imbalances by discounting Exchange Fund Bills (EFBs). Measures of the degree to which the HKMA has sterilised the monetary effects of balance of payments flows were reported in Table 7.1. It was argued in section 7.3 that the very high degree of sterilisation implied by these estimates is probably at least partly spurious. It is hard to know how much is spurious, but it is certain that the HKMA has used sterilisation to a much greater extent than a textbook currency board. Before the reform of the system in 1998, the HKMA operated a 'liquidity adjustment facility' (LAF) that allowed banks that were short of liquidity at the end of each day to borrow overnight against their holdings of EFBs and other short-term money market instruments. There were rules to discourage repeated borrowing from the LAF, but the definition of a 'repeated borrower' was vague and the penalty rates charged for frequent borrowing were not high enough to make it profitable for banks to hold more than token clearing balances at the HKMA. At the end of September 1997, the aggregate clearing balance of the licensed banks was only HK$4 billion, whereas the monetary base, which was then defined as notes and coin plus the aggregate clearing balance, was HK$97 billion.

As long as the official exchange rate at which the HKMA will redeem CIs remains at HK$7.80, the possibility of arbitraging the wholesale and retail markets places some bound on the amount by which the price of US dollars in the inter-bank foreign exchange market could ever rise above HK$7.80. But because of the great inconvenience of dealing in notes in the retail market, the HKMA has kept the exchange rate in the foreign exchange market close to the official rate, but slightly on the strong side of it.[12] On an hour-to-hour basis, the exchange rate is set, not by the willingness of the HKMA to exchange base money for foreign exchange, but by its willingness, in normal circumstances, to buy and sell foreign exchange on credit by allowing the banks to make purchases of foreign exchange in excess of their small clearing balances.

The most severe test of Hong Kong's linked exchange rate system came shortly after the beginning of the Asian financial crisis.[13] On 20 October 1997, the New Taiwan dollar was allowed to float and immediately depreciated by 6 per cent. This triggered a speculative attack on the Hong Kong dollar on 21 October and 22 October.[14] Speculators sold HK dollars forward to the banks, using the technique of matching swap and spot transactions which was described in section 2.1. The commercial banks bought US dollars from the HKMA in the spot market in order to reduce their oversold positions in foreign exchange. These spot purchases of foreign exchange exceeded the banks' clearing balances at the HKMA; however, the banks were not obliged to settle the purchases of foreign exchange made on 21 October and 22 October until 23 October and 24 October, respectively.

At the close of trading on 22 October, despite the two days of extreme pressure in the foreign exchange market, the overnight Hong Kong Interbank Offered Rate on HK dollars (HIBOR) was 5.75 per cent, which was close to the rate that had applied before the speculative attack. The banks presumably expected to be allowed to settle their foreign exchange purchases by borrowing from the LAF against their EFBs. However, on the morning of the 23 October, the HKMA issued a circular to warn the banks against repeated borrowing from the LAF. The circular stated that repeated borrowers would face penal rates, different from the advertised LAF offer rates, that would be determined on a case-by-case basis. One rumour was that the HKMA would set the penal interest rate on LAF borrowing at 1000 per cent. The rumours and the circular created a panic in which the interest rate on overnight money rose in thin trading to a rate equivalent to 280 per cent per year at noon on 23 October. Since the overnight rate only remained at this high level for a few hours, the annualised rate exaggerates the severity of the crisis: an equivalent, but less dramatic description of the tightness of liquidity is that the price for the use of overnight money was HK$0.37 per day per HK$100. The banks began to sell foreign exchange back to the HKMA during the afternoon of 23 October and the HKMA agreed to settle these trades that day. This allowed the banks to restore their liquidity and the inter-bank overnight rate closed at 100–150 per cent on 23 October and fell back to 5 per cent the next day.

The fact that interest rates did not rise and fall in line with the speculative purchases of foreign exchange on 21 October and 22 October, but did rise very dramatically on 23 October, when the banks realised that the HKMA was planning to deny them easy access to the LAF, shows that the rise in interest rates was the result of a misunderstanding between the commercial banks and the HKMA about the extent to which the HKMA would sterilise a capital outflow rather than being directly associated with changes in the expectation of devaluation. Until 23 October, the banks appear to have expected to be able to borrow from the LAF to finance any sudden shortfall in liquidity, whereas the HKMA regarded requests to borrow from the LAF to finance a shortfall in liquidity caused by financing speculation against the HK dollar as an attempt to abuse the LAF.[15]

Under a pure currency board system, the board would not accommodate demands for liquidity by expanding domestic credit. Instead, the banks would have to meet sudden demands for liquidity by borrowing from abroad. To allow time for settlement, they would therefore need substantial clearing balances. For about two months after 23 October 1997, this appears to correspond to how the banks believed Hong Kong's system operated: the banks increased their clearing balances from HK$3.5 billion, at the end of August 1997, to HK$26 billion at the end of November. Then, in the first half of 1998, the aggregate clearing balances fell sharply before levelling off in the second half of 1998 at between HK$2 billion and HK$3 billion. The 1998 decline in clearing balances indicates the banks' growing confidence that the HKMA would never allow a liquidity shortage as severe as that of October 1997 to occur again. This intention was confirmed in September and November 1998 when the HKMA introduced 'technical measures' to reform the way in which it would conduct monetary and exchange rate policy.

Options for the Reform of the HKMA's Monetary Policy

In order to minimise the likelihood of a repetition of the events of October 1997, a group of Hong Kong academics made two proposals for the reform of the HKMA's monetary and exchange rate operations. The first was that the HKMA should stand ready to accept base money and EFBs as collateral for US dollar loans to resident banks at a small premium over the going world interest rate on US dollar deposits, as measured by LIBOR. The second was that banks that have borrowed US dollars from the HKMA should have the right to repay either in US dollars or in HK dollars at HK$7.80 per US dollar.[16]

The essence of the academics' proposals can be put more simply: to a close approximation, it amounts to the HKMA agreeing to sterilise balance of payments outflows, as long as the stock of outstanding EFBs remains positive, by setting a ceiling on the HK dollar interest rate at the world interest rate on US dollars plus the small premium. To see this equivalence, ignore bid–ask spreads and assume initially that although the HK dollar might be devalued, there is no possibility that it will be revalued. Given these plausible approximations, the option to repay loans from the HKMA in US dollars is worth nothing, and a bank that borrows in US dollars from the HKMA may as well contract to repay in HK dollars. At the time the loan is taken out, it makes no difference to the bank that borrows from the HKMA whether it receives dollars or HK dollars: either currency can be exchanged for the other at the fixed spot rate on the day the loan is taken out. The proposals therefore amount to allowing banks to sell their HK dollar-denominated EFBs to the HKMA for HK dollars at a discount given by the world interest rate on US dollars plus the proposed small premium. Therefore, as long as bank holdings of EFBs remain positive, the HK dollar interest rate could never go above the US dollar interest rate plus the small premium. To the extent that the probability that the HK dollar will be revalued is not literally zero, the proposals amount to setting the HK dollar interest rate ceiling slightly below the US dollar interest rate plus the small premium.[17]

The HKMA's pre-October 1997 monetary policy – that is, the discounting facilities offered by the LAF – was well towards the full sterilisation end of the spectrum of monetary strategies under a fixed exchange rate that was described in section 7.1. However, its refusal on 23 October 1997 to sterilise capital outflows was an unannounced move to a position close to the pure currency board end of that spectrum. The academics' proposals would have returned policy to a position close to the pre-October 1997 LAF. In one sense, these proposals were even closer to full sterilisation than the LAF: whereas the LAF allowed the HKMA to raise interest rates rather than fully sterilise outflows, the academics' proposals would have guaranteed that HK dollar interest rates could not rise above LIBOR plus a small premium as long as some EFBs remained outstanding. However, the academics' proposals did limit the amount of domestic credit that could be created to sterilise a balance of payments outflow to the amount of EFBs outstanding, whereas before October 1997 banks were allowed to discount not just EFBs, but also other short-term HK dollar instruments.

The 'technical measures' adopted in September and November 1998 set out rules describing how the HKMA would allocate liquidity to commercial banks. The LAF was renamed the 'discount window'; the definition of a 'repeated borrower' was formalised; the kinds of securities eligible for discounting were restricted to EFBs; and a formula was announced that makes the discount rate equal to the higher of the US Federal Funds rate plus 1.50 percentage points and a five-day moving average of overnight and one month interbank rates (HIBOR).[18] Relative to the pre-October 1997 policies, the 'technical measures' are a move towards currency board purity: the weighted average formula allows the discount rate to rise in response to a capital outflow and EFBs are now the only securities that are eligible for discounting. However, relative to the refusal to sterilise the speculative outflow of October 1997, the new measures are a sharp move away from currency board purity: the weighted average formula for the discount rate commits the HKMA to sterilising outflows as long as some EFBs remain outstanding and if interest rates would otherwise rise above the weighted average formula.

As well as clarifying the rules on discounting, the 1998 reforms also redefined the monetary base to include the banks' holdings of EFBs. Even on the new expanded definition, base money is less than 30 per cent of foreign exchange reserves.[19] Although the reforms move the system away from the unexpected currency board purity of October 1997, the redefinition of base money will make the system look like a very pure currency board policy of non-sterilisation. To see why, consider a speculative attack on the HK dollar in which the banks buy HK$10 billion of foreign exchange from the HKMA and suppose that, before making these purchases, they held clearing balances of HK$3 billion and EFBs of HK$100 billion. Suppose also that the HKMA buys HK$9 billion of EFBs from the banks, thus adding HK$9 billion to their clearing balances, so that the net effect of the banks' foreign exchange purchases and EFB sales is to reduce their clearing balances by HK$1 billion. Under the old definitions, the HKMA's purchase of EFBs would have counted as an HK$9 billion expansion of domestic credit. The HKMA's foreign exchange reserve loss of HK$10 billion would therefore have appeared to be matched by a fall in base money of HK$1 billion and by sterilisation of HK$9 billion. Under the new definitions, purchases of EFBs by the HKMA with clearing balances are defined to be a mere rearrangement of the components of an unchanged volume of base money. The reserve loss of HK$10 billion will therefore be matched by an HK$10 billion fall in measured base money and by no change in domestic credit, which is exactly the outcome under a pure textbook currency board system.

Another proposal for reform, made by the Nobel laureate Merton Miller, was that the HKMA should issue formal guarantees that HK dollar notes can be redeemed for US dollars at HK$7.80. This proposal was rejected by the government. It resembles the other academic proposals discussed above in that the right to redeem HK dollars for US dollars at HK$7.80 can be thought of as a put option, but in this case the put option applies only to HK dollar notes and cannot be separated from them. The prohibitive costs of paying interest on small denomination notes results in less than the optimal quantity of notes being held. The merit of the proposal to guarantee that HK dollar notes can be redeemed in US dollars is that it partially overcomes this inefficiency by increasing the incentive to hold HK notes. By reducing the capital gain that would accrue to the HKMA from devaluing, it also reduces the incentive to devalue; however, this latter effect is relatively trivial, since the capital gain that the HKMA would derive from devaluing would presumably never be an important motive for devaluation. Issuing put options as a way of adding to the credibility of the authorities' commitment to a fixed exchange rate is the obverse of the point made in section 7.2 that sterilising a capital inflow reduces the credibility of the authorities' commitment not to devalue: in both cases, credibility is enhanced by reducing the amount of the authorities' liabilities that is denominated in the domestic currency.

The HKMA's Intervention in the Stock Market, August 1998

Although the speculation against the HK dollar in October 1997 did not break Hong Kong's link to the dollar, the jump in interest rates contributed to a stock market slump. In January, June and August 1998, speculators short-sold both the Hong Kong dollar and the shares that make up the Hang Seng stock market Index (HSI). By combining forward sales of the HSI for HK dollars with forward sales of HK dollars for US dollars, they effectively sold the HSI forward for US dollars, and therefore stood to gain from a fall in the US dollar value of Hong Kong stocks, regardless of whether it came from a devaluation of the HK dollar, or from a slump in the stock market, or both. In August 1998, the HKMA successfully countered this 'double play' by defending the exchange rate and using some of its foreign exchange reserves to buy equities. In effect, the HKMA sterilised the capital outflow by buying shares rather than EFBs.[20] Speculators hoping for a double gain suffered a double loss and the HKMA earned a profit on its equity portfolio of HK\$35 billion.[21]

While it is hard to argue with success, stock market trading is clearly a dangerous course of action for a currency board. Reserves that initially exceeded the stock of base money might fall short of it if the currency board suffered large losses. This is not a serious worry in Hong Kong's case, because the HKMA's foreign exchange reserves are so much larger than the stock of base money that even very large stock market losses would not jeopardise the 100 per cent backing of the monetary base. It is probably also sensible for the Hong Kong government's large stock of assets to be diversified to include equities, and not concentrated entirely in foreign exchange reserves. Perhaps a better solution than to have the HKMA operating in the stock market would be to transfer reserves in excess of the monetary base to an independent asset management fund to invest as it felt best. This formal separation of functions would increase the transparency of the currency board arrangement and reduce the risk of an attack on the HK dollar being triggered by losses on the government's share portfolio. However, the HKMA is unlikely to favour relinquishing control of over 70 per cent of its assets.

8.4   THE CREDIBILITY OF A FLOATING EXCHANGE RATE SYSTEM

Floating exchange rate regimes have often been criticised on the ground that they allow governments to exercise discretionary monetary policy and that this power is frequently misused to fund budget deficits by excessive credit creation.[22] But the use of credit creation to finance public sector spending has been practised in countries with both fixed and floating exchange rate regimes. Under either regime, excessive domestic credit creation eventually leads to inflation and the depreciation of the domestic currency, but the process is usually more costly under a fixed exchange rate regime where it involves periodic exchange rate crises during which the central bank sells foreign exchange reserves at the pre-devaluation exchange rate; these crises may be accompanied by financial crises and by the imposition of exchange controls.

Under a floating exchange rate system, the demand for domestic base money, and hence the price level and the level of the exchange rate, depend on expectations about the growth of the money supply. The central bank must therefore make a credible commitment to limit future inflation and monetary growth, or risk producing hyperinflation. Most economists who support floating exchange rates have also supported Milton Friedman's well-known proposal that the central bank should adopt a single target – to keep the rate of growth of the money supply to a slow steady rate, compatible with low inflation – and that it should not attempt to fine-tune monetary policy for stabilisation purposes. A closely related possibility (which, as described below, has been adopted by New Zealand) is to target inflation directly.

Just as the credibility of a central bank's commitment to a fixed exchange rate may be challenged, so may the credibility of a commitment to the various possible targets which can be pursued under a floating exchange rate system. First, the problem of multiple objectives can reduce the credibility of a money supply, inflation or nominal GDP target under a floating rate system, just as it can reduce the credibility of a commitment to a particular rate under a fixed rate system. In particular, the need to bail out distressed banks, or to engage in expansionary macroeconomic policy, may directly conflict with money supply, inflation or nominal GDP goals. Second, a government always faces a temptation to engage in one last round of monetary expansion before promising to pursue monetary restraint ever afterwards.

Once a central bank's determination to restrain the rate of monetary growth loses credibility, floating exchange rate regimes can produce rapid depreciation of the currency and rapid inflation. Indonesia's failure to make credible commitments to slow monetary growth in 1997–98 is documented in section 8.5 below. Before the Asian crisis, the example that was most often used by critics of floating exchange rate regimes to argue that they are potentially unstable was France's rapid inflation in the early and mid-1920s. In analysing this episode, Nurkse (1944, p. 118) argued that under a floating exchange rate, anticipations of exchange rate depreciation 'are apt to bring about their own realization'. He explained this as follows:

It is true that in the French experience of 1922–26 ... there was an expansion of domestic currency. This expansion, however, was not a cause but sometimes rather a consequence of the violent and uncontrolled exchange rate fluctuations. France emerged from the war with a large internal floating debt. When the decline in the exchange value of the franc began to create anticipations of further decline causing a strong desire to transfer capital abroad, the capital owners obtained the necessary liquid funds by refusing to renew the short-term treasury bills. It was this rather than the current budget deficit that forced the Treasury to borrow from the Bank of France (*ibid.*, p. 122).

Interpreted generously, Nurkse's analysis can be viewed a precursor of the second-generation models of self-fulfilling currency crises. The model exposited in section 5.3 provided a possible explanation of a self-fulfilling crisis in an initially fixed exchange rate system, but it can equally be applied to a floating exchange rate system in which the exchange rate is initially constant because the money supply is constant and the exchange rate is expected to remain constant. A government might respond to a rise in the nominal interest rate by increasing the rate of monetary growth because it would otherwise face an increase in the real interest rate and in the real burden of its debt. In this situation, an expectation of exchange rate depreciation would be self-fulfilling: it would raise the nominal interest rate, induce an increase in monetary growth and validate the expected depreciation. This minor variant on the model of section 5.3 is at least very similar to Nurkse's analysis.

Defenders of flexible exchange rates have criticised Nurkse's analysis on the ground that when the exchange rate is flexible, the government has the power to prevent an excessive expansion of the money supply; provided that it uses this power, a descent into rapid deflation and depreciation will not occur.[23] According to Nurkse, the French authorities responded to a rise in interest rates – in the above quotation this corresponds to the refusal of capital owners to renew their short-term bills – by adding to domestic credit. If they had been able to make a credible commitment not to do this, a self-fulfilling attack on the franc would not have been possible.

The modern second-generation models of self-fulfilling currency crises provide a possible resolution of this old debate: if the government is expected to react in the way posited by Nurkse, a self-fulfilling attack on a flexible exchange rate system is possible; but if the government can make a credible commitment to slow and steady monetary growth, no such instability can arise. If a government cannot make a commitment to slow and steady monetary growth under a flexible exchange rate regime, it is unlikely to be able to make a commitment to avoid excessive creation of domestic credit under a pegged exchange rate regime administered by a central bank.

The Indonesian crisis of August 1997 to July 1998, which is analysed in the next section, is closely analogous to that of France in the 1920s. In each case, the instability of the flexible exchange rate system appears to have arisen from the fact that the authorities responded to a rise in interest rates by expanding domestic credit, thus easing interest rate pressures in the very short run, but adding to expectations of inflation and depreciation in the medium and long run. Whereas in France in the 1920s, the motive for this response appears to have been the government's reluctance to force up interest rates on its short-term debts, the motive in the Indonesian case was the authorities' reluctance to exacerbate the weaknesses of the commercial banks.

The best way to ensure the credibility of a central bank's commitment to monetary stability under a floating exchange rate system is for there to be legislation which gives it a clearly defined responsibility for controlling a single nominal target and the means to do so.[24] New Zealand provides an interesting example of this approach.[25] Under the Reserve Bank of New Zealand (RBNZ) Act, 1989, the RBNZ's 'primary function' is defined to be 'achieving and maintaining stability in the general level of prices'. The Act gives the Governor of the RBNZ complete responsibility for monetary policy, subject to meeting a 'policy targets agreement' which must include a specific target for inflation and which has to be negotiated periodically between the Governor and the Minister of Finance. Since December 1996, the rule has been that annual inflation must be kept between zero and 3 per cent. Before December 1996 the range was from zero to 2 per cent.

The RBNZ's independence is limited both because the government could repeal or amend the Act and because the Act allows the government to override the RBNZ's statutory monetary policy objective and substitute some other objective by issuing an order in council. The overriding order would expire after a year, but could in principle be renewed again and again. Nevertheless, because the responsibility for achieving price stability is delegated to an agency that controls most of the levers that are relevant to achieving this goal, and whose main job is to achieve it, the Act makes the government's commitment to low inflation much more credible than it otherwise would be.[26] While the government could override the RBNZ, this could only be done in a very explicit way, which would cause the government a great deal of embarrassment.

Under a floating exchange rate, as under a fixed rate, the credibility of the monetary authorities' commitments to their stated targets is weakened by the added responsibility of having to provide safety nets for banks and finance companies. Even in the case of New Zealand, where the government has denied that it would bail out depositors in failed banks, the Governor of the RBNZ has noted that the Bank 'retains a wide-ranging capacity to respond to financial distress or bank failure where a bank's financial condition poses a serious threat to the banking system'.[27] If a financial crisis occurred in New Zealand, it is not clear how the RBNZ would balance the trade-off between its low inflation target and its responsibility for the safety of the financial system.

8.5   CREDIBILITY: MONETARY TARGETS AND THE PROPOSAL FOR A CURRENCY BOARD IN INDONESIA

Monetary Targets after the Floating of the Rupiah in August 1997[28]

For 10 months after floating the rupiah in August 1997, Bank Indonesia (BI) failed to keep to the rule that a country with a flexible exchange rate system must make a credible commitment to avoid excessive monetary growth. The need for a clear and credible commitment is particularly important if, as in Indonesia's case, the government has been forced to float the exchange rate because of a speculative attack driven in part by fears that money creation will be used to finance a bail-out of financial institutions.

BI did not make any announcement about monetary targets at the time it floated the rupiah in August 1997 and the exchange rate, which had been Rp. 2615 per dollar at the end of July, depreciated to Rp. 2980 by 18 August. Alarmed by this depreciation, the government implemented a very abrupt tightening of monetary policy by requiring public sector enterprises to shift their deposits from the commercial banks to BI itself. In effect, BI took over some of the commercial banks' deposits and a large amount of their reserves, but none of their loans.[29]

As a result of this liquidity squeeze, commercial banks' deposits at BI fell by 66 per cent during August – an amount equivalent to 20 per cent of the total base money supply at the beginning of the month.[30] Because currency in circulation rose slightly, the overall fall in the supply of base money during the month was a more modest 16.5 per cent. Many banks' deposit balances at the central bank became negative. The annualised interest rates on inter-bank call money jumped from 16 per cent in July to 65 per cent in August, before falling to around 40 per cent in October and November.[31] *Ex post*, these interest rates were not sufficient to compensate depositors for the collapse of the rupiah, but the extent of this collapse was not anticipated at the time.

The rise in domestic interest rates and the depreciation of the rupiah – 17 per cent in August alone – made it impossible for heavily indebted corporations to maintain debt service payments on either domestic or foreign currency loans.[32] As a result, non-performing loans became a severe problem for the banks, which also lost their access to offshore money markets. In early November 1997, BI closed down 16 private banks; since the criteria for closing them were not transparent, and since the soundness of the remaining banks was not known to depositors, there was a run on the private banks and a transfer of deposits to the state banks.[33]

Indonesia's first policy agreement with the IMF, announced on 31 October 1997, contained targets for base money for the coming 12 months. Table 8.1 summarises these targets and those set out in Indonesia's subsequent plans. The October 1997 target was to restrict the growth of base money in the nine months starting from the end of September 1997 to 7.5 per cent. The actual increase over this period was 92.1 per cent. The margin by which the target was missed was so wide that any anti-inflationary effects of the earlier monetary contraction were more than undone.

At the time of drawing up the revised plan announced on 15 January 1998, the failure to meet the 31 October monetary targets was already apparent. Without addressing the reasons for this failure, the revised plan dropped the quantitative target for base money. The new target was to keep inflation in 1998 to less than 20 per cent. This was to be achieved by using base money to contain the growth of broad money to 16 per cent in 1998. In the event, the consumer price index rose by 20.7 per cent in only the first two months of 1998, and broad money grew by 26.7 per cent during the month of January 1998 alone.

In its plans of 10 April and 24 June, the government again avoided addressing the reasons for its failure to keep to its earlier targets. In these plans it reverted to quantitative targets for base money. In each plan, however, these targets were set only for the next three months. Instead of remaining constant during the second quarter of 1998, as envisaged in the April plan, base money actually rose by 18 per cent – an annual growth rate of 96 per cent. However, the situation greatly improved after mid-1998. The June targets were only narrowly exceeded, and in July the planning horizon was extended to the end of March 1999 by which time base money was targeted to be 26 per cent above the level of March 1998 and 13 per cent above the level of July 1998. In the event, it grew by only 22 per cent between March 1998 and March 1999 and declined by 3 per cent between July 1998 and March 1999. Bank Indonesia continued to publish and keep to base money targets throughout 1999. In the second half of 1998 the rupiah steadied. From a low point of about Rp. 15 000 to Rp. 17 000 per dollar in mid-1998 it appreciated and was within the range Rp. 6500 to Rp. 8500 per dollar for most of 1999 and early 2000.

The immediate cause of BI's failure to keep to its monetary targets between October 1997 and June 1998 was its massive last resort lending to the commercial banks. In theory, last resort lending in a banking panic need not be inflationary: the broad money supply (M2), defined as the cash and bank deposits of the non-bank sector, can be kept constant – or allowed to grow in line with the underlying rate of growth of real output and the authorities' targeted rate of inflation – while the central bank expands the supply of base money (M0) by providing the commercial banks with the cash that they need to meet demands for withdrawals by depositors. This increase in the supply of base money would not be inflationary if it merely accommodated the public's desire, at existing prices, to hold cash rather than deposits. However, if the public wishes to transfer

Table 8.1   *Indonesia: base money targets in successive plans, 1997–98 (Rp. trillion)*

Plan	31 Oct. 1997	10 Apr. 1998[a]	24 June 1998[a]	29 July 1998	11 Sept. 1998	19 Oct. 1998	13 Nov. 1998	Actual
July 97								39.9
Aug. 97								33.3
Sept. 97	41.1							36.6
Oct. 97								33.6
Nov. 97								33.8
Dec. 97	42.7							46.1
Jan. 98								56.0
Feb. 98								49.6
Mar. 98	42.7	59.4		61.8				59.4
Apr. 98		59.4						61.1
May 98		59.4	68.0					68.0
June 98	44.2	59.4	68.0					70.3
July 98			68.0	68.6	72.6			75.4
Aug. 98			68.0	68.9				71.4
Sept. 98	45.8		68.0	69.7	69.7	69.9	69.9	71.4
Oct. 98					71.5	71.5	71.5	75.9
Nov. 98					73.0	73.0	73.0	78.4
Dec. 98				74.3	74.3	74.3	74.3	74.1
Jan. 99							75.4	73.4
Feb. 99							76.5	74.5
Mar. 99				77.6				72.8

Notes: Data on the various plans are taken from the letters of intent and memoranda of economic and financial policies sent by the government to the IMF at the dates indicated in the column headings. These letters and memoranda are available on the IMF web site. The starting points for the plans regularly differ from the actual levels in the final column because of revisions.

a.   These 'targets' were not explicitly stated in the government's memoranda to the IMF. Rather, the targets reported here are derived from the statements in Indonesian Government (1998a) and (1998b) that both the domestic and foreign components of base money would be broadly constant during the second and third quarters, respectively.

deposits from weak to strong banks, and if the authorities bail out the weak ones, it is hard to avoid an expansion of broad money. If there is no change in the public's demand for cash relative to deposits, the authorities must stop the broad money supply expanding by selling an amount of securities equal to the amount of last resort loans to the weak banks. In other words, the authorities must borrow from the strong banks to lend to the weak ones. If they borrow and lend at the same interest rates as the market, they might as well not make last resort loans at all, and leave the weak banks to negotiate their own loans from the strong ones. If they lend to the weak banks at more favourable rates than the market, they are providing them with a subsidy and can expect to make a loss, unless they have superior information to the market, or really can arbitrage opportunities that strong banks are too small to arbitrage. In any case, the test of non-inflationary last resort lending is that there must be a fall in the amount of broad money created by the commercial banks, which is equal to the excess of the broad money supply over base money, M2 – M0.

The non-inflationary benchmark policy just described is referred to here as 'accommodative' last resort lending. Under this policy, M2 – M0 will contract during a bank run in which the public withdraw deposits from the commercial banks and the central bank does no more than replenish the banks' cash reserves. However, when the exchange rate varies, M2 – M0, becomes an unsatisfactory indicator of whether last resort lending to banks is merely accommodative. Because M2 includes foreign currency deposits, exchange rate depreciation would cause it to rise, even in the absence of any banking sector transactions. The revaluation effects on the broad money supply of exchange rate changes can be avoided by focusing on M2R, which is defined here as the domestic currency-denominated components of M2.[34]

Although M2 – M0 continued to grow during the Indonesian banking crisis of October 1997 to January 1998, this growth was attributable to the revaluation of foreign currency deposits: the amount of rupiah broad money created by the banks, M2R – M0, did indeed decline during this period. However, in the next six months, from the end of January to the end of July 1998, M2R – M0 grew from Rp. 186 trillion to Rp. 282 trillion, which is an annualised growth rate of 130 per cent. This very rapid creation of broad money by the commercial banks proves that BI's last resort loans did not merely accommodate a contraction of commercial banks caused by a bank run. Rather, these loans allowed the commercial banks to expand their assets and liabilities very rapidly.

Over the period from the end of January to the end of July 1998, commercial bank borrowings from BI grew by Rp. 102 trillion from Rp. 23 trillion to Rp. 125 trillion.[35] These borrowings added directly to base money, but over this period base money grew by 'only' Rp.19 trillion. Sales by BI of its own certificates of deposit (*Sertifikat Bank Indonesia,* or SBI) absorbed Rp. 56 trillion of the Rp. 102 trillion of last resort loans; much of the remaining Rp. 27 trillion (that is, 102 – 19 – 56) was probably used to buy BI's shrinking foreign exchange reserves.

What induced BI to make such excessive loans? Even if a central bank could observe all the monetary aggregates accurately and without lags, it would be hard for it to know whether requested last resort loans are really needed to keep a solvent but illiquid bank afloat, or whether they will be used by a failing bank to gamble on resurrection. In the first half of 1998, the interest rates paid by the strongest and weakest Indonesian banks on inter-bank loans regularly differed by more than 100 percentage points: while the strongest banks were borrowing at 40–50 per cent, the weakest had to pay 150 per cent or more.[36] The conventional recommendation that the central bank should lend freely but at a penalty rate to banks that would be solvent in normal times would have been a poor guide to BI in 1998: how was it supposed to know which of the weak banks were really solvent? Was the appropriate penalty rate 70 per cent or 170 per cent? Any attempt at last resort lending in such circumstances faces a massive problem of adverse selection: the banks that the market judges to be insolvent will be the ones most anxious to borrow from the central bank.

The theoretical niceties of how to distinguish between insolvent and solvent, but illiquid banks, were not BI's only problem. The process of mopping up the state banks' bad debts in late 1999 revealed that President Soeharto intervened personally to pressure BI to channel $1.35 billion to the textile group Texmaco through a state bank, in the form of subsidised pre-shipment export finance, although the loan was reported to have been used to pay off short-term foreign debts.[37]

BI's attempts to overcome the problems of adverse selection and lend to banks that were potentially solvent, but merely illiquid, were spectacularly unsuccessful. By January 2000, the government had been forced to issue it with bonds worth Rp. 165 trillion (about $23 billion at the exchange rate of January 2000) to replace the emergency liquidity support that it had provided to commercial banks that were subsequently closed or taken over.[38] Because banks had dissipated depositors' funds, as well as BI's last resort loans, this amount is much less than the gross cost of the bail-out to the government. Before allowing for recovery of assets, this gross cost is estimated to be about $90 billion, or 51 per cent of GDP in the financial year 1999–2000.[39] Since the entire assets and liabilities of the commercial banking system were 65 per cent of GDP in 1999/ 2000, it appears that, by keeping insolvent banks afloat, BI's emergency liquidity support allowed them to dissipate an amount not much less than the *gross assets* of the whole commercial banking sector.

There was a sharp contrast between the monetary strategies of Indonesia, on the one hand, and of Thailand and Korea on the other. Soon after floating their exchange rates, both the latter countries announced tight limits on their targeted rates of monetary growth which extended almost 12 months into the future. Actual monetary growth in both countries was kept well below these targets. Thailand's plan of 4 August 1997 was for 10 per cent growth of base money between September 1997 and September 1998; Korea's plan of 7 February 1998 was for 14 per cent growth of base money between December 1997 and December 1998. In both cases, base money actually declined over these periods.

The Proposal to Create a Currency Board in Indonesia in February 1998

In February 1998, the Indonesian government floated the idea of creating a currency board and Professor Steve Hanke, a prominent advocate of currency boards, was engaged as a special adviser to President Soeharto. Hanke proposed that the government should announce that a currency board would be established and that the exchange rate would be fixed against the dollar at an average of the market rates observed in a specified, brief period between the announcement and the commencement of the board's operations; during this transition period Bank Indonesia would not intervene in the exchange market.[40] Rumours that a currency board was about to be introduced were probably responsible for the appreciation of the rupiah from Rp. 10 375 per dollar at the end of January to Rp. 8750 at the end of February. The currency board proposal was eventually abandoned because of the opposition to it from the IMF and some of the governments that were participating in the IMF-organised credit package for Indonesia including, in particular, the US government.

Few economists found anything to praise in the proposal for an Indonesian currency board, and several argued that it would worsen the banking crisis. On 27 January 1998, the government had announced a blanket guarantee to all depositors and creditors (other than holders of subordinated debt) of banks incorporated in Indonesia. The main argument used against the currency board proposal was that Indonesia did not have sufficient foreign exchange reserves to meet the guarantee to bank depositors and creditors if they all tried to convert their holdings into foreign exchange. Some critics also argued that a currency board might have been used to finance capital flight by the President and his family. Many argued that the middle of a banking and exchange rate crisis was not a good moment at which to introduce a currency board.

There is no completely unambiguous answer to the question of how much foreign exchange the monetary authorities would need to operate both a currency board and a blanket guarantee of bank deposits. One possible answer is that they might need liquid foreign exchange reserves equal to the broad money supply, which is defined as the non-bank private sector's holdings of notes and coins, plus its holding of bank deposits. If the non-bank private sector decided to convert its entire holdings of domestic money into foreign exchange and if the banks held no foreign currency assets, this is the amount of foreign currency that would be demanded from the authorities. However, even if the authorities held foreign exchange reserves in excess of broad money, they could not be sure that it would remain sufficient, since the commercial banks might always increase the broad money supply, independently of any action by the central bank, by making new loans that might be used to buy foreign exchange. To be certain of being able both to bail out all bank depositors and to ensure the convertibility of the currency at the specified exchange rate, the authorities would

Table 8.2   *Indonesia: contingent rupiah liabilities, due to the*
government's guarantee to bank creditors, and reserves at
various exchange rates (end of February 1998)

1. Exchange rate, Rp./$	8750	5000	4000
2. BI's foreign assets, Rp. trillion	143.8	82.2	65.8
3. Base money, M0, Rp. trillion	49.6	49.6	49.6
4. Narrow money, M1, Rp. trillion	92.5	92.5	92.5
5. Banks' foreign currency deposits, Rp. trillion	165.3	94.4	75.5
6. Rupiah broad money, M2R, Rp. trillion	265.0	265.0	265.0
7. Broad money, M2, Rp. trillion	430.2	359.4	340.5
8. BI's foreign assets as % of M0	290%	166%	133%
9. BI's foreign assets as % of M2	33%	23%	19%

Notes: The exchange rate of Rp. 8750/$ is the actual exchange rate for the end of February 1998, as given by series ae from IMF, *International Financial Statistics* CD-ROM. The other two rates in row 1 are presented for illustrative purposes. Data in the first column for rows 2, 3, 4, 5 and 7 were downloaded from the web site of Bank Indonesia: http://www.bi.go.id/statistik. Row 5 is the sum of commercial banks' foreign currency demand deposits and foreign currency time deposits. Row 6 is row 7 minus row 5. For rows 3, 4 and 6, which are denominated only in rupiah, the column 2 and 3 estimates are equal to those in column 1. For items denominated only in foreign currency (rows 2 and 5), the column 2 and 3 estimates are derived from the column 1 data by multiplying by the ratio of the exchange rates. The column 2 and 3 estimates for row 7 are obtained by summing the corresponding estimates in rows 5 and 6.

therefore need foreign exchange reserves equal to the maximum amount to which the commercial banks could expand the broad money supply, but there is no precise way of knowing exactly what this maximum amount is.

While even the broad money supply does not place an upper bound on the amount of foreign exchange reserves that the authorities would need to meet all the contingent liabilities resulting from guaranteeing both all bank deposits and the exchange rate, it is far more than the amount of foreign exchange reserves that is held by other currency boards or that is ever likely to be needed in practice. In Argentina, at the end of December 1994, just before the unsuccessful speculative attack that followed the Mexican crisis, the monetary authorities' foreign assets were only 30 per cent of broad money, even though the Central Bank of Argentina uses a very broad definition of international reserves which includes its holdings of US dollar-denominated Argentine government bonds.[41] At the end of September 1997, just before the unsuccessful speculative attack on the Hong Kong dollar of October 1997, the foreign exchange reserves of the HKMA were only 20 per cent of broad money.[42]

Table 8.2 presents data which are relevant to judging the adequacy or inadequacy of Bank Indonesia's foreign exchange reserves at the end of February 1998 at three hypothetical exchange rates, which are shown in the last three columns. These are the actual rate at the time, which was Rp. 8750 per dollar, and two stronger rates – Rp. 5000 and Rp. 4000 per dollar – which had been suggested as possible rates that a currency board might have tried to defend. Table 8.2 shows that at the actual exchange rate at the end of February 1998, BI's foreign assets were 33 per cent of broad money, which is higher than the corresponding ratios given above for either Argentina or Hong Kong. Even at the hypothetical exchange rate of Rp. 5000 they would have been 23 per cent of broad money, and therefore higher than the corresponding figure for Hong Kong. And even at an exchange rate of Rp. 4000 per dollar, their ratio to M2 would have been only slightly below the corresponding ratio in Hong Kong.

Of course the banks in Hong Kong in 1997 and in Argentina in 1994–95 were much stronger and better able to resist a prolonged period of high interest rates than those of Indonesia in 1998. However, by February 1998 Indonesia's banks were backed by the government's blanket guarantee of all credits other than subordinated debts. Besides, the fragile state of Indonesia's banks was not uniquely a problem for a currency board regime. The weakness of the criticisms of the currency board proposal is that, with minor amendments, they apply with equal or greater force to any other monetary option that Indonesia might have implemented. This is obviously true of the argument that the severity of the banking crisis made early 1998 a most unpropitious time at which to introduce a currency board: it was an equally unpropitious time at which to try to establish the credibility of the government's stated intention to restrain monetary growth under the flexible exchange rate system, which had been adopted at the outbreak of the crisis in August 1997.

The critics of the currency board emphasised the logical possibility that depositors could have precipitated a banking collapse by rushing to withdraw all rupiah time and savings deposits from the commercial banks, in order to convert them to dollars at the new fixed exchange rate as soon as the board commenced operations. The logical possibility of bank runs exists in any system in which banks hold less than 100 per cent reserves; it was noted in section 5.2 that currency board systems actually have a better record for financial stability than those managed by central banks. Besides, provided that the new fixed rate for the rupiah had been determined in the way proposed by Hanke, those speculators who believed that the board could not defend it would already have had both the incentive and the opportunity to convert their rupiah deposits to dollars at about the same rate during the period of clean floating before the board began operating.

In the absence of a currency board, the government could only give an absolute guarantee over the nominal value of bank deposits: it could not provide a guarantee of the exchange rate or of the real value of bank deposits. Holders of rupiah deposits (including members of the President's family) therefore had even more reason to try to withdraw their deposits and convert them to dollars under the actual system – in which, as the previous subsection showed, the authorities failed to provide credible monetary targets until mid-1998 – than they would have had under a currency board system.

The previous subsection showed that the cost of bailing out Indonesia's banks is unlikely to be much less than half of annual GDP. Under a currency board system this cost would have been much smaller provided that the board had kept to the textbook rule of not making last resort loans. Guaranteed deposits in banks that failed could still have been transferred to a solvent state bank without any losses to depositors, as they were under the arrangements actually adopted. Since a currency board would have avoided the 42 percent expansion of base money that actually occurred between the end of February and the end of June 1998, it would probably have been able to defend an exchange rate of about Rp. 5000 per dollar. Had this happened, Indonesia's corporate and financial debts would now be much easier to resolve than they actually are. And so would the government's.

8.6   OVERVIEW: EXCHANGE RATE REGIMES AND CREDIBILITY

Most developing countries have tried to manage their nominal exchange rates. A few have aimed to fix them against one of the major currencies – usually the dollar. Most have aimed at steady depreciation against a basket of the currencies of their main trading partners. Each of these managed exchange rate strategies is risky if the monetary authorities are also responsible for preventing the traded goods sector becoming uncompetitive at the managed exchange rate, because speculators will be justified in short-selling the currency whenever a devaluation would restore competitiveness.

In addition, if the authorities use domestic credit contraction to reduce what is perceived to be excessive domestic demand, and if they are unwilling to allow balance of payments deficits to raise interest rates for fear that weak banks might collapse, the effects on official foreign exchange reserves of changes in world interest rates and changes in perceptions of domestic economic prospects will be magnified. Table 7.1 showed the very large extent to which many developing countries have tried to sterilise the monetary effects of balance of payments flows. The authorities' weak commitment to a supposedly fixed exchange rate will be exacerbated if they follow such policies, because they risk creating situations in which they lack the reserves necessary to defend the exchange rate, even if they wish to do so.

If a country chooses a managed exchange rate system, there is a strong case for making its commitment as strong as possible either by adopting full dollarisation, or by setting up a currency board. The ability of currency board systems to avoid speculative attacks, and to resist those that nevertheless occur, can be readily understood in terms of the discussion of speculative attack models in Chapter 5. In the 'first generation' models, discussed in section 5.2, the attacks are a consequence of excessive creation of domestic credit, which typically occurs when the government forces the central bank to lend to it to finance deficit spending. Under a currency board system, this does not happen: the currency board only adds to the supply of base money supply by providing it in exchange for foreign currency. By creating a currency board, a government deprives itself of the opportunity and thus the temptation to finance deficit spending by excessive credit creation.

The possibility of multiple equilibria, which gives rise to the speculative attacks described by the 'second generation' models of section 5.3, can occur only if the authorities' promise to defend the exchange rate lacks credibility. This is less likely under a currency board than under a central bank for two reasons. First, a well-designed currency board has a single, clearly specified responsibility: to defend the convertibility of the currency at the fixed rate. Second, although actual currency boards use monetary policy to a much greater extent than the textbook model recommends, they engage in significantly less sterilisation than central banks, as Table 7.1 confirms, and therefore face a much smaller risk of running out of the foreign exchange reserves necessary to defend the exchange rate. The risk of a speculative attack on a currency is greatly increased, as explained in section 5.2, if the authorities are expected to attempt to sterilise capital flows.[43]

If the sole aim of policy was to avoid speculative crises, the two best options for a small country that does not already have a strong reputation for monetary stability would be either a currency board peg to a country that does have such a reputation, or the adoption of a floating exchange rate managed by a central bank with a legislated responsibility to maintain low inflation and with the independence needed to pursue this responsibility.

Section 8.5 showed that last resort lending can easily undermine the credibility of any exchange rate system, whether fixed or flexible. Far from keeping the expansion of base money to what was required by merely accommodative last resort lending, BI financed an expansion of bank lending that was used to speculate against the rupiah. Both base money and broad money almost doubled in the year from mid-1997 to mid-1998, and the rupiah lost 82 per cent of its dollar value in the year to the end of July 1998. It was argued in section 8.5 that there was probably no way in which BI could have undertaken large-scale last resort lending in 1998 without incurring large losses. The conventional rule that the central bank should lend at penalty rates to banks that are basically solvent but temporarily illiquid is not one that can be implemented in conditions like those that existed in Indonesia in 1998, when banks were segmented into very weak ones and relatively stronger ones. BI tried to prop up the weak ones, but they failed anyway and in the process generated debts for taxpayers equal to almost half of annual GDP.

With deposit insurance in place, the least bad strategy for a central bank operating a floating exchange rate when confronted by a collapsing financial sector is to refuse to make last resort loans, but merely to expand base money to accommodate demands by the public to switch from deposits to cash. Base money should not be expanded so rapidly that it causes the growth of broad money to accelerate. Faster growth of base money merely leads to excessive inflation, and trying to direct credit by last resort lending to weak banks on more favourable terms than those on which stronger banks can borrow is a recipe for large losses for the central bank, for the government's deposit insurance scheme, and for taxpayers.

Under this strategy, illiquid banks would have to borrow from the money market and would be closed down if their capital fell below the minimum permitted operating level, as discussed in Chapter 6. It would obviously be much easier to implement such a policy if all banks were initially well capitalised and if deposit insurance was in place. This strengthens the case made in Chapter 6 for making deposit insurance compulsory and for increasing minimum CARs far above the current conventional limit of only 8 per cent.

It would obviously be important that banks should be aware of the proposed rules well in advance of a crisis, so that they could raise their liquidity and arrange lines of credit to draw on in emergencies. The discussion of Hong Kong's experience in late 1997 shows that banks will rapidly raise their holdings of base money if their access to easy credit from the monetary authorities is barred. It also shows that a sudden unannounced change in access to official credit can cause a very undesirable liquidity squeeze.

The case for a currency board is particularly strong when a country's reputation for monetary discipline is poor. It was argued in section 8.5 that a currency board would probably have helped Indonesia avoid the massive currency and financial collapse that it suffered in 1998. However, the credibility of a government's commitment to a fixed exchange rate (or any other policy target) comes at a price, in terms of loss of flexibility, which may not always be worth paying. Admittedly, if the authorities make a very credible, and therefore inflexible, commitment to maintain the exchange rate, prices and nominal wages are likely to become more flexible than if unions and employers believe that the authorities will devalue in response to a rise in unemployment. However, the recessions in Hong Kong in 1997–98 and in Argentina after 1995 show that even in the countries with the strongest commitments to fixed exchange rates, prices and wages can be sufficiently inflexible that a large capital outflow, or a fall in demand and prices in export markets can lead to a recession.

Given that the volatility of capital flows is one of the most important sources of shocks facing small open economies, and given the argument in section 7.1 that the effects on aggregate demand and employment of any given change in capital flows is much larger under a fixed exchange rate system than under a flexible exchange rate system there is a strong case in normal circumstances for preferring a rigid commitment to low inflation, or low monetary growth, under a flexible exchange rate system, rather than a rigid commitment to a fixed exchange rate. Finally, because a flexible exchange rate system is better able than a fixed rate system to stabilise aggregate demand in the face of volatile capital flows, it is easier to achieve credibility if the monetary authorities promise to keep to stable low inflation under a flexible exchange rate system than if they promise to fix the exchange rate.

If the exchange rate is allowed to float, at least relatively free mobility of short-term capital is needed to allow the banks that operate the foreign exchange market to finance short-term imbalances in flows of goods and long-term investments, without excessive exchange rate volatility.

NOTES

1. Base money is defined in section 2.2. See also section 7.1.
2. Schuler (1992, Chapter 5). The currency boards of Hong Kong, Brunei and Singapore revalued against sterling, to which they were previously pegged, when sterling was devalued against the dollar in 1967.
3. Seigniorage is discussed in more detail in section 4.3. Even under a currency board, some of the seigniorage accrues to the foreign country to whose currency the domestic currency is pegged. This happens because, if the currency board is to be sure of meeting demands for foreign currency, it must hold its reserves in very liquid forms, which usually offer relatively low returns.
4. Baliño and Enoch (1997, note 5, p. 2).
5. A useful summary of currency board episodes is given by Hanke *et al.* (1993, pp. 172–80). The list of small countries that have currency boards includes Bermuda, Brunei Darussalam, the Cayman Isles, Djibouti, the Faeroe Islands, the Falkland Islands, Gibraltar and the countries that belong to the East Caribbean Central Bank.
6. The consumer price inflation data are obtained by chain linking series from IMF, *International Financial Statistics* CD-ROM.
7. Gavin and Hausmann (1996, p. 46).
8. Santiprabhob (1997, pp. 4–5, 25).
9. Caprio *et al.* (1996, p. 4).
10. I wish to thank Guy Meredith, Kurt Schuler and K.K. Tang for helpful comments on an earlier draft of this section. Obviously they are not responsible for the opinions expressed here, nor for any remaining errors.
11. For more details see Yam (1997).
12. The price at which the HKMA will intervene in the foreign exchange market to support the HK dollar is being moved by HK$0.0001 per day from HK$7.75 per dollar in April 1999 to HK$7.80 in August 2000. This policy will implement one of the 'technical measures' announced in September 1998.
13. The discussion of this episode is based on Hong Kong Government (1998, Chapter 3) and Meredith (1999).
14. The speculation was also fuelled by Morgan Stanley's recommendation to sell Hong Kong and other Asian shares (Hong Kong Government, 1998, para. 2.4).
15. In a letter to the banks of 12 November 1997 (Annex 3.3 of Hong Kong Government, 1998), the Chief Executive of the HKMA stated that: 'Clearly, LAF should not be abused by the banks for the purpose of funding speculative Hong Kong dollar positions. I am sure you will appreciate that it is inappropriate for the HKMA to provide cheap Hong Kong dollar funding to those shorting the Hong Kong dollar'.

16. See, for example, Cheng *et al.* (1999).
17. Suppose that LIBOR plus the small premium is 6 per cent. If the probability of revaluation of the HK dollar is zero, the academics' proposal is equivalent to allowing banks to exchange EFBs that will yield $780 on 31 December for $100/1.06 = HK$780/1.06 on 1 January. If the probability of revaluation of the HK dollar is not zero, the bank discounting EFBs on 1 January receives both HK$780/1.06 and also an option to put $100 at HK$7.80 per dollar on 31 December. To the extent that the value of this option exceeds zero, the implied HK dollar interest rate is less than 6 per cent.
18. Meredith (1999).
19. At the end of December 1998, base money (which by then included EFBs) was HK$192 billion or US$24.7 billion, whereas the foreign exchange reserves of the HKMA were US$89.6 billion.
20. I am grateful to Max Corden for suggesting this helpful way of describing the policy.
21. HKMA (1998a, p. 80).
22. See, for example, Calvo (1996, pp. 66–7).
23. See, for example, Tsiang (1959) and Grissa (1983).
24. Attempts to correlate economic performance with the independence of the central bank – as measured by legal features of its charter and by the rate of turnover of its governors – find that independence is correlated with relatively low inflation (Grilli *et al.*, 1991; Cukierman, 1992, Chapter 20). However, although their coefficients are statistically significant, the explanatory power of these variables is low. Grilli *et al.* (1991) do not find a statistically significant association between central bank independence and real GDP growth in their sample of industrialised countries. Cukierman *et al.* (1993) confirm this finding for industrialised countries, but find that independence is associated with faster than average real GDP growth in developing countries.
25. See Kirchner (1995).
26. It might be very hard for the RBNZ to ensure price stability if the government persistently ran large budget deficits. The ability to avoid inflation by selling bonds in such circumstances depends on a belief among investors that there is little risk that a future government will use inflation to erode the real value of its debts.
27. Brash (1997, p. 360).
28. Some parts of this subsection are taken from Fane and McLeod (1999).
29. This crude method of monetary contraction had been used to counteract speculation against the rupiah in June and July 1987 and again in March 1991 (Cole and Slade, 1996, pp. 53, 59, 67).
30. McLeod (1998, pp. 922–3).
31. Bank Indonesia (1997, p. 27).
32. Indonesian banks undertook a large volume of foreign currency lending prior to the crisis: foreign currency loans accounted for 20 per cent of the total in June 1997.
33. One of the main criteria for closure was having breached the legal limits on lending to related firms. However, it was widely believed that most Indonesian banks had breached these limits and it was not clear what distinguished the 16 closed banks from the rest. Bank Indonesia (1999a, p. 93) reports that 56 banks were in breach of their legal lending limits in December 1997 and that by December 1998 this total had risen to 137.
34. The foreign currency-denominated components of M2 were estimated as the sum of the foreign currency demand deposits and foreign currency time deposits of commercial banks. See Bank Indonesia (1999b, Tables 1.30, 1.33).
35. Bank Indonesia (1999b, p. 15).
36. Bank Indonesia (1999a, p. 62).
37. *Jakarta Post*, 31 November 1999.
38. Bank Indonesia (2000).

39. The gross cost of bank restructuring is being financed by issuing government bonds to the banks. As of January 2000, Bank Indonesia (2000, p. 23) estimates that the total amount of bonds that the government will have to issue to recapitalise the banks is Rp. 639 trillion. This exceeds the true cost of the bail-out to the government by the amount that will be recouped by eventual privatisation of newly acquired bank shares and by sales of assets originally owned by failed banks. The latter are scheduled to raise Rp. 33 trillion in the first two financial years. The proceeds from privatisation are unlikely to be very large: only Rp. 38 trillion of the Rp. 639 trillion of government bonds issued were used to raise CARs from zero to 4 per cent. GDP in the financial year 1999/2000 is forecast by BI to be Rp. 1224 trillion.
40. See Hanke (1998).
41. For a summary of assets counted as being foreign exchange reserves in Argentina, see Enoch and Gulde (1997, note 20, p. 17). At the end of December 1994, the Argentine peso was approximately at parity with the US dollar, the foreign assets of the monetary authorities were $16.0 billion and M2 was 53.47 billion pesos (Source: IMF, *International Financial Statistics* CD-ROM).
42. At the end of September 1997, the foreign assets of Hong Kong's Exchange Fund were $71.4 billion (source: spreadsheet supplied by HKMA); the HK$ was at 7.738 per US$ and M2 was HK$2786 billion (source: HKMA, 1998b, Table 1.2, p. 9).
43. Flood and Marion (1998).

9. Reforming the international financial architecture

The Mexican crisis of 1994–95 inspired the setting up of working parties of officials from the IMF and other international financial institutions and the central banks and finance ministries of the major industrial countries to search for ways to strengthen 'the international financial architecture', that is, to reduce the frequency and cost of financial and balance of payments crises. The eruption of the Asian crisis in 1997, and its spread to Russia and Brazil in 1998, greatly increased the resources devoted to this task. There has also been no shortage of unofficial advice on global financial reform.

Aside from the Tobin tax, which is discussed in section 9.4, most of the proposals for the reform of the international financial system seek to provide governments of developing countries with safety nets that are analogous to those provided by national governments to domestic financial institutions: last resort loans and deposit insurance. In these analogies, the roles of commercial banks at the national level are played by governments of developing countries at the international level and that of the domestic central bank, or the government deposit insurance agency, is played by the IMF, or some other international agency.

Section 9.1 deals with IMF last resort lending to governments facing financial and exchange rate crises and section 9.2 deals with George Soros's proposal for an international agency to guarantee loans to developing countries. The former is closely analogous to central bank lending to commercial banks experiencing bank runs, the latter is closely analogous to deposit insurance. Section 9.3 deals with proposals by various working parties of experts and officials from the main industrial countries to try to induce private lenders in the industrialised countries to share in the cost of financial crises in developing countries. Under these proposals, private lenders would effectively have to provide either insurance against financial crises, or standby lines of credit, or both. There are therefore similarities between these proposals at the international level and the proposal at the national level, which was briefly mentioned at the beginning of section 6.4, that government organised deposit insurance of banks should be replaced or supplemented by privately provided deposit guarantees.

9.1   THE IMF AS INTERNATIONAL LENDER OF LAST RESORT

In 1944, the Bretton Woods agreement among the World War II allies laid down the framework of a system of fixed exchange rates, which was designed to prevent the competitive devaluations and exchange rate crises of the 1930s.

The IMF was created to coordinate this system and to lend to members facing temporary balance of payments difficulties on current account, subject to conditions designed to prevent borrowers from adopting excessively expansionary financial policies. Each member paid into the Fund an amount equal to an assigned quota; 25 per cent of the quota had to be contributed in the form of gold and the rest in the member's own currency.

The IMF's role as an international lender of last resort was initially very limited; countries could not borrow more than their quotas and in the exchange rate crises of the 1950s and 1960s, international last resort loans mainly took the form of swaps of reserves among the major central banks that belong to the Bank for International Settlements in Basle.

The abandonment of the Bretton Woods fixed exchange rate system in 1971 removed what had been the main reason for the IMF's existence. In the next two decades it enlarged its role as adviser on economic liberalisation to the governments of developing and formerly communist countries. Then in the recent Mexican and Asian financial crises, it became the preferred conduit for international last resort lending by the USA.

The Case for an International Lender of Last Resort

Since the provision of IMF loans to help a central bank to defend a fixed exchange rate is closely analogous to that of domestic last resort lending by a national central bank to a commercial bank trying to meet a run by depositors, it is not surprising that the arguments for and against an international lender of last resort closely mirror the debate on domestic last resort lending: the proponents point to the same types of market failure, collective action problems and externalities that are used to justify domestic last resort lending to banks, while the opponents emphasise the creation of moral hazard.

The need for the IMF to act as the international lender of last resort has been argued not only by those, such as Fischer (1999), who have defended its handling of recent crises, but also by some of those, such as Sachs (1995) and Feldstein (1998a, 1998b), who have been among its most severe critics.[1] Others, such as Schwartz (1998) and Calomiris (1998), argue that its attempts to act as international lender of last resort have done more harm than good. Schwartz (1998) argues that it should be abolished.

Sachs (1995, p. 2) argues that there is a need for an international lender of last resort because 'international financial markets and monetary arrangements are subject to instabilities and inefficiencies' due to the possibility of multiple equilibria and to the collective action problems that bankruptcy and possible bankruptcy can create. He cites three types of multiple equilibria: speculative attacks on a currency, bank runs and the possibility that a potentially solvent non-bank borrower may be forced into bankruptcy because each potential lender knows that this will indeed happen if other potential lenders shun the borrower. Since devaluation is a form of partial default, all the grounds for an international lender of last resort cited by Sachs can be regarded as variants on a single ground: the need to overcome the collective action problems arising from the risk of partial, or total, default. This is, of course, one of the traditional justifications, set out in section 6.2, for a domestic lender of last resort.

The other main argument used to justify domestic last resort lending – the externalities associated with financial panics – can also be used as a potential justification for international last resort lending. This argument underlies the justification of last resort lending offered by Kindleberger (1989) who collected evidence to show that international monetary crises in which an international last resort lender has taken an active lead have generally been followed by less severe recessions than those in which no such lead was taken. He attributes the severity of the Great Depression of the 1930s to the refusal by the US government and the Federal Reserve during the inter-war period to shoulder the burden of international last resort lending which the Bank of England was no longer able to bear.

Differences between Domestic and International Last Resort Lending

The IMF's ability to act as a lender of last resort is sometimes challenged on the ground that, unlike a domestic central bank, it cannot create money. In fact, as Fischer (1999) points out, an institution can operate as an effective lender of last resort even without the ability to create money, provided that it has been endowed with sufficiently large financial resources; besides, the IMF can add to global international reserves because, subject to the consent of its members, it can increase special drawing rights (SDRs) and draw on lines of credit – the General and New Arrangements to Borrow, described below. SDRs must be distributed in proportion to members' quotas, but funds borrowed through the lines of credit can be lent as the IMF chooses.

The bulk of the IMF's funds come from members' quotas. These amounted to $7.8 billion when the IMF was created and have been increased at roughly five-year intervals since then.[2] After a 45 percent increase in quotas had become effective in January 1999, they amounted to about $283 billion.[3] However, since up to 75 per cent of quota contributions can be in the form of the member's own currency, rather than hard currencies, much of the amounts contributed by developing countries cannot be used to finance IMF lending. To supplement the funds provided by quotas, the Articles of Agreement of the IMF were amended in 1960 to provide it with lines of credit from the major industrialised countries for dealing with systemic crises. These credit lines are referred to as the 'General Arrangements to Borrow' (GAB). As of January 2000, the GAB provides the IMF with access to about $23 billion from 11 countries. In November 1998, an additional $23 billion became available with the implementation of the 'New Arrangements to Borrow' (NAB) with a further 14 member countries.[4]

It would be hard for an international last resort lender to implement the traditional recommendation that domestic last resort loans should be made quickly and freely to all that bring good security. Although it does not secure its loans against collateral, the IMF does impose policy conditions that borrowing governments must accept to qualify for its loans. These policy conditions are the analogue, at the international level, of the prudential regulations imposed on commercial banks by national governments.

Because the details of policy conditions attached to each loan take time to negotiate, and because loans are disbursed in tranches as a way of making sure that the policy conditions are fulfilled, IMF loans are not made quickly and freely. However, since a speculative attack can be halted if speculators can be convinced that the government has an incentive to follow the newly agreed policies, and that these policies are consistent with the maintenance of the current exchange rate, the gradual disbursement of loans need not be an insurmountable problem.

The IMF's procedure for negotiating and disbursing loans have sometimes succeeded in halting speculative attacks and sometimes failed. The loan package negotiated between the US Treasury and Mexico in December 1994 initially failed to halt speculation against the peso, despite a 35 per cent fall in its dollar value during December. In early 1995, additional loans, which brought the total package to $52 billion, were coordinated by the IMF. This expansion of the package, and the fact that the dollar value of the peso fell by a further 22 per cent in the first three months of 1995, finally restored confidence in the peso and in the government's ability to meet its debt repayments.

Successive crises have prompted successive reforms to the IMF's lending procedures. In September 1995, following the Mexican crisis, the IMF set up an Emergency Financing Mechanism (EFM) to try to speed-up the process of loan negotiation and disbursement in crisis situations. In 1997, the EFM was used to provide the IMF's emergency loans to Thailand, Indonesia and Korea.[5] These three loan packages were described as amounting to $17 billion, $43 billion and $58 billion, respectively. However, these figures greatly exaggerate the true size of the last resort loans actually made available. Between 64 per cent (Korea) and 77 per cent (Thailand and Indonesia) of the total packages comprised loans from the World Bank, the Asian Development Bank and 'second tier' loans promised by various governments. The second tier loans made up the bulk of the non-IMF part of the packages, but very little of these loans was ever made available. Most of the loans from the World Bank and ADB were not disbursed in the first year, and some of the amounts that were disbursed would presumably have been lent even in the absence of any crisis.

The loans to Thailand and Indonesia in 1997–98 were disbursed so slowly that the amounts received in the first 10 months following the granting of these loans – $3 billion for Thailand and $6 billion for Indonesia – did not make a large difference to the funds available to counter the crises in either country. In Thailand's case, the IMF's approval of its policies helped to reassure international investors. In Indonesia's case, the public dispute between the government and the IMF contributed to the collapse of confidence in the rupiah. In sharp contrast to Thailand and Indonesia, Korea received over $10 billion from the IMF and an additional $5 billion from the World Bank and the ADB in the first month after the negotiation of its loan. Like Mexico in 1994–95, it appeared to receive relatively favourable treatment because of its relatively close links with the USA.

Part of the delay in the disbursement of the Indonesian loan can be blamed on the Indonesian government's failure to meet agreed targets. But this was itself partly due to the toughness of the policy conditions imposed on it. Many of these conditions – for example, the liberalisation of trade and investment, the privatisation of state enterprises, the elimination of domestic monopolies, the removal of special tax concessions to the designated producer of the national car and the introduction of competition policy – had no obvious connection with raising the likelihood that the IMF would be repaid in full and on time, however desirable they may have been on other grounds.

Some loss of independence is one of the inevitable costs of borrowing, but it is in the interest of lenders themselves to limit the conditions imposed on borrowers to those that increase the probability that loans will be repaid. The IMF should require the governments that borrow from it to limit their budget deficits and to avoid building up large contingent liabilities. But it is counterproductive to insist on policies that have little, if any, effect on the probability of loan repayment. Even when a very strong case can be made for such policies, outsiders should limit their advocacy to setting out this case and should not try to force the governments of independent countries to adopt them against their will. The industrialised countries are themselves very far from adopting the *laissez-faire* policies that the IMF tried to force on Indonesia.

A refinement to the IMF's emergency lending proposals was made in December 1997, when the Supplemental Reserve Facility (SRF) was set up. This facility is intended to provide loans for balance of payments support that can be disbursed rapidly to countries that suffer sudden large speculative capital outflows. To provide borrowers with an incentive to repay as soon as a crisis is over, the interest rate rises if the loan has not been repaid after one year, and continues to rise over the next year and a half.

The delays and disputes over the disbursement of the IMF's loans to the Asian crisis countries led to two competing proposals for more fundamental reforms. The first proposal is that the IMF should lend against collateral, rather than conditions. The second is that it should negotiate conditions with potential borrowers in advance of crises. The first proposal was made by Feldstein (1998b), who advocated the creation of an IMF credit facility that would not insist on the kinds of detailed policy reforms that the IMF has traditionally demanded, but would instead set just one main condition, that the borrowing government must pledge future export receipts as collateral:

> A country that borrows from this facility would automatically trigger a legislated diversion of all export receipts to a foreign central bank like the Federal Reserve or the Bank of England, with exporters then paid in a mixture of foreign exchange and domestic currency. Any country that contemplates such collateralized borrowing at some future time must embody such an arrangement in both domestic legislation and international agreements well in advance (Feldstein, 1998b, p. A22).

This proposal has strong similarities to the condition in the US Treasury's loan to Mexico in 1995, which stipulated that the Mexican government had to assign future oil revenues to the US Treasury. The crucial difference is that in the Mexican case the assigned oil revenues already belonged to the Mexican government, whereas Feldstein proposes the assignment of private as well as government export revenues as collateral for loans to governments. To force private exporters to surrender their foreign exchange receipts, the government would have to impose exchange controls.[6] If a country accepted the conditions proposed by Feldstein, the incentives to invest in its export industries would be reduced because investors would know that in a crisis, they would risk receiving less than the open market price for the foreign exchange which they earn. In addition, the collateral against which exporters are able to borrow on their own account can only be made less secure if the government has announced that it will nationalise export receipts in the event of a crisis.

Williamson (1998) proposed the creation of an IMF facility to which countries could apply to have their economic policies endorsed in advance of any crisis, so that if one did occur the IMF would be able to disburse emergency loans to them much more quickly than would otherwise be possible. This idea built on earlier proposals from within the IMF and was adopted in April 1999, when the IMF announced an amendment to the SRF to create Contingent Credit Lines (CCL), available to approved countries to overcome balance of payments problems due to 'international financial contagion'.[7] Subsequently, amendments to this idea were proposed by two groups of US experts – one group was an independent task force sponsored by the Council on Foreign Relations (CFR, 1999); the other was the International Financial Institution Advisory Commission (IFIAC, 2000) set up by the US Congress.

To qualify for fast disbursing loans under the CCL initiative, countries must demonstrate to the IMF that their international reserves and external debts are satisfactory, that they have made arrangements to involve private creditors in combating a potential balance of payments crisis, that they are following sound fiscal and financial policies, and that they are conforming with various codes of best policy practice drawn up by the IMF and the Basle Committee on Banking Supervision.

The IMF adopted a Code of Good Practices on Fiscal Transparency in 1998 and an analogous code for transparency in monetary and financial policies in 1999. To improve the quality of publicly available economic and financial data, the IMF has established the Special and General Data Dissemination Standards.[8] The Basle Committee on Banking Supervision has drawn up a code of best practice for the prudential supervision of financial institutions – the Basle 'Core Principles'.[9] The fact that the criteria for CCL loans do not explicitly include free trade, competition policy, privatisation, capital account liberalisation, and the elimination of special tax or regulatory concessions for favoured business groups suggests that the IMF now accepts that attempts to insist on such policies can undermine the effectiveness of its crisis lending.

The IMF indicated that the amount of credit actually made available to a country in a crisis under the CCL would normally be between three and five times the amount of its IMF quota, but it could be more or less. The precise amount is not guaranteed in advance, but must be requested by the country and approved by the IMF when a crisis occurs. The CCL initiative will therefore not eliminate the need for negotiations between the IMF and approved borrowers should a crisis occur.

The CCL arrangements are open to the criticism that they will be available only to approved countries, and if the approval process has been done correctly, the approved borrowers should never experience crises. One response to this criticism is that even if no country ever borrowed under the CCL arrangements, they would have been useful if they had encouraged countries to improve their policies so as to gain approval. A second response is indicated by the fact that the IMF proposes to provide loans to approved countries that suffer attacks brought on by 'international financial contagion'. In everyday language, the CCL arrangements will be triggered when crises are blamed on irrational markets rather than on policies that the IMF has just approved. In more theoretical terms, the IMF's approval process could be rationalised as an attempt to ensure that a country's policies will not lead inevitably to a speculative attack, of the kind surveyed in section 5.2, but does not require that they be so sound as to rule out the possibility of a self-fulfilling crisis of the type surveyed in section 5.3.

Both the criticism and the suggested responses are partly correct: the CCL arrangements and the new codes of international best practice will probably help to improve national policy making and to speed up the negotiation and disbursement of IMF loans. But since many of the countries that are most likely to need last resort loans will not rapidly qualify for the CCL facility, delays in negotiating and disbursing loans are likely to remain a problem.

The IFIAC (2000) report was not unanimous, but the majority position was highly critical of the CCL arrangements. The main criticisms were embodied in the differences between the CCL arrangements and the IFIAC majority's own recommendations for crisis lending by the IMF. First, the majority recommended that IMF loans should only be for very short terms, for example, 120 days or less, with at most, one rollover of the loan. Second, it recommended that the interest rate on IMF loans should be above the yield on the borrower's sovereign bonds immediately before its application for IMF help. Third, it recommended that its scheme should be the only kind of lending that the IMF undertakes. Fourth, it recommended somewhat different eligibility criteria, including the requirements that potential borrowers would have to open their financial sectors fully to foreign entry and impose high minimum CARs. Subject to the specified eligibility criteria for membership of the scheme, IMF loans would be immediately available up to specified credit limits and would not be conditional on additional policy reforms.

The first and third of these conditions would mean that all IMF loans would have to be repaid in eight months or less. The majority argued that 'liquidity crises typically last for a matter of weeks or, in extreme cases, for several months.' However, if loans are not conditional on policy reforms, and if they must be repaid very rapidly, they might well be insufficient to restore market confidence in the borrower. The IFIAC report does not explain what is to prevent a continuation of capital outflows that would leave the borrower unable to repay the IMF loan in full within eight months.

In contrast, CFR (1999) recommended that the IMF should continue to use policy-conditional loans in cases in which crises are judged to be the fault of the country's own policies, but set up a new 'contagion facility' that would lend without imposing policy conditions to victims of contagion. Drawing this distinction would involve highly subjective judgements that would place the IMF in an invidious position, and when policy conditionality is deemed necessary the unresolved problems of possible delays in loan negotiation and disbursement would reappear.

CFR (1999) also recommended a large reduction in the scale of IMF lending except in crises that threaten the functioning of the international financial system or the performance of the global economy. The report sums this up as 'less can be more'. The reasons offered were 'that many emerging economies will not build the crisis prevention framework that is critical to greater resilience until they believe that they are more "on their own" in country crises and that smaller IMF loans are a necessary part of sending that message.' If these reasons are valid – and the next subsection argues that they may well be – they imply that the effects of IMF loans on increased risk-taking as a result of moral hazard in the long run exceed the crisis-alleviating effects of these loans in the short run. If so, no IMF lending at all would be even better than reduced IMF lending: 'nothing can be most'.

International Last Resort Lending and Moral Hazard

The availability of international last resort loans creates moral hazard in two ways: governments have incentives to hold lower international reserves and to pursue riskier policies than they otherwise would, and private lenders and borrowers have reduced incentives to avoid excessively risky projects. The second effect is widely acknowledged, but the first is often denied.[10] For example, in the context of the Mexican crisis of 1994–95, Williamson (1998) asks: 'what country would deliberately risk getting itself into a situation like that in which Mexico found itself because of a belief that this would entitle it to some bailout finance?'[11] Since Williamson argues that Mexico's policies in 1994–95 were not sustainable, it is not unreasonable to suggest that the expectation that a bailout would be available allowed and encouraged the government to continue pursuing these policies longer than it otherwise would have.

The argument that governments would not deliberately provoke crises in order to qualify for foreign assistance misses the point that moral hazard exists because someone protected by insurance does not bear the *full* cost of any loss, and therefore has a diminished incentive to take precautions to avoid loss. This can and generally does happen even though the purchaser of insurance shares in losses and therefore certainly does not have any incentive to provoke them deliberately. The fact that the IMF believes that it is necessary to impose conditions on the countries that it lends to shows that it believes that they might otherwise take the kinds of risk that can lead to financial and exchange rate crises. Such risks include protecting a weak financial sector from foreign competition, forcing banks to make soft loans to favoured borrowers, using money creation to finance budget deficits, building up large debts, sterilising balance of payments deficits and not holding enough foreign exchange reserves to be able to defend a supposedly fixed exchange rate.

As with domestic last resort lending, international last resort lending helps cure crises in the short run, but magnifies risk-taking in the longer run unless the moral hazard that it encourages can be tightly limited by effective prudential controls on the risks that borrowers can take. Whether international last resort lending by the IMF does more to cure than to create crises therefore depends on the effectiveness of its policy conditionality in preventing imprudent behaviour by governments and private borrowers and lenders.

Even if IMF lending has not increased the frequency and severity of crises, it is unlikely that it has had a large net effect on alleviating them. The reason is that last resort loans operate by increasing a country's effective foreign exchange reserves – which exceed its official reserves by the amount that it can be sure of being able to borrow in a crisis – and IMF lending has been quite small relative to the differences among countries in official reserve holdings. The $3 billion disbursed by the IMF to Thailand and the $6 billion disbursed to Indonesia in the first 10 months after the negotiation of each country's 1997 loan were small relative to the foreign exchange reserves which each held before the start of the crisis: in December 1996, Thailand's foreign exchange reserves, excluding gold, were $38 billion and Indonesia's were $18 billion. Even the amounts lent to Mexico and Korea are modest relative to the gaps between the reserves held by the principal borrowers from the IMF and those held by the most prudent countries: at the end of December 1996, Taiwan's reserves (excluding gold) were $88 billion, whereas Mexico's and Korea's were only $19 billion and $34 billion, respectively. Besides, the net effect of IMF lending on a country's effective reserves is smaller than the amount that it can expect to be able to borrow from the IMF because the availability of last resort loans reduces the country's incentive to hold high reserves of its own. The effect on raising the likelihood of avoiding currency and financial crises is further diminished (and may become perverse) because additions to effective reserves encourage governments to take greater risks than they otherwise would.

If it were quite certain that the IMF's international last resort lending really did diminish the likelihood of crises, and if its cost were small, there would be a case for greatly expanding its last resort lending. But since neither assumption holds, it is important to find other ways of strengthening financial systems. The main ones recommended throughout this study are, of course, higher minimum CARs for financial institutions, improved bankruptcy procedures and increased openness of financial sectors to foreign entry.

An Asian Monetary Fund?

In 1997, Japan raised the possibility of setting up an Asian Monetary Fund, which would have supplemented the IMF and presumably competed against it. This proposal was tentatively abandoned in 1997 in response to opposition from the US government and the IMF itself. However, Japanese dissatisfaction with the current Washington-based arrangements for international last resort loans, under which the austerity of loan conditions and the rate of disbursement seem to depend mainly on the borrower's importance to the USA, resulted in renewed interest in an Asian Monetary Fund. The idea is supported by Wade and Veneroso (1998) on the ground that the IMF's fiscal and interest rate policies for handling the Asian crisis were too restrictive.

In 1998, the Japanese Finance Minister, Mr Kiichi Miyazawa, announced a Japanese loan package for Asia of $30 billion, half in medium and long-term programmes and half in swap arrangements to meet short-term crisis needs. By May 1999, about $12 billion had been disbursed to Indonesia, Korea, Thailand, Malaysia and the Philippines. In February 1999, the Japanese government announced that a revised proposal for a $100 billion fund was being prepared and would be presented to the G–8 (that is, the G–7 plus Russia) meeting in Tokyo in 2000.[12] Subsequently, Japan abandoned this plan, at least temporarily.

Ultimately, decisions on the provision of international last resort loans will be driven more by competition among the major economic powers for influence in their chosen spheres than by a search for efficiency. However, on efficiency grounds alone, having two international last resort lenders would make no more sense than having two official domestic last resort lenders, or two domestic agencies for the prudential regulation and supervision of banks. Although problems inevitably arise when any debtor contracts debts to more than one creditor, they need not be insuperable if the debtor's reputation, or collateral, is sufficiently good, or if the penalties for default are sufficiently large. However, for a sovereign country to need a last resort loan, its reputation must already be in doubt, and in the case of international last resort loans, the penalties for default are very limited and the only collateral is the package of policy conditions imposed by the lender. If two lenders tried to impose policy conditions, the scope for delay and confusion would be even greater than it is at present.

9.2 OFFICIAL GUARANTEES FOR LOANS TO DEVELOPING COUNTRIES

The analogy between international last resort loans to governments and domestic last resort loans to banks prompts the question whether an international analogue to deposit insurance would be feasible. Soros (1997, 1998) has proposed such a mechanism. He recommends the creation of an International Credit Insurance Corporation (ICIC), which would work in tandem with the IMF and would guarantee international loans for 'a modest fee'. It would set a ceiling on the total amount of loans to each country that it was willing to insure. Borrowers in any particular country would not be barred from obtaining loans in excess of the limit for that country, but in the case of such non-guaranteed loans, 'creditors would have to beware'. All borrowing countries that belonged to the scheme would be required to report all borrowings to ICIC; this requirement would apply to private as well as to public borrowings and would also cover borrowings that were not guaranteed.

There are two main difficulties with Soros's proposal. The first is to decide how the total ICIC limit for each recipient country would be allocated among the potential domestic borrowers. Soros (1997) warns that: 'Special care must be taken not to give governments discretionary power over the allocation of credit, because that could foster corrupt dictatorships'. If the ICIC proposal is to have any effect, the 'modest fee' for its guarantees must be less than the price at which private loan guarantees can be purchased under existing market arrangements; but if limited amounts of loan guarantees are to be allocated at a subsidised price, no amount of special care will get round the fact that some agency and its officials must control the allocation process.

The second difficulty is that, like deposit insurance for domestic banks, the provision of subsidised loan guarantees would generate moral hazard and adverse selection. If the guarantee fee was uniform, the value of the guarantees would be highest if they were allocated to the riskiest projects. Allocating the guarantees by auction would therefore not be sensible, because they would be bought by the firms with the riskiest projects, thus maximising ICIC's expected losses. If the guarantees were allocated by government officials in each country, the probable losses to ICIC would again be very large.

Suppose that ICIC had been in existence before the Asian crisis, and that it had guaranteed half the foreign loans made to emerging Asian countries. Such guarantees might have prevented the crisis, but would more probably have delayed it, and perhaps even magnified its eventual size. In the case of Indonesia alone, foreign loans to private sector borrowers amounted to about $84 billion in 1998 and most of these loans are now non-performing.[13] If ICIC had guaranteed half these loans, it would now have to pay out a sum more than three times the size of the loan that the IMF actually provided to Indonesia. The IMF loan will presumably be repaid, and was subject to strict policy conditions. In contrast, ICIC would have provided guarantees, rather than loans, and its only means of recouping any part of its outlays would have been through a bankruptcy system that scarcely functions at all. Its position in each of the other emerging market countries hit by the crisis would have been only slightly better. Had ICIC been operating before the crisis, and had it guaranteed a substantial fraction of the loans made to the countries widely regarded as being economic miracles until 1997, the foreign banks that lent to these countries would be owed so much that ICIC would now be bankrupt, and the G–7 countries would have had to bail it out on a massive scale.

To limit its exposure to moral hazard, adverse selection and outright fraud, ICIC itself could allocate the guarantees in each country. If its guarantees covered a significant fraction of total international lending to developing countries, this would presumably involve making ICIC into a bureaucracy far bigger than the World Bank or the IMF. Even with its own massive bureaucracy of loan assessors, ICIC's losses – had it been operating before the Asian crisis – would probably exceed those incurred by foreign lenders to the Asian crisis countries: unlike the foreign lenders, whose losses have been at their own expense, ICIC's losses would be borne by taxpayers in the industrialised countries, not by the staff that it employed to allocate its guarantees.

Besides generating adverse selection problems of its own, the creation of ICIC would exacerbate the moral hazard problems associated with the inadequate bankruptcy procedures which, as argued in Chapter 6, have greatly contributed to the severity of the Asian crisis. If ICIC had been in existence before the Asian crisis, borrowers and lenders would now have even less incentive than they actually have to restructure loans. Rather than seek remedies from formal bankruptcy procedures, or out of court settlements of non-performing loans, lenders would simply demand that ICIC make good its loan guarantees.

9.3 INTERNATIONAL PROCEDURES FOR DEALING WITH SOVEREIGN DEFAULT

A thread which runs through all the reports of the various official working parties set up to investigate ways of reforming the international financial system is the desire of governments to make private sector lenders share in the cost of crises in emerging markets. One suggested way of achieving this is that the IMF should be able to condone the unilateral suspension of debt service payments by governments, so as to make it harder for creditors to take legal action against them. This proposal has been defended as a partial substitute, at the international level, for national bankruptcy laws, which can prevent one creditor seizing the assets of a debtor that has defaulted, if it is judged by the domestic bankruptcy court that seizure would be harmful to creditors as a group, because the debtor is potentially solvent.

The merits and defects of such proposals can be clarified by distinguishing between two possible motives for preventing creditors from taking legal action against a debtor that has unilaterally suspended contracted debt service payments. In the first case, the restriction on individual creditors is designed to help creditors as a group, by allowing the debtor to work its way out of a situation of temporary illiquidity, free from legal harassment by some individual creditors. In the second case, the restriction is designed to force all creditors to share in some unforeseen misfortune that has befallen the debtor. The role of a bankruptcy court is, or should be, limited to the first objective. The second is a form of insurance and those that want insurance should enter into explicit insurance contracts and pay for it.

Proposals designed to increase total repayments to all creditors – the first type – are referred to here as 'anti-creditor grab' proposals. The test of these proposals is whether they operate as intended and are not too expensive. Proposals that are designed to reduce total repayments – the second type – are referred to here as 'attempts to get free insurance'. Although such proposals have no merit, they have some similarities to a third type of proposal, which might sometimes be efficient: these are proposals designed to facilitate the purchase of insurance by governments of emerging market countries.

Collective Action Clauses

The report of an official working party on international responses to sovereign liquidity crises, Group of 10 (1996), henceforth the G–10 Report, recommended that the contracts used in bond issues by sovereign governments should be amended to include collective action clauses designed to facilitate bargaining between a group of creditors and a debtor unable, or unwilling, to repay in full.[14] To make it harder for a few bond holders to block proposals to reduce or restructure debts, when such proposals are acceptable to most others, the report proposed that bond contracts should explicitly provide for collective representation of creditors to permit majority action to change the terms of the contract and to compel all creditors to share in a proposed debt reduction or restructuring.

Collective action clauses in bond and syndicated bank loan contracts offer a possible partial substitute, at the international level, for the ability of national bankruptcy courts to impose collective solutions on recalcitrant creditors. In terms of the classification set out above, they are therefore potentially desirable attempts to prevent creditor grabs. However, if they pass the test of providing benefits in excess of their costs they will be adopted without the need for regulations that try to force borrowers and lenders to adopt them.

In April 1998, the Group of 22 countries (G–22) set up a working group to study ways to reduce the disruption caused by capital outflows in the event of a crisis.[15] This working group supported the G–10 Report's proposals for loan contracts that include collective action clauses. It recommended that the G–22 governments should examine the use of such clauses in their own loan contracts and engage in educational efforts to promote their use in bond issues by other governments and by organisations that borrow with government guarantees.[16] The working group also encouraged governments of emerging market countries to explore the use in loan contracts of clauses that would provide them with partial insurance by specifying that in certain clearly defined situations repayments are to be reduced, or new loans are to be provided. The working group suggested that collective action and insurance clauses might also play a useful role in debt instruments issued by private borrowers, but did not recommend that they be made mandatory (G–22, 1998a, p. 21).

Given its very cautious approach, the G–22 working group's proposals are sensible; but, as the group itself noted, they are certainly not a panacea for solving crises. It may well be that the complexity of the proposed contracts, the difficulties of enforcing them and the interest rate premia that would be demanded for providing insurance usually outweigh the potential benefits. The report's recommendation that borrowers 'consider' the use of such clauses is therefore more likely to lead to consideration than to implementation.

Sachs (1995) and Williamson (1998) have proposed that the IMF should perform some of the functions of a bankruptcy court with respect to governments that are in arrears on their debt service obligations. Sachs (1995) notes that a bankrupt US firm under court supervision may be able to attract new loans, because Chapter 11 of the US Bankruptcy Code allows courts, in certain circumstances, to assign administrative priority to the repayment of new loans ahead of existing loans. He proposes that, in certain circumstances, the IMF should be able to give formal approval to the suspension of debt service payments by a government and to assign administrative priority to the repayment of new debts ahead of existing ones. To extend the IMF's powers in this way would require the amendment of its Articles of Agreement.[17] If the IMF could grant priority to the repayment of new loans, the need for last resort lending by the IMF itself would be reduced, because governments in financial difficulties would be better placed to borrow from the international capital markets:

> Like a bankruptcy court, the IMF could supervise the extension of "administrative priority" for new private-market borrowing for a liquidity-strapped member government. For example, [it] would authorize that Mexico could borrow $20–30 billion of new funds on a priority basis vis-à-vis the pre-December 1994 debt. The IMF would impose traditional conditionalities on the priority borrowing, so that Mexico would not simply squander the new funds to the detriment of the pre-existing creditors (Sachs, 1995, p. 18).

Sachs's proposals for more formal international bankruptcy arrangements were considered and rejected by the G–10 Report (1996), which argued that it would not be feasible to create a formal mechanism for signalling the official community's approval of a suspension of debt service payments by a government, but instead recommended that the IMF should consider extending the circumstance in which it grants tacit approval of such unilateral actions by lending to a country that is continuing to accumulate arrears on its debts to private creditors.[18]

The background to this proposal is that the IMF used once to insist that governments clear their existing arrears to other creditors before it would lend to them. In the debt crisis in the 1980s, IMF loans were widely used to allow governments to maintain flows of debt service to commercial banks, thus allowing the banks to avoid having to classify the loans as non-performing. However, since the late 1980s, the IMF has sometimes lent to countries that have not cleared their arrears on repayments of commercial bank loans. The G–10 Report suggested that the IMF should also consider lending to a country that is in arrears to 'other groups of private creditors' – bond holders are the most obvious example – provided that it is making 'very strong' efforts to implement an IMF-approved adjustment programme and 'reasonable' efforts to negotiate with its creditors.[19] The Report did not suggest that the suspension of debt service payments to G–10 governments should be condoned, even in exceptional circumstances. It is argued here that the IMF should not use either formal or informal means to make it easier for governments to reduce contracted debt service payments. In principle, temporary protection of debtors from individual creditors can be justified as a way of raising aggregate repayment to all creditors, but the frequent references in official reports to 'burden sharing' by private lenders show that this is not the objective of these reports.

The G–10 Report offered three arguments for rejecting Sachs's proposal for formal international bankruptcy procedures: first, while the IMF can impose policy conditions on countries to which it lends, its powers are far weaker than those of a bankruptcy court, which can replace the management of a bankrupt firm (G–10, 1996, para. 26). Second, sovereign debtors generally have little need for protection against creditors because they 'have few assets located outside their own territories, and some of these benefit from sovereign immunity' (G–10, 1996, para. 91). Third, it would be difficult to obtain the agreement necessary to amend the IMF's articles. Since the first two arguments emphasise the relative impotence of the international community when confronted by a government that defaults on its contracted debt service payments, it is ironic that the G–10 working party should have recommended that the IMF consider extending the circumstances in which it lends to countries in arrears, thus further undermining attempts to penalise default.

Besides making it easier for contracts to be broken, either a formal or an informal mechanism for facilitating unilateral standstills on debt service payments would exacerbate moral hazard. This point is made by Cline (1998, pp. 18–20) who notes that the cases of Poland and Peru in the early 1990s demonstrate that countries that follow policies that are consistent with strict IMF conditions may also make aggressive demands for debt forgiveness.

The analogue at the national level of IMF lending to a government that forces private creditors to forgive part of their debts is central bank lending to the owners and managers of a bank that reneges on some of its contracted debts. Facilitating the unilateral reduction of contracted debt service payments is therefore inconsistent with the G–10 Report's first broad conclusion, that 'it is essential to maintain the basic principles that the terms and conditions of all debt contracts are to be met in full and that market discipline must be preserved'.[20] The report immediately qualifies this principle by stating that temporary suspension of debt payments may be unavoidable in exceptional circumstances; but, lending into arrears not only encourages temporary suspension, but also strengthens the ability of debtors to obtain permanent partial debt forgiveness. The G–10 Report implicitly acknowledge this by noting that the proposed IMF lending would 'improve the bargaining position of the debtor substantially' and 'signal to the unpaid creditors that their interests are best served by quickly reaching an agreement with the debtor'.[21]

The defect of the G–10 Report's proposal for IMF lending to countries that have not maintained contracted repayments is that it is an attempt to get ex post insurance for free, rather than to purchase it *ex ante*. Argentina, Indonesia and Mexico have purchased explicit insurance against unexpected capital outflows by negotiating contingent lines of credit from major international banks.[22] Under Argentina's Contingent Repurchase Facility the central bank can, at its own discretion, swap up to $6.2 billion of government securities for dollars with international banks. Private firms in developing countries can involve foreign lenders in the risks of the projects they undertake by issuing convertible bonds, preference shares, or ordinary shares.

In principle, bonds could also be used to provide insurance. For example, a new special category of 'insurance bonds', to be issued by governments of developing countries, might specify that debt service payments would be permanently reduced, or temporarily rescheduled, by specified amounts in specified circumstances involving adverse economic events for the debtor. The details would differ from issue to issue. The IMF, or some other agency, would be appointed in advance to decide whether the specified circumstances had occurred. Debt service reduction in the specified circumstances would not involve default, but would be like a pay-out by an insurance company to compensate for the occurrence of the event insured against, with the IMF as the judge of whether the event had occurred. The contract could even specify that the debtor would only have the right to reduce debt service payments if it accepted policy conditions to be specified by the IMF.

The interest rates charged on such 'insurance bonds' would obviously be higher than those on bonds without explicit insurance. Specifying the adverse events would be difficult, and judging whether they had occurred would be costly. It therefore seems entirely possible that the interest rate premia demanded by lenders would be higher than the amount that borrowers would be willing to pay. The main reason that these hypothetical contracts are discussed here is not to argue that they would do much, if anything, to help solve international financial crises; rather, it is to argue that they at least clearly dominate IMF-sanctioned partial default by debtor governments. If insurance bonds were created, the G–10 governments might suffer the embarrassment of finding that no countries would choose to pay the interest rate premia that lenders would demand as compensation for their additional risk. The more limited choice provided by the G–10 Report's actual proposal would avoid this possible embarrassment by forcing all developing country borrowers to be in the category that almost all would probably have avoided had they been given the choice.

CFR (1999) goes beyond even the G–10 Report: a large majority of the task force members argued that the IMF should make its crisis loans conditional on the borrowing country forcing private creditors to reschedule their debts. This is a euphemism for making IMF loans conditional on the borrower agreeing to default on its private debts. The report tries to have its cake and eat it too by adding the qualification that: 'The intent should not be to permanently affect creditors' rights but rather to provide a "breathing space" to bring more order into the negotiation process'. This qualification is disingenuous given that the stated aim of the proposal is 'to obtain better private-sector burden sharing'. The weakness in the CFR's logic is its failure to explain why it is desirable to insert what amount to *ex post* insurance clauses into loan contracts that have been freely entered into and that do not contain any insurance element. The CFR's implicit answer seems to be that interest rates on such loans often carry risk premia that reflect the probability of partial default. This amounts to arguing that because loan contracts are sometimes hard to enforce, governments or the IMF should further hinder efforts to enforce them.

9.4   THE TOBIN TAX

Tobin (1974, 1978, 1996) recommended that all countries, acting in concert, should impose a uniform turnover tax at a low rate on all spot conversions of one currency into another. Even though Tobin regrets having to tax trade in goods and services, he suggests that, to prevent evasion by disguising currency transactions by inserting a non-currency denominated asset or service into a currency transaction, it would also be necessary to apply the tax to all payments by a resident of one currency area for goods, services, real assets and equity securities supplied by a resident of another currency area.[23] Otherwise, the sale of sterling by B, for dollars supplied by A, could be disguised as the sale of oil by B, for dollars supplied by A and the sale of oil by A for sterling supplied by B. He suggested a rate of 1 per cent in the original and 1978 versions of his proposal, but in the 1996 version used an illustrative rate of 0.1 per cent on each purchase or sale of foreign currency, and thus 0.2 per cent of the principal amount on a round trip. The proposal has attracted both prominent supporters and prominent critics.[24]

Tobin (1996) states that two principal objectives of the tax are 'to make exchange rates reflect to a larger degree long-run fundamentals relative to short-range expectations and risks', and 'to preserve and promote autonomy of national macroeconomic and monetary policies'.[25] According to Tobin, his proposal would negligibly affect the incentives for commodity trade and long-term capital investments, but would penalise short-horizon round trips quite heavily: at the proposed rate of 0.1 per cent of the principal per transaction, the revenue from the tax on a round trip repeated every business day for a year would be roughly 50 per cent of the principal.

Macroeconomic and Monetary Autonomy

Unavoidable transactions costs, whose effects on financial markets are exactly analogous to those of the Tobin tax, already provide some scope for autonomous national macroeconomic and monetary policies in the very short run. The Tobin tax would very substantially increase the scope for deviations from covered interest parity on short-term securities with maturities of, say, a week to a month, but would only mildly increase the scope for such differentials to occur on securities with maturities of a year. Ignoring other transactions costs, a Tobin tax at 0.2 per cent per round trip would remove the incentives for arbitrageurs to intervene if deviations from covered interest parity on one-year securities were less than 0.2 percentage points per year; but for securities with a maturity of one week, deviations from covered interest parity could exceed 10 percentage points per year.[26]

The Tobin tax would therefore add substantially to the ability of a government with a fixed exchange rate to conduct independent monetary policy in the short run, but not in the long run. If governments wanted genuine monetary autonomy they would still have to adopt floating exchange rates.

Long-run Fundamentals Relative to Short-run Expectations and Risk

The most obvious weakness of the Tobin tax is that it would add only a negligible amount to the cost of borrowing to speculate against a weak currency. The interest rates observed during the Asian crisis clearly illustrate the force of this criticism. At the height of the speculative panic in Korea in 1997, offshore speculators wishing to short-sell the won had to pay swap premia that rose to 32 per cent on one-year contracts and to 55 per cent, at annualised rates, on three-month contracts.[27] The latter rate is equivalent to 11.6 per cent over three months. At the proposed rate of 0.2 per cent per round trip, the Tobin tax would have raised the premium on borrowing won for a year from 32 per cent to 32.2 per cent and the premium on borrowing won for three months from 11.6 per cent to 11.8 per cent over the three-month life of the contract. At the height of the Thai crisis in June 1997, offshore speculators had to pay a premium for three-month baht borrowing of 60.5 per cent per year, that is, 12.6 per cent over three months.[28] The Tobin tax would have raised this cost from 12.6 per cent to 12.8 per cent. The addition that the Tobin tax would have made to the cost of speculating during these crises is utterly trivial compared to the day-to-day variations in these interest differentials.

Another powerful and frequently made criticism of Tobin's proposal is that transactions costs in foreign exchange markets (and stock markets) in developing countries are large and have exactly the same effects as a tax on transactions would have. Since volatility remains high, despite these transactions costs, there is no reason to expect that it would be reduced much, if at all, by the imposition of additional transactions costs in the form of a Tobin tax. The tax would however inhibit the efficient division of activities among specialist financial intermediaries because, like any cascading turnover tax, its burden could be reduced by vertically integrating firms which trade with each other.

Even if reducing speculation were desirable, the fundamental defect of the Tobin tax as a way of trying to do this is that it is not a tax on speculation *per se*, but just a cascading turnover tax on all foreign exchange transactions. This is demonstrated by the fact that some forms of speculation would entirely escape it. If a devaluation of the domestic currency is expected, exporters have an incentive to delay converting export receipts into domestic currency; domestic investors planning to draw down foreign loans have an incentive to delay converting loan proceeds into domestic currency; importers have an incentive to bring forward their payments; and those investing abroad have an incentive to obtain the necessary foreign exchange as early as possible. All such leads and lags in foreign payments deplete the reserves of a central bank trying to defend its currency against a speculative attack, but none of these forms of speculation would increase liabilities for the Tobin tax.

Tobin states (1996, p. xii) that 80 per cent of foreign exchange transactions involve round trips of seven days or less, and most occur within one day. He seems to take it for granted that transactions that involve round trips completed within a very short period mainly involve speculation, and cites anecdotal evidence that active traders in foreign exchange markets regard the long run as being 'the next ten minutes'. In fact, speculative attacks on currencies often involve transactions with time horizons of several months. For example, Soros (1998, p. 136) states that when his funds short-sold the Thai baht and Malaysian ringgit in early 1997, they operated in maturities ranging from six months to a year. This is hardly surprising since even the cleverest and most powerful speculator could scarcely hope to predict (or trigger) the timing of a devaluation to within one day, let alone ten minutes. In contrast, arbitrage opportunities in the most highly organised and efficient financial markets may well last only for a matter of minutes.

The empirical evidence from securities markets suggests that transactions taxes actually raise the volatility of share prices rather than lower it. This is the conclusion of Aitken and Swan (1998) who study the effects on price volatility of the halving of the security transactions tax in Australia in May 1995 from 0.6 per cent to 0.3 per cent per round trip. Their measure of daily price volatility is the standard deviation of trade-to-trade price changes on the given day. If transactions taxes reduce volatility, as assumed by Tobin, halving the tax should have raised the standard deviation of Australian share price changes. In fact, Aitken and Swan's econometric point estimates imply that it contributed to a reduction in the standard deviation by 13 per cent in the short run and by 26 per cent in the long run.[29]

Lindgren (1994) studied the cross-country relationship between transactions taxes and stock market volatility. Using quarterly data for 14 stock markets over 11 years, he also found a significant *positive* effect of transactions taxes on volatility within the group of countries that impose transactions taxes of between 0.50 per cent and 2 per cent. This is also the opposite of the effect assumed by Tobin. At lower tax rates, Lindgren found no relationship, either positive or negative, between volatility and the tax rate. He also found no significant relationship if he tried to estimate a linear relationship between volatility and the tax rate for all the countries in his sample.

The empirical findings which suggest that transactions taxes raise price volatility, rather than lower it, are not particularly surprising: first, speculation may usually be stabilising, as argued by Friedman (1953); second, transactions taxes do not directly tax speculation, but do reduce investor liquidity and discourage the efficient sharing of risks by raising bid-ask spreads.

Besides all its other weaknesses, the Tobin tax would be very hard to administer. If it were applied simply to exchanges of one currency for another, speculators could avoid it almost completely by using NDF forward and swap contracts, since, as explained in Chapter 2, the only foreign currency actually exchanged under these contracts is the amount needed to net out the difference between the forward rate in the contract and the spot rate on the day the contract matures. If only these net differences were taxed, the effects on large-scale speculation would be utterly trivial. In the case of simple derivative contracts, it would be possible to overcome this type of avoidance by estimating and taxing the 'notional' amounts that would have been exchanged under the equivalent underlying direct transactions. Drafting the legislation to deduce these notional amounts for complicated packages of contracts that combine swaps, forward transactions, borrowing, lending and options would appear to be very difficult, if not impossible. To avoid creating loopholes that could be exploited by conducting some parts of a package of interrelated contracts in one country and the rest in another, the legislation would have to be written and interpreted consistently in all.

9.5 OVERVIEW

The provision of international last resort loans by the IMF (section 9.1) and the guaranteeing of developing country debts by an international agency (section 9.2) are closely analogous to the two main safety nets that national governments provide for commercial banks: domestic last resort loans and deposit insurance. Chapter 6 reached pessimistic conclusions about the usefulness of bank safety nets, but argued that their worst abuses can be discouraged by setting high capital adequacy ratios. The grounds for pessimism are multiplied when the guaranteed institution is a developing country government rather than a domestic bank: the ultimate sanction of a national government over a domestic bank – to replace the management, take over its debts, and take away its licence – is not available to the IMF and the G–10. Similarly, the 'equity' of a national government, defined as the excess, over its debts, of the value of the physical resources that it controls and its ability to levy taxes, cannot provide a secure buffer to its creditors and guarantors because few if any of its assets can be seized if it defaults on its debts.

It was argued in Chapter 6 that high capital adequacy requirements offer the only good prospect of controlling the moral hazard created by national safety nets for banks. Trying to design effective international safety nets is like trying to design national safety nets without being able to use capital adequacy requirements to control moral hazard.

The codes of best practice that the IMF is encouraging national governments to adopt resemble the prudential regulations used by domestic last resort lenders and deposit insurance agencies as protection against moral hazard. These codes will probably help many countries to improve policy making but, being voluntary, they will be even weaker than domestic prudential regulations on banks, which are often ineffective, despite being backed by legal sanctions.

International last resort lending resembles domestic last resort lending in that it alleviates today's crisis at the cost of building up problems for the future. Judging whether the IMF's last resort lending has a beneficial or harmful long-run influence on global financial stability is inevitably a matter of opinion and conjecture. It was suggested in section 9.1 that the IMF's last resort lending probably does not make much difference to the rate at which financial and exchange rate crises occur: the availability of last resort loans makes effective foreign exchange reserves larger than official reserves by the amount of the loans expected to be available. But IMF lending is on too small a scale to make much difference to the disparities between the effective reserves of the most and the least prudent countries. IMF loans helped solve the Mexican and Asian crises once they had begun, but the knowledge that IMF loans would be available probably encouraged Mexico, Thailand and Korea to continue to try to prop up weak banks and to sterilise balance of payments deficits for longer than would otherwise have been the case. The costs of delay will be largely met by taxpayers in these countries over many years to come.[30]

If outsiders share in the risks of financial crises in developing countries, they are providing them with a form of insurance. The apparent wish of governments, officials and experts to make the private sector lenders in industrialised countries share in these costs is sensible only to the extent that they are proposing that the private firms that would provide this insurance would explicitly contract to provide it and be appropriately paid for doing so.

The official proposals for 'involving the private sector' face a dilemma: if, like G–10 (1996) and CFR (1999), they seek to force private sector lenders to provide disaster insurance without being paid for doing so, the result is likely to be evasion, inefficiency and reduced lending, but very little free insurance. But if, like G–22 (1998a) and IMF (1999), they merely recommend that borrowers and lenders 'consider' types of loan contract that they can already consider, they will amount to little.

Soros's proposed agency to guarantee international loans, ICIC, would have strong similarities to deposit insurance since they are both forms of loan guarantee. In the USA, the FDIC and the Federal Savings and Loan Insurance Corporation set the premia for deposit insurance which banks are legally obliged to pay, and their exposure to moral hazard is limited both by legally binding prudential regulations on insured institutions and by the existence of a sophisticated bankruptcy system. Even so, taxpayers had to pay for the bail-out that was needed to resolve the S&L debacle. ICIC is not a viable proposal because it lacks all the safeguards that are needed to keep losses to official deposit insurers within reasonable bounds. It would have no safeguards to take the place of prudential regulations and would probably become a black hole that would absorb whatever resources the governments of the industrialised countries were willing to pour down it. If it tried to charge fees high enough to cover these foreseeable costs, it would find it had few, if any, clients.

Viewed as a tax on destabilising speculation, the Tobin tax has three major defects, any one of which alone would destroy the case for it. First, empirical evidence suggests that, far from reducing price volatility in the markets to which they are applied, transactions taxes raise it. This result is not especially surprising since transactions taxes are cascading turnover taxes, not taxes on speculation. Second, at the proposed rate of 0.1 per cent per transaction and 0.2 per cent per round trip, the tax would have negligible effects on the costs that speculators already face when they borrow in currencies that are expected to depreciate. Third, it would be very hard to administer.

The pessimistic conclusions of this chapter reinforce the case, argued in Chapter 6, for strengthening financial systems by at least doubling the minimum required capital adequacy ratios of insured financial institutions, by making national bankruptcy procedures effective and by opening the domestic financial sectors of developing countries to free entry by international banks.

NOTES

1. Feldstein (1998a, 1998b) criticised the IMF's handling of the Asian crisis on the grounds that it imposed excessively contractionary monetary and fiscal policies, undermined the confidence of global investors and unnecessarily usurped the sovereignty of debtor countries.
2. Kindleberger (1989, p. 222).
3. IMF (2000a).
4. See IMF (1998a, b) and IMF (2000b).
5. See Nellor (1998, pp. 246–9).
6. This criticism of Feldstein's proposal is made by Dorrance (1998).
7. IMF Press Release no. 99/14, 25 April 1999.
8. In April 1999, 47 countries belonged to the IMF's Special Data Dissemination Standard, which is designed for countries seeking to borrow from international capital markets and requires the provision of detailed data on foreign exchange reserves and external liabilities, as well as on the real sector, the financial sector and the fiscal situation. These countries can gradually phase in their compliance with the designated standards over several years. The General Data Dissemination Standard is intended to improve the quality of the economic and financial data provided by all members of the IMF.

9.   Basle Committee on Banking Supervision (1997).
10. See, for example, Camdessus (1995).
11. Williamson (1998, note 2, p. 195).
12. *Australian Financial Review*, 12 February 1999.
13. Bank Indonesia (2000).
14. Group of 10 (1996, paras. 53–65). This report is often referred to as the 'Rey Report', after the chairman of the working party that wrote it.
15. The report of this working group is Group of 22 (1998a). The G–22 set up two other working groups at the same time. One studied ways to improve the transparency and accountability of governments and financial institutions; the second studied proposals for tighter prudential controls, deposit insurance and rules for the resolution of the debts of insolvent banks and finance companies. Summaries of all three reports are given in G–22 (1998b).
16. Group of 22 (1998a, pp. 19–21).
17. Sachs suggested that it might already be possible for the IMF to achieve much the same outcome using its existing powers: under Article VIII 2(b) it can approve exchange restrictions that are then not subject to court challenge in the member countries. 'It is possible that priority lending, debt restructurings, and debt standstills could be designed as forms of exchange control, that would then be given legal protection against challenges by disgruntled creditors' (Sachs, 1995, p. 19). However, the Group of 10 (1996, para. 89) argued that this Article 'could not easily be construed as covering the case in which a sovereign debtor interrupts its own payments'. Without either supporting or opposing the proposal, IMF (1999, pp. 21–2) mentions the possibility of amending this article to allow the IMF to sanction a temporary stay on litigation by creditors, that would not permanently affect their rights.
18. Group of 10 (1996, Executive Summary, para. 9).
19. Group of 10 (1996, Executive Summary, para. 9 and main report, paras. 92–5).
20. Group of 10 (1996, Executive Summary, para. 2).
21. Group of 10 (1996, para. 94).
22. IMF (1999, pp. 10–12, 32–5).
23. Tobin (1978, pp. 155, 158–9).
24. Summers and Summers (1989) are cautious supporters. Those who argue that the Tobin tax would be ineffective include Garber and Taylor (1995), Eichengreen (1999) and Dornbusch (1998).
25. Tobin (1996, pp. xii, xiii).
26. Suppose that the annualised interest rates on one-week US dollar and Hong Kong dollar securities were 5 per cent and 15 per cent, respectively, but that the forward premium on the US dollar was zero, so that there was a divergence of 10 percentage points from covered interest parity. If the rate of the Tobin tax is 20 cents per $100 on a round trip, it would just exceed the gross of tax arbitrage profit of 19 cents, that is, ($15 – $5)/52, per $100 per week from borrowing at 5 per cent per year to lend at 15 per cent per year.
27. Data on the offshore swap premia for the dollar relative to the won were supplied by the BOK and by a private bank.
28. As reported in note 8 of Chapter 2, the offshore implied yield on three-month baht on 18 June 1997 was 69.8 per cent. Since the three-month LIBOR was then 5.8 per cent, the swap premium on the dollar, relative to the baht, was 60.5 per cent per year, or 12.6 per cent per quarter.
29   The actual reduction was only 3 per cent. According to Aitken and Swan's estimates, the difference arose because changes in other exogenous variables partially offset the effects of the halving of the transactions tax. These other variables are the term structure of interest rates, the volume of trading on the New York Stock Exchange, changes in the Dow Jones index and changes in the bank bill rate.
30. Calomiris (1998).

References

Adams, Charles, Donald J. Mathieson, Garry Schinasi and Bankim Chadha (1998). *International Capital Markets: Developments, Prospects, and Key Policy Issues*, Washington, DC: International Monetary Fund.

Aitken Michael J. and Peter L. Swan (1998). 'The Impact of a Transactions Tax on Security Market Traders: The Case of Australia's Tax Reduction', *Working Paper*, Department of Finance, University of Sydney, Australia.

Aizenman, Joshua (1989). 'Country Risk, Incomplete Information and Taxes on International Borrowing', *Economic Journal*, **99**, (March), 147–61.

Applegate, Craig (1999). 'How Much Can the Eurobond Market Teach Us About Whether Or Not Australia and the South-East Asian Countries Have Excessive Levels of Foreign Debt?', Paper presented at the *28th Annual Conference of Economists*, La Trobe University, Australia.

Arndt, Heinz W. (1974). 'Survey of Recent Developments', *Bulletin of Indonesian Economic Studies*, **10**, (2) (July), 1–34.

Bagehot, Walter (1866). 'One Banking Reserve or Many?', *The Economist*, **24**, (1 September), 1025–6.

Bagehot, Walter (1873; new edn 1920). *Lombard Street: A Description of the Money Market*, London: Murray.

Balassa, Bela (1964). 'The Purchasing Power Doctrine: A Reappraisal', *Journal of Political Economy*, **72**, 584–96.

Baliño, Tomás J.T. and Charles Enoch (1997). 'Currency Board Arrangements: Issues, Experiences, and Implications for IMF-Supported Programs', *IMF Occasional Paper 151*, Washington, DC: International Monetary Fund.

Banerjee, Abhijit V. (1992). 'A Simple Model of Herd Behavior', *Quarterly Journal of Economics*, **CVII**, (3) (August), 797–817.

Bank Indonesia (1975). *Report for the Financial Year 1974/1975*, Jakarta: Bank Indonesia.

Bank Indonesia (1997). *Weekly Report*, (no. 2000) (23 December), Jakarta: Bank Indonesia.

Bank Indonesia (1999a). *Report for the Financial Year 1998/99*, Jakarta: Bank Indonesia.

Bank Indonesia (1999b). *Indonesian Financial Statistics*, **32**, (12) (December), Jakarta: Bank Indonesia.

Bank Indonesia (2000). 'Indonesia's Recent Economic and Monetary Development', *Mimeo*, Jakarta: Economic Research and Monetary Policy Department, Bank Indonesia.

Bank Negara Malaysia (1994). *Exchange Control Notices*, Kuala Lumpur: Bank Negara Malaysia.

Bank Negara Malaysia (1998a). 'Measures to Regain Monetary Independence', Press Release, 1 September, Kuala Lumpur: Bank Negara Malaysia.

Bank Negara Malaysia (1998b). *Annual Report*, Kuala Lumpur: Bank Negara Malaysia.

Bank of Thailand (1996). *Annual Economic Report 1996*, Bangkok: Bank of Thailand.

Bartolini, Leonardo and Allan Drazen (1997). 'Capital-account Liberalization as a Signal', *American Economic Review*, **87**, (1) (March), 138–54.

Basle Committee on Banking Supervision (1997). *Core Principles for Effective Banking Supervision*, online at: http://www.bis.org.

Basle Committee on Banking Supervision (1999). *A New Capital Adequacy Framework*, Basle: Bank for International Settlemements.

Benge, Matthew (1999). 'Notes on Applied Tax Policy: International Taxation', *Mimeo*, Canberra: Australian National University.

Benston, George J. and George G. Kaufman (1993). 'Deposit Insurance Reform: A Functional Approach. A Comment', *Carnegie-Rochester Conference Series on Public Policy*, **38**, 41–50.

Benston, George J. and George G. Kaufman (1997). 'FDICIA After 5 Years', *Journal of Economic Perspectives*, **11**, (3) (summer), 139–58.

Benston, George J., Robert A. Eisenbeis, Paul M. Horvitz, Edward J. Kane, and George G. Kaufman (1986). *Perspectives on Safe & Sound Banking. Past, Present, and Future*, Cambridge, MA and London: Massachusetts Institute of Technology Press.

Berg, Andrew and Catherine Pattillo (1998). 'Are Currency Crises Predictable? A Test', *Working Paper 98/154*, Washington, DC: International Monetary Fund.

Berger, Allen N., Richard J. Herring and Giorgio P. Szegö (1995). 'The Role of Capital in Financial Institutions', *Journal of Banking and Finance*, **19**, 393–430.

Bhagwati, Jagdish (1985). 'Investing Abroad', Esmée Fairbairn Lecture, University of Lancaster, UK.

Bhagwati, Jagdish (1998). 'The Capital Myth: The Difference between Trade in Widgets and Dollars', *Foreign Affairs*, **77**, (3), 7–11.

Brash, Donald T. (1997). 'Banking Soundness and the Role of the Market', Chapter 16, pp. 355–68 in Enoch and Green (eds.) (1997).

Brecher, Richard and Carlos Díaz-Alejandro (1977). 'Tariffs, Foreign Capital and Immiserizing Growth', *Journal of International Economics*, **7**, (November), 317–22.

Browne, Christopher (1997). 'Comment', pp. 349–52 in Enoch and Green (eds) (1997).

Bruce, Neil (1992). 'A Note on the Taxation of International Capital Income Flows', *Economic Record*, **68**, (202) (September), 217–21.

Cagan, Phillip (1956). 'The Monetary Dynamics of Hyperinflation', Chapter II, pp. 25–117 in Milton Friedman (ed.), *Studies in the Quantity Theory of Money*, Chicago and London: Chicago University Press.

Cairncross, Alec K. (1973). *Control of Long-term International Capital Movements*, Washington, DC: The Brookings Institution.

Calomiris, Charles W. (1998). 'The IMF's Imprudent Role as Lender of Last Resort', *Cato Journal*, **17**, (3) (winter), 275–94.

Calvo, Guillermo A. (1991). 'The Perils of Stabilization', *IMF Staff Papers*, **38**, (4) (December), 921–6.

Calvo, Guillermo (1996), 'Commentary to Part II', pp. 66–7 in Hausmann and Rojas-Suárez (eds) (1996).

Calvo, Guillermo A., L. Leiderman and C.M. Reinhart (1993). 'Capital Inflows and Real Exchange Rate Appreciation in Latin America: The Role of External Factors', *IMF Staff Papers*, **40**, (1) (March), 108–51.

Calvo, Sara and Carmen M. Reinhart (1996). 'Capital Flows to Latin America: Is There Evidence of Contagion Effects?', Chapter 5, pp. 151–71 in Guillermo Calvo, Morris Goldstein and Eduard Hochreiter (eds), *Private Capital Flows to Emerging Markets After the Mexican Crisis*, Washington, DC: Institute for International Economics and Vienna: Austrian National Bank.

Camdessus, Michel (1995). Address at the Zurich Economic Society, Zurich, Switzerland, (14 November).

Caprio, Gerard, Michael Dooley, Danny Leipziger and Carl Walsh (1996). 'The Lender of Last Resort Function Under a Currency Board: The Case of Argentina', *Open Economies Review*, **7**, (July), 617–42.

Casserley, Dominic and Gregg Gibb (1999). *Banking in Asia: The End of Entitlement*, Singapore: John Wiley and Sons (Asia).

CFR (Council on Foreign Relations) (1999). *Safeguarding Prosperity in a Global Financial System: The Future International Financial Architecture. Report of an Independent Task Force*, on line at http://www.foreignrelations.org

Cheng, Leonard K., Yum K. Kwan and Francis T. Liu (1999). 'An Alternative Approach to Defend the Hong Kong Dollar', Paper presented at the *American Economic Association and American Finance Association Meetings*, 3–5 January, New York.

Chiu, Paul C.H. (1999). 'Financial Policy Responses to the Asian Financial Turmoil and Future Reform of the ROC', Paper presented at the *7th Pacific Basin Rim Conference on Finance, Economics and Accounting*, Taipei, 28–29 May.

Claessens, Stijn, Michael P. Dooley and Andrew Warner (1995) 'Portfolio Capital Flows: Hot or Cool?', *World Bank Economic Review*, **9**, (January), 131–51.

Cline, William R. (1998). 'Crisis Management in Emerging Capital Markets', pp. 18–20 in Fischer *et al.* (1998).

Cole, David C. (1995). 'Financial Sector Development in Southeast Asia', Chapter 5, pp. 223–60 in Shadid N. Zahid (ed.), *Financial Sector Development in Asia*, Oxford and New York: Oxford University Press.

Cole, David C. and Betty F. Slade (1996). *Building a Modern Financial System: The Indonesian Experience*, Cambridge: Cambridge University Press.

Cooper, Richard N. (1998). 'Should Capital Account Convertibility be a World Objective?', pp. 11–19 in Fischer *et al.* (1998).

Corden, W. Max (1984). 'Booming Sector and Dutch Disease Economics: Survey and Consolidation', *Oxford Economic Papers*, **36**, (3) (November), 359–80.

Corden, W. Max and J. Peter Neary (1982). 'Booming Sector and De-industrialisation in a Small Open Economy', *Economic Journal*, **92**, (368) (December), 825–48.

Cukierman, Alex (1992). *Central Bank Strategy, Credibility, and Independence: Theory and Evidence*. Cambridge, MA and London: The MIT Press.

Cukierman, Alex, Pantelis Kalaitzidakis, Lawrence H. Summers and Steven B. Webb (1993). 'Central Bank Independence, Growth Investment and Real Rates', pp. 95–140 in Allan H. Meltzer and Charles I. Plosser (eds), *Carnegie-Rochester Conference Series on Public Policy*, **39**, (December), Amsterdam: North-Holland.

de Krivoy, Ruth (1996). 'Crisis Avoidance', pp. 171–92 in Hausmann and Rojas-Suárez (eds) (1996).

de Vries, Margaret G. (1969a). 'Progress Towards Liberalization', Chapter 12, pp. 249–79 in Horsefield (ed.) (1969, Vol. II).

de Vries, Margaret G. (1969b). 'A Convertible Currency World', Chapter 13, pp. 280–96 in Horsefield (ed.) (1969, Vol. II).

Diamond, Douglas W. and Philip H. Dybvig (1983). 'Bank Runs, Deposit Insurance, and Liquidity', *Journal of Political Economy*, **91**, (June), 401–19.

Díaz-Alejandro, Carlos (1985). 'Good-Bye Financial Repression, Hello Financial Crisis', *Journal of Development Economics*, **19**, 1–24.

Djiwandono, J. Soedradjad (1997). 'The Banking Sector in an Emerging Market: The Case of Indonesia', Chapter 15, pp. 335–48 in Enoch and Green (eds) (1997).

Dooley, Michael P. (1995a). 'A Retrospective on the Debt Crisis', Chapter 7, pp. 262–87 in Peter B. Kenen (ed.), *Understanding Interdependence: The Macroeconomics of the Open Economy*, Princeton, NJ: Princeton University Press.

Dooley, Michael P. (1995b). 'Capital Mobility and Economic Policy', Chapter 10, pp. 247–63 in Sebastian Edwards (ed.), *Capital Controls, Exchange Rates, and Monetary Policy in the World Economy*, Cambridge: Cambridge University Press.

Dooley, Michael P. (1996) 'A Survey of Literature on Controls over International Capital Transactions', *IMF Staff Papers*, **43**, (4) (December), 639–87.

Dornbusch, Rudiger (1998). 'Capital Controls: An Idea Whose Time Is Past', pp. 20–7 in Fischer *et al.* (1998).

Dorrance, Graham (1998). *Australian Financial Review*, (14 October).

Drazen, Allan (1989). 'Monetary Policy, Capital Controls, and Seigniorage in an Open Economy', in Marcello De Cecco and Alberto Giovanni (eds), *A European Central Bank? Perspectives on Monetary Unification After Ten Years*, Cambridge: Cambridge University Press.

Edwards, Sebastian (1984). 'The Order of Liberalization of the External Sector in Developing Countries', *Essays in International Finance no.156*, Princeton, NJ: International Finance Section, Princeton University.

Edwards, Sebastian (1987). 'Sequencing Economic Liberalization in Developing Countries', *Financial Development*, **24**, (1) (March), 26–9.

Edwards, Sebastian (1989). *Real Exchange Rates, Devaluation, and Adjustment. Exchange Rate Policy in Developing Countries*, Cambridge, MA: The MIT Press.

Edwards, Sebastian (1998). 'Capital Flows, Real Exchange Rates, and Capital Controls: Some Latin American Experiences', *Working Paper 6800*, Cambridge, MA: National Bureau of Economic Research.

Edwards, Sebastian and Alejandra Cox Edwards (1991). *Monetarism and Economic Liberalization: The Chilean Experiment*, Chicago: University of Chicago Press.

Eichengreen, Barry (1999). *Towards a New International Financial Architecture: A Practical Post-Asia Agenda*, Washington, DC: Institute for International Economics.

Eichengreen, Barry, Andrew Rose and Charles Wyplosz (1995). 'Exchange Market Mayhem: The Antecedents and Aftermath of Speculative Attacks', *Economic Policy*, **21**, (October), 249–312.

Eichengreen, Barry, Andrew Rose and Charles Wyplosz (1996). 'Contagious Currency Crises: First Tests', *Scandinavian Journal of Economics*, **98**, (4), 463–84.

Enoch, Charles and John H. Green (eds) (1997). *Banking Soundness and Monetary Policy: Issues and Experiences in the Global Economy*, Washington, DC: International Monetary Fund.

Enoch, Charles and Ann-Marie Gulde (1997). 'Making a Currency Board Operational', *IMF Paper on Policy Analysis and Assessment PPAA/97/10*, Washington, DC: International Monetary Fund.

Fane, George and Ross H. McLeod (1999). 'Lessons for Monetary and Banking Policies from the 1997–98 Economic Crises in Indonesia and Thailand', *Journal of Asian Economics*, **10**, (3), 395–413.

Fane, George and John Nash (1998). 'Georgia's Economic Collapse, 1991–1994: The Role of State Orders and Inflation', *Policy Reform*, **2**, 247–67.

FDIC (Federal Deposit Insurance Corporation) (1999). *Memorandum to the Board of Directors on Bank Insurance Fund Assessment Rates for the Second Semiannual Assessment Period of 1999*, on line at: http://www.fdic.gov.

Feldstein, Martin S. (1998a). 'Refocusing the IMF', *Foreign Affairs*, **77**, (2) (March/April), 20–33.

Feldstein, Martin S. (1998b). 'Reforming the International Monetary Fund: Focus on Crisis Management', *The Wall Street Journal*, 6 October.

Ffrench-Davis, Ricardo (1981). 'Exchange Rate Policies in Chile: The Experience with the Crawling Peg', pp. 152–74 in John Williamson (ed.), *Exchange Rate Rules*, New York: St. Martin's Press.

Fischer, Stanley (1982). 'Seigniorage and the Case for a National Money', *Journal of Political Economy*, **90**, (April), 295–313.

Fischer, Stanley (1998). 'Capital-Account Liberalization and the Role of the IMF', pp. 1–10 in Fischer *et al.* (1998).

Fischer, Stanley (1999). 'On the Need for an International Lender of Last Resort', Revised version of paper presented at the *American Economic Association and American Finance Association Meetings*, 3–5 January, New York, online at: http://www.imf.org/external/np/speeches/ 1999/010399.htm.

Fischer, Stanley, Richard N. Cooper, Rudiger Dornbusch, Peter M. Garber, Carlos Massad, Jacques J. Polak, Dani Rodrik and Savak S. Tarapore (1998). 'Should the IMF Pursue Capital-account Convertibility?', *Essays in International Finance no. 207*, Princeton, New Jersey: International Finance Section, Princeton University.

Flannery, Mark J. (1994). 'Debt Maturity and the Deadweight Cost of Leverage: Optimally Financing Banking Firms', *American Economic Review*, **84**, (1), 320–31.

Flood, Robert P. and Peter Garber (1984). 'Gold Monetization and Gold Discipline', *Journal of Political Economy*, **92**, (1) (February), 90–107.

Flood, Robert P. and Nancy P. Marion (1998). 'Perspectives on the Recent Currency Crisis Literature', *IMF Working Paper* 98/130, Washington, DC: International Monetary Fund.

Folkerts-Landau, David F.L. (1985). 'The Changing Role of International Bank Lending in Development Finance', *IMF Staff Papers*, **32**, (June), 317–63.

Folkerts-Landau, David F.L. (1996). 'Comment', pp. 103–5 in Hausmann and Rojas-Suárez (eds) (1996).

Folkerts-Landau, David, Takatoshi Ito *et al.* (1995). *International Capital Markets: Developments, Prospects, and Policy Issues*, Washington, DC: International Monetary Fund.

Frankel, Jeffrey A. and Andrew K. Rose (1996). 'Currency Crashes in Emerging Markets: An Empirical Treatment', *Journal of International Economics*, **41**, 351–66.

Friedman, Milton (1953). 'The Case for Flexible Exchange Rates', pp.157–203 in *Essays in Positive Economics*, Chicago: University of Chicago Press.

Friedman, Milton (1960). *A Program For Monetary Stability*, New York: Fordham University Press.

Garber, Peter and Mark P. Taylor (1995). 'Sand in the Wheels of International Finance: A Sceptical Note', *Economic Journal*, **105**, (January), 173–80.

Gavin, Michael and Ricardo Hausmann (1996). 'The Roots of Banking Crises: The Macroeconomic Context', pp. 27–63 in Hausmann and Rojas-Suárez (eds) (1996).

Goldstein, Morris (1998), *The Asian Financial Crisis: Causes, Cures, and Systemic Implications*, Institute for International Economics, Washington, DC.

Goldstein, Morris and John Hawkins (1998). 'The Origins of the Asian Financial Turmoil', *Reserve Bank of Australia Discussion Paper 980*, Sydney: Reserve Bank of Australia (May).

Goldstein, Morris and Philip Turner (1996). *Banking Crises in Emerging Economies: Origins and Policy Options*, BIS Economics Papers no. 46, Basle: Bank for International Settlements.

Greenspan, Alan (1998). 'Understanding Today's International Financial System', Remarks Before the *34th Annual Conference on Bank Structure and Competition of the Federal Reserve Bank of Chicago*, 7 May, online at: http://www.bog.frb.fed.us/boarddocs/speeches/1998/19980507.htm.

Grilli, Vittorio and Gian Maria Milesi-Ferretti (1995). 'Economic Effects and Structural Determinants of Capital Controls', *IMF Staff Papers*, **42**, (September), 517–51.

Grilli, Vittorio, Donato Masciandaro and Guido Tabellini (1991). 'Political and Monetary Institutions and Public Financial Policies in the Industrial Countries', *Economic Policy*, **6**, (13) (October), 341–92.

Grissa, Abdessatar (1983). 'The French Monetary and Exchange Rate Experience in the 1920s', Chapter 11, pp. 261–80 in Emil Claasen and Pascal Salin (eds), *Recent Issues in the Theory of Flexible Exchange Rates*, Amsterdam, New York and Oxford: North-Holland Publishing Company.

Group of 10 (1996). *The Resolution of Sovereign Liquidity Crises: A Report to the Ministers and Governors*, Basle: Bank for International Settlements; Washington, DC: International Monetary Fund.

Group of 22 (1998a). 'Report of the Working Group on International Financial Crises, 1998', online at: http://www.ustreas.gov/menu/html.

Group of 22 (1998b). 'Summary of Reports on the International Financial Architecture', online at: http://www.ustreas.gov/menu/html.

Hanke, Steve H. (1998). 'Reflections on Asian Exchange Rates', paper presented at the conference on *Asia: Meeting the Challenge*, Hong Kong, 25–27 March.

Hanke, Steve H., Lars Jonung and Kurt Schuler (1993). *Russian Currency and Finance: A Currency Board Approach to Reform*, London and New York: Routledge.

Harberger, Arnold C. (1980). 'Vignettes on the World Capital Market', *American Economic Review*, **70**, (May), 331–7.

Harberger, Arnold C. (1985). 'Lessons for Debtor Country Managers and Policymakers', Chapter 9, pp. 236–57 in Gordon W. Smith and John T. Cuddington (eds), *International Debt and the Developing Countries*, Washington, DC: The World Bank.

Hart, Oliver D. and David M. Kreps (1986). 'Price Destabilising Speculation', *Journal of Political Economy*, **95**, (5) (October), 927–52.

Hartman, David G. (1985). 'Tax Policy and Foreign Direct Investment', *Journal of Public Economics*, **26**, 107–21.

Hausmann, Ricardo and Liliana Rojas-Suárez (eds) (1996). *Banking Crises in Latin America*, Washington, DC: Inter-American Development Bank.

Helleiner, G.K. (ed.) (1998). *Capital Account Regimes and the Developing Countries*, Basingstoke and London: Macmillan Press Ltd.

Hong Kong Government (1998). *Report on the Financial Market Review*, online at: http://www.info.gov.hk/fsb/finance/index.htm.

HKMA (Hong Kong Monetary Authority) (1998a). *Annual Report 1998*.

HKMA (Hong Kong Monetary Authority) (1998b). *Monthly Statistical Bulletin*, (45) (May).

Horsefield, J. Keith (ed.) (1969). *The International Monetary Fund, 1946–65, Twenty Years of International Monetary Cooperation. Volume I: Chronicle*, by J. Keith Horsefield; *Volume II: Analysis*, by Margaret de Vries, J. Keith Horsefield *et al.*; and *Volume III: Documents*, Washington, DC: International Monetary Fund.

Hymer, Stephen and Robert Rowthorn (1970). 'Multinational Corporations and International Oligopoly: The Non-American Challenge', Chapter 3, pp. 57–91 in Kindleberger (ed.) (1970).

IFIAC (International Financial Institution Advisory Committee) (2000). *Report*, on line at: phantom-x.gsia.cmu.edu/IFIAC/Report.html.

IMF (International Monetary Fund) (1959). *10th Annual Report on Exchange Restrictions*, Washington, DC: International Monetary Fund.

IMF (International Monetary Fund) (1993). *Balance of Payments Manual*, 5th edn, Washington, DC: International Monetary Fund.

IMF (International Monetary Fund) (1995). *Exchange Arrangements and Exchange Restrictions. Annual Report 1995*, Washington, DC: International Monetary Fund.

IMF (International Monetary Fund) (1996). *International Capital Markets, 1996*, Washington, DC: International Monetary Fund.

IMF (International Monetary Fund) (1998a). 'How We Lend', online at: http://www.imf.org.

IMF (International Monetary Fund) (1998b). 'The General Arrangements to Borrow', online at: http://www.imf.org.

IMF (International Monetary Fund) (1999). *Involving the Private Sector in Forestalling and Resolving Financial Crises*, online at: http://www.imf.org.

IMF (International Monetary Fund) (2000a). 'IMF Quotas and Quota Reviews', online at: http://www.imf.org.

IMF (International Monetary Fund) (2000b). 'The General Arrangements to Borrow (GAB). The New Arrangements to Borrow (NAB) ', online at: http://www.imf.org.

Indonesian Government (1998a). *Supplementary Memorandum of Economic and Financial Policies, April 10*, online at http://www.imf.org.

Indonesian Government (1998b). *Second Supplementary Memorandum of Economic and Financial Policies, June 24*, online at http://www.imf.org.

Johnson, Harry G. (1970). 'The Efficiency and Welfare Implications of the International Corporation', Chapter 2, pp. 44–55 in Kindleberger (ed.) (1970).

Johnson, R. Barry, Salim M. Darbar and Claudia Echeverria (1997). 'Sequencing Capital Account Liberalization: Lessons from the Experiences in Chile, Indonesia, Korea, and Thailand', *Working Paper 157*, Washington, DC: International Monetary Fund.

Jones, Ronald W. (1967). 'International Capital Movements and the Theory of Tariffs and Trade', *Quarterly Journal of Economics*, **81**, 1–38.

Kaminsky, Graciela L. and Carmen M. Reinhart (1999). 'The Twin Crises: The Causes of Banking and Balance-of-Payments Problems', *American Economic Review*, **89**, (3) (June), 473–500.

Kaminsky, Graciela L. Saul Lizondo and Carmen M. Reinhart (1998). 'Leading Indicators of Currency Crises', *IMF Staff Papers*, **45**, (1) (March), 1–48.

Kane, Edward J. (1995). 'Three Paradigms for the Role of Capitalization Requirements in Insured Financial Institutions', *Journal of Banking and Finance*, **19**, (3–4) (June), 431–59.

Kaufman, George C. (1994). 'A Proposal for Deposit Insurance Reform that Keeps the Put Option out of the Money and the Taxpayers in the Money', Chapter 18, pp. 493–510 in Charles A. Stone and Anne Zissu (eds), *Global Risk Based Capital Regulations. Volume 1: Capital Adequacy*, Burr Ridge, IL: Irwin Professional Publishers.

Kawai, Masahiro (1999). 'The Resolution of the East Asian Crisis: Financial and Corporate Sector Restructuring', Paper presented at the conference on *Reforms and Recovery in East Asia: The Role of the State and Economic Enterprise*, Australian National University, Canberra, Australia, 21–22 September.

Kemp, Murray C. (1964). *The Pure Theory of International Trade*, Englewood Cliffs, NJ: Prentice-Hall.

Kenen, Peter (1993). 'Financial Opening and the Exchange Rate Regime', pp. 237–62 in Helmut Reisen and Bernhard Fischer (eds), *Financial Opening. Policy Issues and Experiences in Developing Countries*, Paris: Organisation for Economic Co-operation and Development.

Kindleberger, Charles P. (ed.) (1970). *The International Corporation*, Cambridge, MA: Massachusetts Institute of Technology Press.

Kindleberger, Charles P. (1987). *International Capital Movements*, Marshall Lectures 1985, Cambridge: Cambridge University Press.

Kindleberger, Charles P. (1989). *Manias, Panics, and Crashes: A History of Financial Crises*, revised edn, New York: Basic Books.

Kirchner, Stephen (1995). 'Central Bank Independence and Accountability: The New Zealand Case', *Agenda*, **2**, (2), 169–80.

Kouri, Pentti J. K., and Michael G. Porter (1974). 'International Capital Flows and Portfolio Equilibrium', *Journal of Political Economy*, **82**, (May/June), 443–67.

Krugman, Paul (1979). 'A Model of Balance of Payments Crises', *Journal of Money Credit and Banking*, **11**, (August), 311–25.

Kydland, F.E. and E.C. Prescott (1977). 'Rules Rather Than Discretion: The Inconsistency of Optimal Plans', *Journal of Political Economy*, **85**, (3) (June), 473–92.

Labán, Raúl and Felipe B. Larraín (1997). 'Can a Liberalization of Capital Outflows Increase Inflows?', *Journal of International Money and Finance*, **16**, (3), 415–31.

Lal, Deepak (1987). 'The Political Economy of Economic Liberalization', *The World Bank Economic Review*, **1**, (2) (January), 273–99.

Le Fort, Guillermo and Carlos Budnevich (1998). 'Capital Account Regulations and Macroeconomic Policy: Two Latin American Experiences', Chapter 2, pp. 45–81 in Helleiner (ed.) (1998).

Lindgren, Ragnar (1994). 'Transactions Taxes and Stock Market Volatility', *Working Paper 59*, Stockholm School of Economics, October.

Lindsey, Timothy (1998). 'The IMF and Insolvency Law Reform in Indonesia', *Bulletin of Indonesian Economic Studies*, **34**, (3) (December), 119–24.

Massad, Carlos (1998). 'The Liberalization of the Capital Account: Chile in the 1990s', pp. 34–46 in Fischer *et al.* (1998).

Mathieson, Donald J. and Rojas-Suárez, Liliana (1993). 'Liberalization of the Capital Account. Experiences and Issues', *Occasional Paper 103*, Washington, DC: International Monetary Fund.

McKibbin, Warwick J. (1998). 'Risk Re-Evaluation, Capital Flows and the Crisis in Asia', Chapter 14, pp. 227–44 in McLeod and Garnaut (eds) (1998).

McKibbin, Warwick J. (1999). 'International Capital Flows, Financial Reform and Consequences of Changing Risk Perceptions in APEC Economies', Paper presented at the Institute of Policy Studies conference on *Experience of Economic Reform within APEC*, Wellington, New Zealand, July.

McKinnon, Ronald I. (1973). *Money and Capital in Economic Development*, Washington, DC: Brookings Institution.

McKinnon, Ronald I. (1991). *The Order of Economic Liberalization: Financial Control in the Transition to a Market Economy*, Baltimore and London: Johns Hopkins University Press.

McKinnon, Ronald I. and Huw Pill (1997). 'Credible Economic Liberalizations and Overborrowing', *American Economic Review*, **87**, (2), 189–93.

McLeod, Ross H. (1998). 'From Crisis to Cataclysm? The Mismanagement of Indonesia's Economic Ailments', *The World Economy*, **21**, (7) (September), 913–30.

McLeod, Ross H. and Ross Garnaut (eds) (1998). *East Asia in Crisis: From Being a Miracle to Needing One?*, London and New York: Routledge.

Meredith, Guy M. (1999). 'Liquidity Management under Hong Kong's Currency Board Arrangements', Paper presented at the *International Workshop on Currency Boards: Convertibility, Liquidity and Exit*, 9 October, Hong Kong.

Merton, Robert C. and Zvi Bodie (1993). 'Deposit Insurance Reform: A Functional Approach', *Carnegie-Rochester Conference Series on Public Policy*, **38**, 1–34.

Miller, Merton H. (1995). 'Do the M&M Propositions Apply to Banks?' *Journal of Banking and Finance*, **19**, 483–9.

Mishkin, Frederic S. (1992). *The Economics of Money, Banking and Financial Markets*, 3rd edn, New York: Harper Collins.

Mohammed, Aziz Ali (1998). 'Issues Relating to the Treatment of Capital Movements in the IMF', Chapter 7, pp. 211–19 in Helleiner (ed.) (1998).

Montgomery, John (1997). 'The Indonesian Financial System: Its Contribution to Economic Performance, and Key Policy Issues', *Working Paper 97/45*, Washington, DC: International Monetary Fund.

Moreno, Ramon (1995). 'Macroeconomic Behavior during Periods of Speculative Pressure or Realignment: Evidence from Pacific Basin Economies,' *Federal Reserve Bank of San Francisco Economic Review*, (3), 3–16.

Mundell, Robert A. (1968). *International Economics*, London: Macmillan.

Musch, Frederick C. (1997). 'Applying Basle Standards in Developing and Transition Economies', Chapter 7, pp. 130–9 in Enoch and Green (eds) (1997).

Nash, John (1990a). 'Export Instability and Long-term Capital Flows: Response to Asset Risk in a Small Economy', *Economic Inquiry*, **28**, (April), 307–16.

Nash, John (1990b). 'Export Risk and Capital Movements: The Theory of Asset Swapping', Chapter 7, pp. 122–37 in Richard O'Brien and Ingrid Iversen (eds), *Finance and the International Economy: The AMEX Bank Review Prize Essays*, Oxford: Oxford University Press for the AMEX Bank Review.

Nellor, David C.L. (1998). 'The Role of the IMF', Chapter 15, pp. 245–65 in McLeod and Garnaut (eds) (1998).

Nurkse, Ragnar (1944). *International Currency Experience: Lessons of the Inter-war Period*, League of Nations, United Nations reprint, 1947.

Obstfeld, Maurice (1986). 'Rational and Self-Fulfilling Balance-of-Payments Crises', *American Economic Review*, **76**, (March), 72–81.

Obstfeld, Maurice (1996). 'Models of Currency Crises With Self-fulfilling Features', *European Economic Review*, **40**, 1037–47.

Organisation for Economic Co-operation and Development (OECD) (1990). *Liberalisation of Capital Movements and Financial Services in the OECD Area*, Paris: OECD.

Padoa-Schioppa, Tommasso (1997). 'Evolving Supervisory Standards in Advanced Market Economies', Chapter 6, pp. 115–24 in Enoch and Green (eds) (1997).

Park, Yung Chul and Chi-Young Song (1998). 'Managing Foreign Capital Flows: The Experiences of the Republic of Korea, Thailand, Malaysia and Indonesia', Chapter 3, pp. 82–140 in Helleiner (ed.) (1998).

Phillips, Ronnie J. (1995). *The Chicago Plan and New Deal Banking Reform*, Armonk, NY: M.E. Sharpe.

Pierce, J.L. (1991). *The Future of Banking*, New Haven, CT: Yale University Press.

Quirk, Peter J., Owen Evans *et al.* (1995). 'Capital Account Convertibility: Review of Experience and Implications for IMF Policies', *Occasional Paper 131*, Washington, DC: International Monetary Fund.

Reisen, Helmut (1994). *Debt, Deficits and Exchange Rates: Essays on Financial Interdependence and Development*, Aldershot, England: Edward Elgar.

Rhee, Yeongseop and Chi-Young Song (1999). 'Exchange Rate Policy and the Effectiveness of Intervention: The Case of Korea', Chapter 5, pp. 69–104 in Stefan Collignon, Jean Pisani-Ferry and Yung Chul Park (eds), *Exchange Rate Policies in Emerging Asian Countries*, London and New York: Routledge.

Rodrik, Dani (1998). 'Who Needs Capital-Account Convertibility?', pp. 55–65 in Fischer *et al.* (1998).

Rojas-Suárez, Liliana and Stephen R. Weisbrod (1996a). 'Achieving Stability in Latin American Financial Markets in the Presence of Volatile Capital Flows', pp. 61–92 in Ricardo Hausmann and Liliana Rojas-Suárez (eds), *Volatile Capital Flows: Taming their Impact on Latin America*, Washington, DC: Inter-American Development Bank.

Rojas-Suárez, Liliana and Stephen R. Weisbrod (1996b). 'Banking Crises in Latin America: Experiences and Issues', pp. 3–21, in Hausmann and Rojas-Suárez (eds) (1996).

Rossi, Marco (1999). 'Financial Fragility and Economic Performance in Developing Countries: Do Capital Controls, Prudential Regulation and Supervision Matter?', *IMF Working Paper 99/66*, Washington, DC: International Monetary Fund.

Ryan, Timothy (1996). 'United States', pp. 243–7 in Hausmann and Rojas-Suárez (eds) (1996).

Sachs, Jeffrey D. (1995). 'Do We Need an International Lender of Last Resort?' Frank Graham Lecture. Princeton University, Princeton, NJ.

Sachs, Jeffrey D., Aaron Tornell and Andrés Velasco (1996a). 'The Collapse of the Mexican Peso: What Have We Learned?', *Economic Policy*, **22**, (April), 15–63.

Sachs, Jeffrey D., Aaron Tornell and Andrés Velasco (1996b). 'Financial Crises in Emerging Markets: The Lessons from 1995', *Brookings Papers on Economic Activity*, (1) (August), 147–98.

Samuelson, Paul A. (1964). 'Theoretical Notes on Trade Problems', *Review of Economics and Statistics*, **46**, 145–54.

Santiprabhob, Veerathi (1997). 'Bank Soundness and Currency Board Arrangements: Issues and Experience', *IMF Paper on Policy Analysis and Assessment 97/11*, Washington, DC: International Monetary Fund.

Schuler, Kurt (1992). *Currency Boards*. Unpublished Ph.D. thesis. George Mason University. First part is online at: http://users.erols.com/kurrency/webdiss1.htm; second part at: ditto/webdiss2.htm.

Schuler, Kurt (1999). 'The Importance of Being Orthodox', *Mimeo*.

Schwartz, Anna J. (1998). 'Time to Terminate the ESF and the IMF', *Mimeo*, online at: http://www.stern.nyu.edu/~nroubini/asia/AsiaHomepage.html

Shaffer, Sherrill (1997). 'Deposit Insurance Pricing: The Hidden Burden of Premium Rate Volatility,' *Cato Journal*, **17**, (1) (spring/summer), 81–90.

Shiller, Robert J. (1981). 'Do Stock Market Prices Move Too Much to Be Justified by Subsequent Changes in Dividends?', *American Economic Review*, **71**, (3) (June), 421–35.

Shiller, Robert J. (1989). *Market Volatility*, Cambridge, MA and London: The MIT Press.

Sieper, E. and G. Fane (1982). 'Exchange Control and Exchange Rate Policy', pp. 129–282 in Australian Financial System Inquiry, *Commissioned Studies and Selected Papers, Part 2 Macroeconomic Policy: External Policy*, Canberra: Australian Government Publishing Service.

Sjaastad, Larry A. (1983). 'International Debt Quagmire – to Whom Do We Owe It?', *The World Economy*, **6**, (3) (September), 305–24.

Soros, George (1997). 'Avoiding a Breakdown: Asia's Crisis Demands a Rethink of International Regulation', *Financial Times*, London, 31 December.

Soros, George (1998). *The Crisis of Global Capitalism: Open Society Endangered*, New York: Public Affairs.

Summers, L. and V. Summers (1989). 'When Financial Markets Work Too Well. A Cautious Case for Securities Transactions Tax', *Journal of Financial Services Research*, **3**, 261–86.

Tang, S.Y. (1995). 'Informal Credit Markets and Economic Development in Taiwan', *World Development*, **23**, (5), 845–55.

Tobin, James (1974). *The New Economics One Decade Older*. Princeton, NJ: Princeton University Press.

Tobin, James (1978). 'A Proposal for International Monetary Reform', *Eastern Economic Journal*, **4**, (July–October), 153–9.

Tobin, James (1996). 'Prologue' pp. ix–xviii in Mahbub ul Haq, Inge Kaul and Isabelle Grunberg (eds), *The Tobin Tax: Coping With Financial Volatility*, New York: Oxford University Press.

Truman, Edwin S. (1996). 'The Risks and Implications of External Financial Shocks: Lessons from Mexico', *International Finance Discussion Papers, 535*, New York: Board of Governors of the Federal Reserve System.

Tsiang, S.C. (1959). 'Fluctuating Exchange Rates in Countries with Relatively Stable Economies: Some European Experiences After World War I', *IMF Staff Papers*, **7**, (October), 75–106.

Velasco, Andrés (1991). 'Liberalization, Crisis, Intervention: The Chilean Financial System, 1975–85', Chapter 3, pp. 113–74 in V. Sundararajan and Tomás J.T. Baliño (eds), *Banking Crises: Cases and Issues*, Washington, DC: International Monetary Fund.

Vernon, Raymond (1966). 'International Investment and International Trade in the Product Cycle', *Quarterly Journal of Economics*, **80**, (May), 190–207.

Wade, Robert and Frank Veneroso (1998). 'The Resources Lie Within', *The Economist*, 7 November.

Warr, Peter G. (1999a). 'What Happened to Thailand?', *The World Economy*, **22**, (July), 631–50.

Warr, Peter G. (1999b). 'Indonesia: Trade Shocks and Construction Booms', pp. 326–54 in Paul Collier, Jan Willem Gunning and Associates (eds), *Trade Shocks in Developing Countries*, Oxford: Oxford University Press.

Williamson, John (1998). 'A New Facility For the IMF?', Chapter 5, pp. 184–95 in Helleiner (ed.) (1998).

Williamson, John and Molly Mahar (1998). 'A Survey of Financial Liberalization', *Essays in International Finance no.211*. Princeton, NJ: International Finance Section, Princeton University.

Wilson, Dominic (1999). 'Managing Capital Flows in East Asia', Paper presented at the conference on *Reforms and Recovery in East Asia: The Role of the State and Economic Enterprise*, Australian National University, Canberra, Australia, 21–22 September.

World Bank (1997). *Private Capital Flows to Developing Countries: The Road to Financial Integration*, New York: Oxford University Press.

Wyplosz, Charles (1986). 'Capital Controls and Balance of Payments Crises', *Journal of International Money and Finance*, **5**, 167–79.

Yam, Joseph (1997). 'Hong Kong's Monetary Scene: Myths and Realities', Speech at Bank of England Seminar. Revised version of 30 April 1997, online at: http://www.info.gov.hk/hkma/system/scene.html.

Yeager, Leland B. (1976). *International Monetary Relations: Theory, History, and Policy*, 2nd edn, New York: Harper and Row.

Index

inability of mild or moderate
controls to avert financial and
currency crises 50–53, 57–9
key features of controls used to
prevent convertibility on capital
account 26–7
prudential purpose of 8, 14–16,
31–3, 38, 56
'real demand principle' for granting
access to forward and swap
foreign exchange markets in
Korea 50
analogous principle in Taiwan
and Malaysia 40–42
restrictions on access of non-
residents to domestic capital
markets 12, 28–33
restrictions on access of residents to
offshore capital markets 12, 27–8
restrictions on domestic currency
lending by residents to non-
residents 11, 18, 31–3
restrictions on forward market
trading in won, rupiah, ringgit
and baht tightened (1997) 19
capital flows
advantage of flexible exchange rate
system relative to fixed rate
system in stabilising output and
employment in the presence of
volatile capital flows 134, 144
defined 10, 35
CAR (capital adequacy ratio)
analogy between bank capital and
the deductible in disaster
insurance 117
Basle 8 per cent CAR too low even
in industrialised countries 125
Basle Committee recommendation
for 8 per cent minimum CAR
115
CAR can be raised without affecting
economies of scope 120
contribution to true capital of
scarcity value of bank licences
reduced by financial
liberalisation 121
deposit guarantees analogous to put-
options 121

efficacy of high minimum CAR in
preventing financial collapse 118,
125–30
increasing minimum CAR unlikely
to induce inefficiency 119–21
minimum CAR as a check on moral
hazard 115, 119
minimum CAR set at only 4 per cent
in Indonesia after crisis 174
need for higher risk weights in
developing than in industrialised
countries 127
problems in assigning appropriate
risk weights 121–3
problems in measuring capital 121–2
proposals to raise minimum CAR
121, 127–30, 182, 184, 197
ratio of book to market value of bank
equity 131
rationalisation for need to measure
CAR of banks in a group on a
consolidated group basis 131
relatively high minimum CAR in
Singapore, Hong Kong and
Argentina 128
rolling over of bad loans 121, 131
self-assessment of risk 122
setting low minimum CAR of
guaranteed banks is a protective
subsidy to banks and to risk-
taking 125
CFR (Council on Foreign Relations),
report of task force on *Safeguarding
Prosperity in a Global Financial
System* 180
argues that scale of IMF lending
should be reduced to counter
moral hazard 182
recommends that IMF continue to
use policy conditional loans
when crises are the fault of the
borrowing government, but create
a special contagion facility to
lend without conditions when
crises are due to contagion 182
recommends that IMF lending be
made conditional on borrowing
country forcing private creditors
to reschedule debts 191
see also lending into arrears by IMF

credibility of monetary and exchange
rate policies
credibility of fixed exchange rate
reduced by sterilisation 138, 170
credibility of inflation or monetary
target diminished if central bank
is responsible for safety of
financial system as well as stated
target 160
enhanced by delegating
responsibility for a single target
to specialised institution 158
flexible exchange rate system and
157–60, 172
Indonesian currency board proposal
and 166–9
Indonesian monetary targets
(1997–98) 161–5
inflation targets and central bank
independence in New Zealand
160
Nurkse's analysis of French inflation
(1922–26) anticipates second
generation models of self-
fulfilling crises 158–9
speculative attacks and 104, 158
currency boards 133, 141–4
ability of currency boards to resist
speculative attacks consistent
with theoretical models 169–70
banks less fragile under currency
boards than under central banks
149–51
case for currency board highest when
need to restore credibility is
greatest 171
currency boards in colonial period
148
devaluations by currency boards
extremely rare 147
modern currency boards 148
objective of is to derive revenue from
issuing own currency while
borrowing the reputation and
credibility of a major
international currency 148
occasional bank failures in currency
board systems 150–51
relative openness to foreign entry of
the financial sector in currency
board systems 151

risk of recession if exchange rate is
pegged 171
role of sterilisation policy and
international bail-out in repelling
the 1995 attack on the Argentine
peso 149
speculative attack on Argentine peso
(1995) 149
success of Argentina's currency
board-type arrangements 148–9
'textbook' currency board system
defined 147
see also Argentina; Hong Kong;
Indonesia
currency crises (*or* balance of payments
crises)
definitions of crises in empirical
studies 98, 105
empirical evidence on 77, 98–105,
131
estimated benefits of high ratio of
FDI to debt in preventing 77
first generation models of inevitable
crises 87–90, 103
frequency of currency crises
positively associated with
controls on capital outflows 131
inability of capital controls to
prevent crises in first generation
models 105
leading indicators of currency crises
100–101
limited ability of existing models to
warn of 1997 Asian crisis 101,
104
second generation models of self-
fulfilling crises 90–93, 103
'tequila crisis' *see* Mexico
see also Asian crisis (1997–99)

debt crisis of 1980s, especially in Latin
America 5–6
debt–equity ratios of banks, before and
after introduction of safety nets 107,
131
default
bargaining costs and 95
contract interest rate is adjusted for
default risk 94
costs of 94–8

speculative attack on HK dollar
(October 1997) 153–4
HKMA policy during the
attack an unexpected
move from partial
sterilisation to textbook
currency board purity 155,
172
timing of interest rate rise
indicates that cause was
misunderstanding between
banks and HKMA about
sterilisation of speculative
outflow 153–4
sterilisation of monetary effects of
balance of payments by HKMA
142, 152; overstated by present
estimates 143–4
stock market speculation an
inadvisable strategy for a
currency board 157
technical measures (1998) a move
away from currency board purity
of October 1997, but closer to
currency board purity than the
system pre-October 1997 or the
academics' proposals 155–6

ICIC (International Credit Insurance
Corporation)
analogous to deposit insurance 175
lacks safeguards needed to limit
losses of government deposit
insurance agencies 197
losses that could have been incurred
in Asia if set up before 1997 186
potential for adverse selection and
fraud because credit guarantees
are most valuable to the most
risky borrowers 186
problem of allocating subsidised
credits 185
proposed by George Soros 175

IFIAC (International Financial
Institution Advisory Commission)
majority recommends that IMF loans
should be for maximum of 120
days with at most one rollover 182
majority report criticises IMF's CCL
arrangements 181

majority report recommends that
IMF lend only to countries that
have opened their financial
sectors to entry by international
banks and imposed high
minimum CAR 182
set up by US Congress 180

IMF (International Monetary Fund) 3
articles of agreement 3, 8, 177, 198
attitude to capital controls 3, 7–9
CCL (Contingent Credit Lines)
introduced to speed up
negotiation and disbursement of
loans by encouraging potential
borrowers to qualify in advance
by adopting IMF-approved
policies 180
Code of Good Practice on Fiscal
Transparency 181
Emergency Financing Mechanism 178
General and New Arrangements to
Borrow 177
Interim Committee recommends
amending articles to promote
capital account liberalisation 8
international last resort lending by
175–85
proposals to speed-up the
disbursement of loans 178–82
quotas of member countries 176–7
relatively rapid disbursement of
loans to Mexico (1995) and to
Korea (1997–98) 178–9
slow disbursement of loans to
Indonesia and Thailand
(1997–98) 178–9
Special and General Data
Dissemination Standards 181, 197
Supplemental Reserve Facility 179–80
see also international last resort
lending; lending into arrears by
IMF

imputation of corporate tax to
shareholders 66–7, 80–81, 84

Indonesia
credit actually created by Bank
Indonesia (BI) in 1997–98
contrasted with 'accommodative'
last resort lending 164–5